The Folk, Country, and Bluegrass Musician's Catalogue

BY HENRY RASOF

St. Martin's Press
New York

Designed by Deborah Bracken
and Carolyn Ogden

Illustrations by Alphonse Tvaryanas

Library of Congress Cataloging in Publication Data

Rasof, Henry.
   The folk, country & bluegrass musician's catalogue.

   1. Folk music—Handbooks, manuals, etc.   2. Country
music—Handbooks, manuals, etc.   3. Bluegrass music—
Handbooks, manuals, etc.   I. Title.
ML102.F66R4   784.5'2   81-14488
ISBN 0-312-29696-7   AACR2

First Printing 1982

TABLE OF CONTENTS

ACKNOWLEDGMENTS

In the course of writing this book I have had the privilege of tapping the knowledge of a great many musicians, instrument builders, and dealers. Special thanks go to Stan Werbin, proprietor of Elderly Instruments, and to Doug Berch, musician and builder, for reading the entire manuscript, and to Jim Garber, multi-instrumentalist par excellence, for lending his hand on numerous chapters. Thanks also to Rick Altman of the Folklore Center in New York for helping me get my feet wet and to the staff at McCabe's Guitar Shop for their patience and wisdom.

I also wish to acknowledge the specialized help of the following: Becky Blackley (Autoharp); Larry Brown (banjo); Bob Zaidman (guitar); Sam Rizzetta, Dennis Dorogi, Peter Tommerup, and Madeline MacNeil (mountain and hammered dulcimer); Molly Mason (string bass); Joseph Gold, Julie Lieberman, and Peter Tatar (violin); Peter Rothe (balalaika); Miles Tager (ukulele); Steve Garcia (harmonica); and Kathy Kaplan and Pat Conte (discographies). I am also grateful for the generosity of Peter Pickow at Oak Publications and Bill Bay at Mel Bay Publications, of Mike Longworth of Martin Guitars, and of the National Council for the Traditional Arts for letting me use their information on festivals. Lawrence Ostrow of Guitars Friend inspired the form of the book, and George Gruhn of Gruhn Guitars in Nashville provided the photographs of vintage instruments.

Finally, my thanks to two people for their interest, encouragement, patience, and help: Jeffrey Weiss, the producer of the book, and Bob Miller, my editor at St. Martin's Press.

INTRODUCTION

A hundred years ago there was little need for a book like this one, that will help you wade through the zillions of brands and models of guitars and banjos, through the countless albums, through the clutter of instruction books, through the myriad kinds of instrument strings. You went to your Sears or Montgomery Ward catalogue, or if you were lucky enough to live in a big city, to a music dealer, and pretty much took what you could get.

All that has changed. Not only is there more to choose from, but more people are able to afford instruments and also to afford really good instruments. And with the advent of books on every aspect of music, and of music teachers to teach you how to play like Earl Scruggs or Doc Watson or David Grisman, more venues of expression are available than ever before. In the good old days, after all, you bought a cheap guitar or banjo and taught yourself off the radio; if you were lucky you had a few records or a relative who would show you a few licks.

Using the *Folk, Country, and Bluegrass Musician's Catalogue* is easy, because starting an instrument can be difficult. Just turn to the chapter whose featured instrument interests you and you will find almost everything you need to know about choosing an instrument; you'll also find lists of records, books, magazines, and festivals, all relevant to the instrument at hand. Later in the book you'll find sections of general interest, regardless of your instrument or the instrument you want to play.

Prices, unfortunately, will have increased on most products by the time you read this, in most cases by a modest 8 to 12%. Because of changes in prices as well as in quality and availability, recommendations and suggestions should not be followed blindly.

Now, hurry up and read this book, buy yourself a guitar, or a ukulele, or whatever, some picks, records, and books, and start making music!

CHAPTER 1

✿ WHERE TO BUY ✿
A MUSICAL INSTRUMENT

The best place to begin a search for nearly all instruments except violins and string basses is with a dealer who specializes in fretted or folk instruments. Such a store is often a folk-music center, featuring concerts and instruction, as well as serving as a hangout for local pickers. *Specialty dealers* cater to a particular audience and sell a limited number of different products, so they are usually quite knowledgeable of folk instruments. Customers demand more from these dealers, too. Such merchants sell out of a store front, through the mail, or through both channels.

General music stores carry a little of everything but may also have a specialty—guitars, or drums, or maybe amplifiers and electric guitars, or band instruments. You may find what you want at a general music store, but most likely the selection and expertise will leave something to be desired.

Department stores often sell inexpensive musical instruments, sometimes through a catalogue (like Sears). Although you can often get instruments more cheaply than at a music store, department stores do not offer a "guitar service center" as they do tire service centers. The possibilities in this kind of store are severely limited, in other words. Department stores do have good refund policies, however.

Pawnshops and other second-hand stores are a last resort for the novice. The new instruments sold in most pawnshops are of the cheapest quality; you will get no service; and what appears to be a low, low price may be equal to—or even greater than—the price at a music store. Used instruments are often terribly overpriced and in poor condition. Treat second-hand stores and their instruments with great caution.

Mail-order dealers are excellent sources of instruments and accessories. Instruments are usually set up and ready to play, guaranteed, and often heavily discounted. Some mail-order dealers carry a wide selection of merchandise, while others specialize more than any specialty store can afford to do. For instance, some dealers sell only strings, or only

Martin guitars, or only banjo parts. The biggest disadvantage of buying by mail is that you can't examine the merchandise before you buy, but to compensate, almost all mail-order dealers let you buy on approval, allowing from forty-eight hours to two weeks to decide whether you want to keep the instrument. Most of these dealers have a minimum order, and all charge extra for shipping.

Manufacturers sometimes sell directly to the customer, and some instruments, like custom models, are largely sold this way, usually through personal contact, in fact. But because most dealers can sell to an individual for less than the manufacturer will (a dealer buys at wholesale—i.e., 40-50% off list—and can mark up the price to the suggested list price or keep it lower), it is probably more advantageous to ask a dealer to order a particular instrument for you than to order it yourself.

Individuals are also sources of instruments, both new and used, but watch your step. First, many people do not know the market value of the instrument they are selling and may overcharge (they may also undercharge, of course). Second, a private party will not guarantee the instrument. Third, manufacturers' warranties almost always cover only the original owner. And fourth, the instrument may need work, whereas most stores fix up what they sell.

SPECIAL CONSIDERATIONS

Banjos. A banjo is one of the most difficult instruments to buy because it often requires extensive adjustments before it plays well. The best sources are specialty stores and mail-order dealers.

Violins. Most fine violins are sold through dealers who buy, sell, appraise, and repair only violins and sometimes other bowed instruments. Violin dealers usually sell instruments in decent condition. Most reputable dealers will write a certificate on a good violin, stating that in their opinion, a particular instrument is, for example, a Stradivarius made in 1714 and owned by such and such famous violinists. Finding an inexpensive violin at a dealer's may be difficult, however, since some dealers will not handle instruments below a certain standard of quality and, therefore, price.

Violins are sold in general music stores, some folk-instrument stores, pawnshops, antique stores, and flea markets, and also through individuals and mail-order dealers. Be very careful when dealing with any of these sources, especially the second-hand stores; although you *may* pay less than from a violin dealer,

there's an excellent chance you will have bought an inferior instrument requiring extensive repairs. If you cannot find what you want at a violin dealer's and you can find nothing by checking newspaper advertisements, try mail-order dealers; some have a broad selection of inexpensive instruments.

If you buy a violin at a garage sale for $25 and invest $75 in fixing it up, there are three possible results: you'll have either a violin worth $100, or an instrument worth more than $100, or an instrument worth *less* than $100. Though now you have an instrument that has cost you $100, the true market value may still be $25: just because the instrument plays does not mean it is any good. Sometimes, however, the garage-sale fiddle may be a gold mine. Peter Tatar, a violin dealer in New York City, had the following experience: "A customer went to New England, paid $25 for a violin, and had me set it up. When I had finished, I told him the instrument was worth $2500."

Mountain and Hammered Dulcimers; Psalteries. These instruments are made primarily in small shops or by individual builders. Many dealers in folk instruments carry both kinds of dulcimers, but sometimes the only means to obtain such an instrument is by directly contacting the manufacturer.

Ukuleles. Ukes are fairly easy to find, old and new, but new Martins may have to be special-ordered; your dealer can do this for you. By the way, it is worth checking the second-hand sources for used ukuleles.

String Basses. Basses are sold in music stores and by dealers of bowed instruments (some of whom sell only string basses, in fact). Although some bowed-instrument dealers may not carry the kind of bass that folk musicians tend to use, they often can direct you to other dealers, public schools, or individuals that may be selling such an instrument. One needn't be quite so fussy when buying an inexpensive bass as when buying an inexpensive violin. Second-hand stores are worth a visit, and the directory of mail-order dealers at the end of this chapter lists one bass dealer that will sell through the mail.

Balalaikas. Few dealers sell inexpensive balalaikas, and only occasionally will you find a really good instrument at a dealer; even then chances are it will be used. The first thing to do is ask around among musicians, dealers, and builders; check the classifieds in your local papers, and if a Russian-language paper is available, find someone who reads Russian to check the classifieds. Then contact the Balalaika and Domra Association of America (3319 W. 3 St., Chester, PA 19103) and ask for their newsletter, which may list instruments for sale. The BDAA also has a directory of balalaika ensembles around the country. One may be near you, and you can call for information.

If you have a chance to visit the Soviet Union, try the tourist stores first; most instruments they sell will be of the souvenir sort, but you may find a good balalaika. Next check the commission stores, where a balalaika maker may have an instrument being sold on consignment. As a last resort, you might try to contact members of a balalaika orchestra, in hopes of locating a builder or an instrument. Be very careful when dealing with a private party, dealer, or musician; because there's no free enterprise (at least officially), certain transactions may be illegal. Get a receipt for any instrument you buy.

THE DEALER

It is important to find a dealer you can trust and who can serve your needs at a reasonable price. Finding the perfect dealer may be impractical or impossible, but here are some points to consider when approaching a dealer.

Service. Does the store service what it sells? If your guitar needs a minor repair in three months, can the store do the job? Does the store guarantee its merchandise? Is the store a factory-authorized service center for one or more of the brands it sells? A music store doesn't have to do or be any of these things, but many stores do.

Knowledge. Do the salespeople know their business? Is the dealer up on trends and developments in the music industry?

Selection. Is there a varied stock in all price brackets? Are there brands and models to choose from (or even *too* many), or is the dealer trying to push one brand?

Price. Are instruments sold at list price or at discount? Although buying at a discount is obviously desirable, it may have some disadvantages. For example, some stores will not let you test heavily discounted instruments. Other stores are in the business of selling a lot of instruments and do not provide follow-up service. Are there hidden costs for shipping and setup? For example, you may save 40%

on a guitar bought through the mail, but if you return it, you pay for round-trip shipping; this can cost up to $40. In the long run you may pay more than if you purchased the instrument in person.

Approval Privilege. Aside from mail-order dealers, who usually let you try an instrument before a sale is final, some violin dealers also let you take home an instrument on approval.

FINDING A DEALER

Mail-order dealers are listed at the end of this chapter. To find local music stores, talk to local musicians. Also, check the Yellow Pages of your telephone directory under the heading "Music—Retailers." Distinguish between different types of stores by their display ads—"Fine Fretted Instruments," "Guitars and Banjos Our Specialty," "Vintage Stringed Instruments," "Peter Tatar and Son: Fine Violins," "Drums and French Horns," "The Dulcimer Shoppe," etc. If you can't tell from the ad, call the store. In case you can't find the right kind of store in your town, and still want to shop in person, check the Yellow Pages of a nearby city. Other ways to locate a dealer are to write to manufacturers and ask who stocks their instruments in your area; write or call mail-order dealers (many also run retail shops and know of other stores around the country); try reading the advertisements in magazines such as *Banjo Newsletter* and *Frets.*

DEALERS (MOSTLY MAIL ORDER*) OF INSTRUMENTS, ACCESSORIES, STRINGS, BOOKS, RECORDS, INSTRUMENT-BUILDING SUPPLIES

Buying books, accessories, strings, records, and supplies involves decisions similar to those involved in buying an instrument: Where should you buy them? How much should you pay for them? Which are the best ones? Mail-order dealers are excellent sources of strings, accessories, and materials, since they often stock a wider variety than most music stores. Prices are good too. However, sometimes a group of people buying in bulk can get a good deal from a local store too, and you save on postage and potential mixups and delays. Records are discounted by many mail-order dealers; then again, some record chains sell more cheaply than anyone. There's a good chance the mail-order specialty dealers will stock

*Many of these dealers also conduct a walk-in trade.

unusual or hard-to-find records, or just records your local store won't stock, such as old-time music or prewar blues. Books are ordinarily not discounted through the mail, though a few dealers do offer small savings.

Key: A dot signals outstanding dealers. However, each dealer has something special to offer, so by no means ignore the other sources. *Italics* signal specialties.

• **Andy's Front Hall,** RD 1, Wormer Road, Voorheesville, NY 12186. *Records, books,* some accessories, *Irish instruments, hammered* (Fogel, Hughes, Bednark, Here, Inc.) and mountain *dulcimers.*

Mike Bailey Music Co., 8937 Drake Parkway, Chattanooga, TN 37416. Banjos, guitars, and mandolins. Strings, accessories, *instruction books and tapes, tablature.*

Bein & Fushi, Inc., Fine Arts Building, Suite 1014, 410 S. Michigan Ave., Chicago, IL 60605. Of interest to fiddlers.

• **Eddie Bell Guitar Headquarters,** 251 W. 30 St., 1B, New York, NY 10001. Guitars, banjos, ukuleles, mandolins, strings, accessories, books. Very good discounts.

Blue Ridge Dulcimer Shop, P.O. Box 2164, Winchester, VA 22601. Mountain and hammered *dulcimers; dulcimer records, books,* strings and accessories. Friendly, helpful. Almost all records and books listed in the dulcimer chapters are available here.

• **Brother Slim's Record Revival,** Richey Records, 7121 W. Vickery, #118, Fort Worth, TX 76116. Well-organized catalogue of *records, tapes,* some books. Discounts.

• **Buck Musical Instrument Products,** 40 Sand Rd., New Britain, PA 18901. Autoharp. *Guitars:* Martin LoPrinzi, Guild, Gibson, Ovation, Yamaha, Ibanez, Madeira, Sigma. Dobro. *Banjos:* Gibson, Ode, Wildwood, Saga. *Mandolins:* Gibson and others. Buck dulcimers. Harmonicas. Ask for other brands. *Records.* Excellent source of *accessories,* wood, *parts,* unusual items (goose quills for dulcimer players). Warranty and setup. Nice, helpful folks. Impressive catalogue: $3. Very good discount.

• **Capritaurus,** P.O. Box 153, Felton, CA 95018. Mountain and hammered *dulcimers,* harps, mando-

lins, mandolas, psalteries, wind instruments, *exotica,* kits, Irish instruments. Records, books, luthiers' supplies (e.g., tools), cases, accessories. Ten-day approval. Knowledgeable staff. Excellent catalogue, sensibly organized. 10-40% discounts.

Casa Folklorica, 1053 N. Johnson, Mineola, TX 75773. "Traditional musical *instruments* of the *Andean* countries," including charangos (small, fretted, stringed instruments), various wind instruments. Books, records.

County Sales, P.O. Box 191, Floyd, VA 24091. *Records.* Well-organized catalogue.

Cowboy Carl Records, P.O. Box 116, Park Forest, IL 60466. *Records:* blues, country, rockabilly. Bimonthly list.

Down Home Music, Inc., 10341 San Pablo Ave., El Cerrito, CA 94530. *Records: blues,* bluegrass, rockabilly, country, rock; some books; newsletter. Blues catalogue: $1.

The Dulcimer Shoppe, Drawer E, Highway 9 North, Mountain View, AR 27560. *Dulcimer* books and records. Catalogue: $1.

The 1833 Shop, P.O. Box 329, Nazareth, PA 18064. Catalogue of accessories includes information about *Martin guitar kits.*

• **Elderly Instruments,** P.O. Box 1795, 541 E. Grand River, East Lansing, MI 48823. Enormous selection of instruments, old and new. Autoharp. *Banjos:* Gibson, Deering, Gold Star, Iida, Ode, Ome, Saga, Stewart-MacDonald, Wildwood. *Guitars:* Martin, Gallagher, Gurian, Guild, Ibanez, Applause, Greven, Takamine, Yamaha. Dobro. *Mandolins:* Gibson, Stiver, Unicorn, Kentucky. Mountain and hammered dulcimers, tin whistles, concertinas, harmonicas, limberjacks, etc. *Accessories, strings, books, records,* tools, *plans,* materials. Expert, friendly help. Free, extensive catalogue. 30-40% discounts on instruments, 15% on books.

Facsimile Book Shop, 16 W. 55 St., New York, NY 10019. Books on, and records of, Irish music.

• **Fiddlepicker,** Box 1033, Mountainside, NJ 07092. *Violins, bows,* cases. Good selection of instruments under $500; bows average $225-250. Trade-in privileges.

• **Fred's String Warehouse,** P.O. Box 7, Temple, PA 19560. *Strings,* harmonicas, electronic devices,

The Dulcimer Shoppe, Mountain View, Arkansas.

accessories. *Guitars:* Ovation, Martin, Gallagher. Other instruments—write for details. Excellent discounts.

• **The Fret Factory,** P.O. Box 541, Ormond Beach, FL 32074. *Banjos:* Stelling, Ome, Ode, Wildwood, Deering, Liberty, Saga, Goldstar, Imperial, Stewart-MacDonald. *Mandolins:* Stelling and Unicorn. Excellent discounts.

• **The Fret Mill,** 114 First St., S.E., Roanoake, VA 24011. *Banjos:* Deering, Goldstar, Stelling, Wildwood, Saga, Stewart-MacDonald. *Guitars:* Guild, Ibanez, Ovation, Washburn, Yamaha. *Mandolins:* Aria Pro II, Washburn. Mountain and hammered dulcimers. Some vintage instruments. Violins. Books, records, strings. Very good discounts.

• **Gewa,** P.O. Box 622, Boston, MA 02215. *Exotic* and other instruments, including *balalaikas.* Catalogue: $3.

• **Gruhn Guitars, Inc.,** 410 Broadway, Nashville, TN 37203. New and *used instruments.* New guitars: Martin and Ovation. New mandolins: Gilchrist. Probably the premier dealer of used instruments in the country. Large discounts on new American instruments.

Guitar Trader, 12 Broad St., Red Bank, NJ 07701. New and *used instruments,* predominantly *electric guitars* but many acoustic stringed instruments too. Good discounts on new instruments.

Guitars Friend, Rt. 1, Box 200, Sandpoint, ID 83864. Autoharp. *Banjos:* Raimi, Saga, Deering, Stelling, Stewart-MacDonald. *Guitars:* Applause, Ovation, Yamaha, Guild, Martin, Givens, Gurian, Franklin. Dobro. Mandolins: Givens, Flatiron. Strings, accessories. Discounts.

• **Gurian Guitars,** Box 595, West Swanzey, NH 03469. Wide selection of *supplies for instrument makers.*

Here, Inc., 29 S.E. Main St., Minneapolis, MN 55414. *Dulcimer* books, records, supplies.

Hughes Dulcimer Co., 4419 W. Colfax Ave., Denver, CO 80204. *Dulcimer* books, records, accessories.

• **Hobgoblin Music,** P.O. Box 5311, South San Francisco, CA 94080. Excellent source of mountain and hammered *dulcimers* and *British instruments* (including Irish).

• **Jean's Dulcimer Shop,** P.O. Box 8, Highway 32,

10

Cosby, TN 37722. Mountain and hammered *dulcimers*, Chromaharp, instrument kits. Builders' supplies. *Records* of, and *books* for, Autoharp, dulcimer, clawhammer banjo.

• **Lark in the Morning,** Box 1176, Mendocino, CA 95460. *Exotica. Harps*, concertinas, and other *instruments used in Irish music.* Hurdy-gurdies, flutes, zithers, French and German dulcimers, lute kits, Turkish and Bulgarian instruments, bouzoukis. Newsletter. Some books and records.

Wm. Harris Lee & Co., Fine Arts Building, 410 S. Michigan Ave., Suite 1029, Chicago, IL 60605. Of interest to fiddlers.

The Liberty Banjo Company, 2472 Main St., Bridgeport, CT 06606. A major supplier of *banjo* parts. Catalogue: $4.

Living Blues Mail Order Catalog, 2165 N. Wilton Ave., Chicago, IL 60614. *Blues records.*

• **Mandolin Brothers,** 629 Forest Ave., Staten Island, NY 10310. New *guitars:* Martin, Ovation, Washburn, Guild, Sigma, Adamas. Dobro. New *banjos:* Gibson, Washburn, Ode. Autoharp. Some accessories and strings. Large selection of *used* instruments. Excellent discounts on new instruments.

• **Metropolitan Music Co.,** Mountain Rd., RD 1, Stowe, VT 05672. *Violins*, cellos, violas, basses. *Strings, accessories,* tools, varnish, some items for fretted instruments. Excellent discounts.

• **Mogish Strings,** P.O. Box 493, Chesterland, OH 44026. Mostly *strings*, at terrific discounts. Guitars:

Lark in the Morning, Mendocino, California.

Yamaha. Biggest selection of stings: Martin, D'Addario, GHS.

Wayne Moskow Musical Instruments of the World, 3095 X Kerner Blvd., San Rafael, CA 94901. *Indian* and *Middle Eastern instruments:* sitars, sarods, ouds, drums, kotos, santurs. Gongs, bells, and strange instruments some of which are built by Mr. Moskow himself (who also builds fine sitars and sarods). Records.

Musician's Supply, P.O. Box 1440, El Cajon, CA 92022. Mostly electronic accessories. *Guitars:* Sigma, Takamine, *Taylor.*

Peripole, Browns Mills, NJ 08015. *Chromaharp,* dulcimers, numerous instruments good for children and schools. Useful for teachers. Large catalogue. Good discounts.

Rare Record Distribution Service, 417 E. Broadway, P.O. Box 10518, Glendale, CA 91205. Rare records.

Saga Musical Instruments, P.O. Box 2841, South San Francisco, CA 94080. Accessories, instrument parts.

Oscar Schmidt, 1415 Waukegan Rd., Northbrook, IL 60062. Good source for anything pertaining to the *Autoharp: parts, strings, books,* records, *cases.*

Southern Record Sales, 5101 Tasman Dr., Huntington Beach, CA 92649. Specialty *records.*

• **Stewart-MacDonald,** Box 900, Athens, OH 45701. *Banjo* and *mandolin parts, accessories, strings, kits,* books. Important source; however, their products cost less when ordered through some dealers.

Swanay Instruments, P.O. Box 2124, Fullerton, CA 92633. *Banjo parts, accessories;* strings, selected items.

Traeger's Bass Shop, 115 Christopher St., New York, NY 10014. Pickups, accessories, amps, strings, cases—all for the *bass. Instruments* too.

Vintage Records, Box 6144, Orange, CA 92667. Record auctions via U.S. Postal Service. Catalogue: $1.

• **Philip Weinkrantz Musical Supply Co.,** 3715 Dickason Ave., Dallas, TX 75219. *Violin strings, cases, accessories, parts.* Instruments, *bows.* Healthy discounts.

CHAPTER 2

SELECTING
AN INSTRUMENT

The musical instrument you buy should depend on your musical interests, budget, experience, commitment, and ambition. Most important for a beginner is an instrument that is not too difficult to learn and that won't discourage you while learning.

Although experienced musicians pay a lot of attention to sound quality, and a beginner is advised to get an instrument that sounds halfway decent, many beginners can ignore this aspect at first. Developing an ear for good tone requires time; also, many beginners are apt to spend more time worrying about their fingering than their tone quality.

A performing musician may require a beautifully finished instrument to flash around on a stage, but a beginner can ignore cosmetics—the physical appearance (and special decorative features—also called appointments) of the instrument—for the simple reason that cosmetics are costly and bear little if any relation to playability and tone. And whereas an experienced, committed musician may be willing to sink a lot of money into a fine instrument, a beginner

probably shouldn't spend too much because 1) it may take time to appreciate the qualities of a fine instrument, 2) expensive doesn't always mean good, and it takes experience to know how to distinguish between the two, and 3) you may lose interest after a while and lose more money on your investment than necessary. As a general rule, spend as much as you need to get an instrument that satisfies you, keep in mind that extremely cheap instruments are invariably junk, and in the beginning try to resist the attitude that only the best will satisfy you. Michael Hoover of McCabe's in Santa Monica, California, tells of a man who bought an expensive Martin guitar but couldn't play it, and wound up buying a much less expensive guitar to learn on.

Each instrument chapter in this book contains a comprehensive section on selecting an instrument. Despite the amount of information, much of it is easily mastered, and even if you have no previous experience you should have little trouble selecting an instrument. If you already play a fretted instrument such as a guitar, you will notice that the procedure for selecting a banjo, for instance, is similar. The hardest instrument to buy is a violin, because most decent, affordable instruments are secondhand; you can't noodle around on a fiddle the way you can on a guitar; and reliable makes aren't commonly available as with other instruments.

All said and done, the *best* way to buy an instrument is to take along someone who plays that instrument or a similar one; for a violin this is almost mandatory. Finding a trustworthy, knowledgeable dealer is also essential.

Once you arrive at the music store, tell the dealer what you want, but try as many instruments as possible, both in and out of your price bracket, so that you can arrive at a basis for comparison.

Setup

There's an excellent chance you won't find an instrument that perfectly meets all the criteria of playability spelled out in each chapter. (This may certainly be the case with a banjo and with a used instrument.) This may vary for a number of reasons:

1. A new instrument may need to be set up, which means putting on strings, positioning the bridge, adjusting the string height—all the things that make an instrument playable. Instruments—especially violins—bought from sources other than specialty dealers may need considerable work, or perhaps just a few adjustments.

2. Most good instruments arrive from the factory or builder already set up and may require only minor adjustments. Cheap instruments often need the most work.

3. A setup can be free or can cost anywhere from $15 to about $60 on a new fretted instrument, more on a violin or used instrument.

4. You must determine whether an instrument is worth being set up. For example, it is not worth $60 to set up a $100 mandolin, but it may be worth $60 on a $1000 mandolin.

5. Repair bills vary between shops. Obtain a second opinion if the price seems high, or buy the instrument elsewhere.

6. Never pay for structural repairs on a new instrument unless you really know what you are doing.

7. Only buy an instrument that is set up or that can be, and that is worth setting up.

8. When in doubt, do not buy.

Left-Handed Players

Left-handed instruments are manufactured; sometimes they are the same price as right-handed instruments, sometimes they cost more—it depends on how the instrument has to be modified and on the company. For most beginners, however, the differences between playing right- and left-handed are negligible and it is advantageous to learn on the right hand. A special instrument is often hard to obtain, even when manufactured; it may have to be special-ordered from the manufacturer or require special work on the part of the dealer. A left-handed instrument may be harder to sell when you are ready to progress to a new instrument. And finally, there's the point expressed by Ed Sulfinger of Buck's County Folk Music Shop in New Britain, Pennsylvania: "If you're at a party and a guy is offering a ten-million-dollar contract for a banjo player and there's a right-handed banjo there, you can't take part in the talent search."

The Politics of Brands

1. Most inexpensive guitars, banjos, and mandolins (and some other instruments too) are built in Japan, Korea, or Taiwan and must say so on a visible sticker. (Sometimes the sticker is gone on used instruments.) The most expensive of these instruments are made in Japan.

2. Never buy on brand name alone. Every instrument a company makes is slightly different, and companies go through changes. They may decide to cut corners, or to stop cutting corners. Companies also change ownership, which may result in better or lesser quality instruments. Also, brand names change hands. The name "Washburn," for example, was recently resurrected by another company from the original Washburn that went out of business over fifty years ago. The new Washburns are good but do not have the same value—whether real or sentimen-

tal—as the originals. Lastly, in the low-price, foreign-dominated market, names come and go, and many instruments appear to be manufactured by the same factory or factories; some of these instruments also have no brand name.

3. Never buy a particular make of instrument because your idol uses it. For one thing, performers have special needs that may not be your needs. Guitarist X may like guitar X because it mikes well, but since you may not be using a microphone, guitar X may be a mistake for you. Furthermore, some musicians are fickle. They change instruments frequently and are sometimes paid to advertise certain brands.

Materials

Materials are chosen for their strength, durability, appearance, workability, acoustic properties, availability, and price, as well as for tradition. Generally, instruments within a given price bracket use pretty much the same materials; some materials, of course, are better than others. Although it is probably true that the better the materials, the more the builder cares about the quality of the instrument, it does not necessarily follow that using all the "right" materials guarantees a quality instrument.

Woods: Solid vs. Laminated. Laminated wood consists of two or more layers of wood, glued together. The very cheap laminated wood called plywood carries the connotation of coarse and thick. Expensive laminated wood may be called veneer and has a thin outer surface of fine wood. Solid wood used for the top, sides, and back of instruments is acknowledged to produce the best sound and should improve over time in much the same way that a good red wine improves with age. Solid wood is also more expensive than laminated wood. Because the top of most stringed instruments is the most important part acoustically, a solid top is more important than a solid back and sides. Laminated wood, though acoustically inferior to solid wood, is stronger, less prone to cracking, and perfectly acceptable—perhaps even preferable—on inexpensive instruments, especially those subjected to rough use or frequent exposure to the elements. On some instruments the top laminate may pull off, either by itself or as a result of the bridge lifting from string tension. In both cases the top is very difficult—or impossible—to repair.

Because they cost more to build and are of better quality, instruments made partially or entirely of solid wood for the top, sides, and back usually command a higher resale and trade-in value than those made of laminated woods. On some instruments, and for certain parts of other instruments, however, laminated wood is preferred for its strength and is perfectly acceptable from the point of view of sound. On chorded zithers, psalteries, harps, hammered dulcimers, and similar instruments (pianos, for example), laminated pin blocks are often used, and are very good; on an instrument like the hammered dulcimer that concentrates enormous tension across the top, a laminated top can work quite well; on fretted instruments a vertically laminated neck is both attractive and strong.

Woods and Other Materials. Softwoods are desirable for the tops of most instruments for acoustic reasons. Spruce is the most frequently used wood for most instruments. Cedar is traditionally used for the tops of flamenco guitars. Some builders and manufacturers use cedar as well as pine and redwood for the tops of other instruments. Hardwoods, such as mahogany, maple, walnut, and rosewood, make strong, stable necks and acoustically good backs and sides; very hard woods, such as ebony and rosewood, make a fingerboard extremely resistant to wear and a strong bridge; other hard materials, such as bone, ivory, plastic, brass, and sometimes ebony and rosewood, make excellent nuts and saddles, which need to resist the bite of the strings and conduct the vibrations from the strings into the body of the instrument. Nickel silver makes excellent frets because it is relatively impervious to the effects of corrosion and oxidation and constant wear. Each instrument and its own set of preferred materials will be covered in the individual chapters.

HARDWOODS

Koa - A tropical wood from Hawaii with an amber color that often possesses some dark streaks. Some koa also has a curly figure. An excellent wood.

Honduras Mahogany - A fine mahogany that works well, is stable and light, and sounds good too. It ranges in color from pinkish tan to brown, sometimes possessing a ribbon figure.

African Mahogany - Another good mahogany for instruments.

Luan or Philippine Mahogany - An inferior mahogany used primarily in cheap instruments and plywood doors.

Flamed Maple - Often called curly maple, tiger maple, or fiddleback maple. The wood has a wild, rippling figure running fairly perpendicular to the grain direction. When properly finished, the "flames" take on a three-dimensional quality that is very attractive.

Quilted Maple - The figure of the wood looks "woven," sometimes almost geometric.

Rock Maple - A hard species of maple, which can be plain or highly figured.

Brazilian Rosewood - The finest rosewood, long preferred by many luthiers. It is hard to obtain these days and therefore very costly.

Indian/East Indian Rosewood - This seems to be the "standard" rosewood of the industry these days. It ranges in color from a reddish brown to an obvious purple.

SOFTWOODS

German Spruce - Very fine, well-textured spruce that is now rare and expensive. Some prefer it to Sitka spruce; others say it makes no difference in the quality of the instrument.

Sitka Spruce - A fine spruce from Alaska and Canada. The most common wood for guitar and mandolin tops.

Western Red Cedar - A lightweight, aromatic wood used for soundboards and occasionally for necks. It ranges in color from a yellowish pink to a rich, reddish brown.

THE FINISH

The finish does three things: it protects the wood, affects the sound, and enhances the appearance. A stain has one purpose: to enhance appearance. On violins, the varnish is colored. The quality of the finish usually reflects the overall quality of an instrument; the best finishes, for example, take an extremely long time to apply. Cheap instruments often appear too slick-looking, with thickly applied lacquer or some other type of finish. Some instruments, like the Adamas guitar, are painted or decorated in other ways than staining or covering with a transparent finish.

Options

Many builders offer a variety of options on their instruments, some costing just a few dollars, others costing hundreds of dollars. Generally, the smaller a business, the easier it is to get special features. Banjos have lots of options, and so do mountain and hammered dulcimers. Many dulcimers are sold with either three or four strings (and a minute price difference) and with a choice of woods (usually quite reasonable). Hammered dulcimer options include a choice of woods, number of strings per course, and decorative work. Guitar and mandolin options are usually minimal, including choice of woods, fingerboard width, and neck inlays.

Concluding Tips and Advice

• If you're a little unsure about buying an instrument or aren't quite sure how serious you are, rent. This is an especially good idea if you're thinking of playing the banjo.

• Always comparison shop. Discounts on some premium-quality instruments run as high as 45%; strings are sometimes discounted still higher.

• Manufacturers sometimes "include" the price of a hardshell case in their list price, and some dealers also "include" a case. Be not misled. You're not getting a free case, you're paying for it: the price is tacked onto the list price of the instrument. Unless you really want or need the case (see Chapter 18), try to buy the instrument without the case; you'll save in the neighborhood of $100.

• The plainest models are the cheapest, and often the only difference between one model and another is some fancy inlaywork and from $50 to $500. Expensive imported instruments tend to be fancier than their domestic counterparts, but *very* expensive domestic instruments are the fanciest of all.

CHAPTER 3

◈ THE GUITAR ◈

Not too long ago, in the 1930s and 1940s, popular music often meant jazz, big bands, and instrumental music dominated by wind instruments like the saxophone. Sometimes the singing one heard seemed almost peripheral, as if the voice were being used as just another instrument. In the world of classical music, the piano and violin were the preeminent instruments, and the guitar was something of a relic left over from past days of glory. Folk musicians regarded the guitar as useful for accompaniment, but when it came to instrumental music and having a good time surely the fiddle was far more interesting to play and to hear. Only some blues and jazz musicians seemed to take the guitar seriously; it is from them that most of today's popular guitar music has emerged: rock 'n' roll, whether English or American, has its roots in guitar blues.

Then things began to change. With the advent of rock 'n' roll in the 1950s, the influence of jazz began to wane. The saxophone lingered on in '50s rock and in rhythm and blues, but by the late 1960s only a few groups (such as Blood, Sweat and Tears) still maintained any link with jazz. Classical musicians began to take the guitar more seriously, and

traditional musicians such as Doc Watson began, toward the late 1950s, to extend the technique of the flattop guitar and make it a far more important instrument than it had been.

By the end of the 1960s there was no doubt that the guitar had reached the top—with room to spare, as skyrocketing guitar sales were to show for almost another decade. The guitar was again important in classical music, it had reasserted its importance in jazz, it was the hottest item among bluegrass musicians, it had been picked up by white musicians who had become interested in the blues, and it was the undisputed king of rock 'n' roll.

The guitar is one of the most diverse of all instruments. Whereas basically the same violin is used to play classical, bluegrass, country, and old-time music and almost all jazz, the guitar has gone through a succession of changes designed to better adapt it to each type of music. From the classic, or Spanish, guitar came the acoustic steel-string guitar, which then got split into flattop and archtop versions. These guitars were amplified, and fully electric guitars were then built. Now some manufacturers are producing electric guitars that don't even look like guitars. Although each type of guitar seems

Classic guitar: Madeira C-60.

Six-string flattop guitar: Martin D-28.

best suited to a different type of music, you can play almost any kind of music on any guitar. Acoustical and structural differences between instruments limit the effectiveness of such a practice, however.

The *classic* guitar has six nylon strings, comes in a fairly standard size, and is the instrument of classical music. A close relative of this guitar is the flamenco guitar, which differs slightly in materials and construction and is the instrument of the passionate Spanish folk music known as flamenco. The fla-

menco guitar also has nylon strings and is built in one standard size and shape (with minor variations between various luthiers).

The *flattop* guitar has either six or twelve metal strings and is built in various sizes and shapes, is constructed differently and more sturdily than the nylon-string guitars, and is used to play almost any kind of nonclassical music, including folk, bluegrass, pop, blues, and country. Steel-string guitars are often played with the bare hands but are more often played with one or more picks.

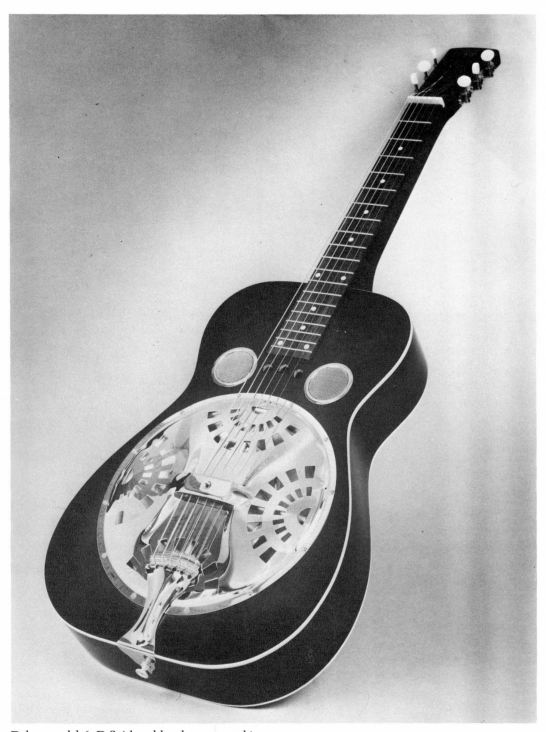

Dobro: model 6oD-S (slotted head, square neck).

The *resophonic guitar* (or "Dobro"*) has six and occasionally more steel strings and incorporates a "resonator" in the top which amplifies and modifies the sound, lending a ring and a twang that are popular in blues, country, bluegrass, and Hawaiian music.

*DOBRO is a registered trademark belonging to the Original Musical Instrument Co., Inc., used by permission.

Resophonic guitars are usually played with finger-picks and a slide. The *pedal steel* guitar is something of a cross between a resophonic guitar and an electric guitar but looks more like a purely electronic instrument than either. The pedals connect to levers holding the strings; the tuning can be changed by working the pedals.

Six-String Flattop Guitars

Archtop acoustic guitar: Epiphone Deluxe.

Flattop guitar: Martin 00–21 Grand Concert. Note twelve-fret neck, slotted head.

The *archtop* guitar has six steel strings, a body that is built the way a violin is built (arched, carved top and back) but that looks like that of a guitar, and is used mostly to play jazz, although sometimes it is used in other kinds of music. (Maybelle Carter, of the Carter Family, used an archtop.) Jazz guitarists usually play an amplified or unamplified archtop or a hollow-body electric archtop.

Martin, the fabled manufacturer of guitars, is responsible for both the names and the specifications of many guitars sold today. Unfortunately for the consumer, however, the Martin-guitar model appellations are extremely loosely used. What one company calls its grand concert model, for example, may be an exact replica of the Martin Grand Concert model, or it may be something else entirely. Perhaps

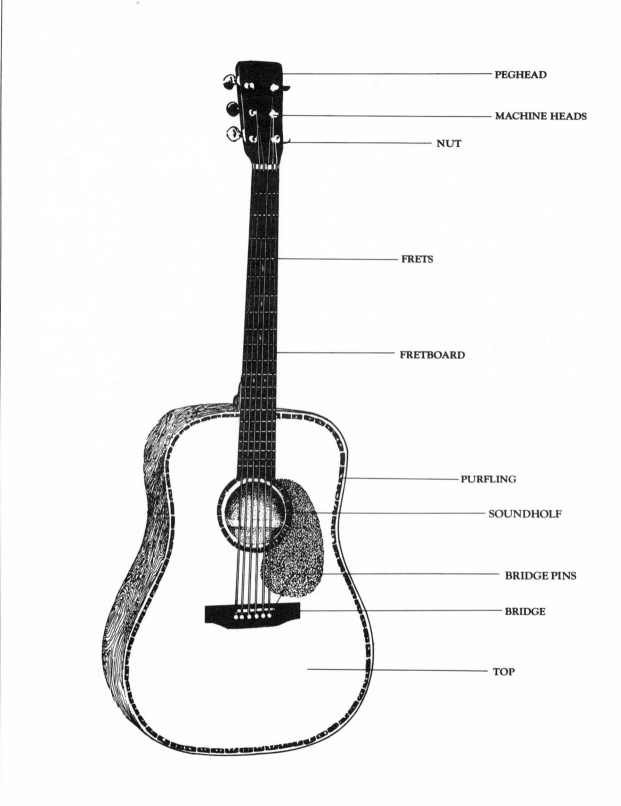

PEGHEAD

MACHINE HEADS

NUT

FRETS

FRETBOARD

PURFLING

SOUNDHOLF

BRIDGE PINS

BRIDGE

TOP

Flattop guitar schematic: Martin D-28 Dreadnought.

the only certainty is the dreadnought, which is Martin's invention and the most popular flattop guitar used. Manufacturers of dreadnought guitars either copy Martin or stick mighty close to the design.

The largest distinction between the various sizes and shapes of instruments is sound. Generally speaking, big guitars are louder than small guitars; guitars with a large bottom bout tend to be bass heavy; smaller or medium-sized guitars tend to sound evenly balanced over both the bass and the treble range.

Flatpickers tend to prefer a big guitar like a dreadnought; bluegrass musicians, especially, favor dreadnoughts, which are good for accompaniment. But a flatpicker who does a lot of solo work may want a big guitar with a more balanced tone, and so some dreadnoughts are specially designed to achieve just this. Fingerpickers often like smaller guitars that have a more balanced tone; they don't need as much volume as a bluegrass guitarist, for example, who is playing in a band.

Twelve-String Flattop Guitars

Twelve-string guitars are also made in various sizes and shapes, but most common are the jumbo and dreadnought pictured on this page. Some twelve-string guitars have a slotted head (as do some six-string guitars), like that on a classic guitar.

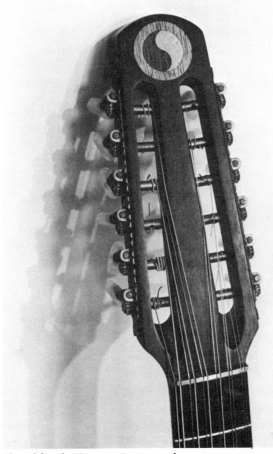

Slotted head, Neptune Rising twelve-string guitar.

Twelve-string flattop guitar: Guild F-512 NT.

Resophonic Guitars

Because by far the most common resophonic guitar is the Dobro, people tend to call all such guitars Dobros, the same way we often call any soft drink Coke, even if it's orange soda. Other resophonic guitars are made by custom builders and now and then by a larger company—which usually goes defunct. For these reasons, only Dobros are going to be discussed. Obtain information about other instruments by contacting the custom builders in the directory of builders and manufacturers at the end of this chapter.

Dobros are built with six, eight, or ten strings and various kinds of bodies, resonator systems, and necks. According to Ron Lazar of Original Musical Instruments, the manufacturer of the Dobro, most wood-bodied instruments with Dobro resonators are used for bluegrass and Hawaiian music; most metal-bodied Dobros with Dobro resonators are used for Hawaiian music; and most metal-bodied instruments with National-type resonators are used for playing bottleneck blues. The square-necked Dobros are used mainly for playing the instrument lap style; the round-necked instrument is suited for other types of playing.

Classic Guitars

Classic guitars are all built pretty much to the same specifications:

Total length - about 39½"
Width - 14–14½"
Depth - 3½–4"
Nut width - 2–2¼"

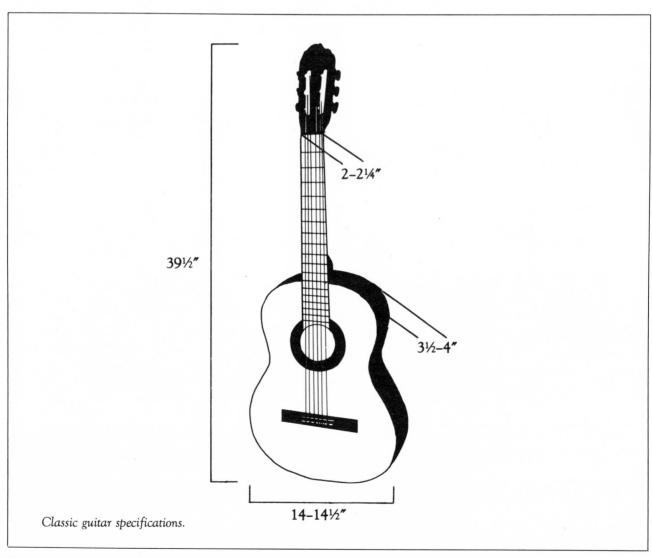

Classic guitar specifications.

INTERVIEW WITH DOC WATSON

In the years since he was "discovered" back in the early 1960s, Doc Watson has inspired countless musicians, guitarists, and nonmusicians with his tasteful, inspiring versions of traditional and modern songs, and has left his mark on the history of the guitar. He was not the first to exploit the virtuoso potential of the steel-string flattop guitar, but he has been the most prominent of those responsible for bringing this guitar into the spotlight. Although Doc's initial appeal is often his dazzling guitar work, he is really a superb all-around musician.

Few of the flashy guitarists he has inspired are as inspiring or play with as much feeling.

Doc played a concert at the Beacon Theater in New York City in February 1981. The audience was large, attentive, and also rather noisy in its appreciation of both the legendary guitarist and the excellent Seldom Scene. About ten minutes before the Seldom Scene went on, Doug Tuchman, the impressario, signaled me to go upstairs, and it was there, in the dilapidated "green room," that I spoke with Arthel "Doc" Watson.

A lot of people play fast these days, but few play with the kind of feeling you have.

Feeling is sixty percent of it. And I don't care technically how good you are. If you don't got a little soul to go with it, I think something's missing. You really have to appreciate what the music says and know that and be able to feel that before you can perform or play that. Some people hear it technically and see it as flashy stuff, but I don't. Occasionally for kicks I'll do something real speeded up for the audience—to get them to sit on the edge of their seats—but the real thing of doing a concert is getting right down there and, as Michael [Michael Coleman, his bass player] says, *play* it.

Even when you're flashy you seem to be reserved, keeping something back.

The bit about reserved and being musical— this may throw you—that's not something you manufacture yourself, it's part of a talent. Every man that's a musician, or an artist in any way, shape, or form, is born with the talent for that particular thing that he might get into. The taste or feeling is there, you just have to develop your abilities. I don't think it's something I could do and then say "Hey, look here at what I did. . . ." You've either got it or you don't. To be truly musical is a talent you're born with, like any other thing you have an aptitude to do.

Do you consider yourself a singer who plays guitar or a guitarist who also sings?

It's just about equal. I love good songs, that say things, whether they're humorous or very serious ballads, or whatever.

What attracts you to a song?

If it has something to say about any given, whether it's joy, sorrow, or the in-betweens, and if the music has feeling along the same lines I might enjoy it and like it.

Do you work out tunes in a certain kind of way?

I seldom ever do it in exactly the same note pattern unless it's an absolute arrangement or something like . . . "Tennessee Stud" will be the same, but just some good old pickin' thing—I might play it different tonight than I played it last night or I'd play it tomorrow night. In other words, I improvise a good bit, especially in the pickin' things.

I've always felt you've exhausted all the possibilities when you've worked out a song.

No, not always. Sometimes it's done spontaneous.

Maybe on your recordings . . .

It would be spontaneous on the recordings, or live—either one. Usually I will have done most of the licks at one time or another before, or note patterns, or phrasings, and I will change it a bit, but not totally. I guess it's all in your head to start with, the notes are unconsciously there and they come out and you get really inspired, you know.

What are your most memorable experiences with other musicians, and the biggest challenges?

The first challenge to me was a big thing, *Just Plain Old Country Boys*, the album I did with Lester and Earl in 1967, and the next big thing was the album with Chet [Atkins]. He's been sort of my ideal for years as a guitar player, and that was a challenge. We wasted one day, totally, of session, and next day we just went and sat down and picked. Neither one of us was afraid to bother the other person's style the next day.... Chet is just an old country boy ... and loves the guitar better than he loves to eat. I don't love the guitar that good.... I love the guitar, but not as good as Chet does. I think he sleeps, eats, and breathes guitar, but as good as I was I was never that devoted to it. In other words, my love of life and living are split among other things.

Have you done everything you've wanted to do with your music?

Now, that one I'll have to leave absolutely sittin' on the fence. I don't know.

Do you have a vision of where you're heading?

No, I just like to play, and if I hear something new that I want to learn, even though it may be an old song, I'd like to learn it. And if a good new lick, improvisation comes along on the guitar that I can memorize after it came out of an inspired moment, I will. I don't think you ever quit learning.

How have you seen your audiences change over the years?

Well, I don't know—they've grown a lot. A lot of the festivals are awfully noisy, but—on the other hand, Wednesday night we had a concert, a sellout, at Harvard, and that audience, you would not believe, they were super attentive ... and there were even people sitting on the stage around us, but you wouldn't know

it until they applauded.

Are concert audiences better than festival audiences?

Concert audiences are always better, college or no, and we still draw quite a few of the same people who came to hear me and Merle in the sixties.... I find concert audiences much more rewarding than festivals. You may have sixty percent of the people who are really there to listen, but you will get that forty percent who are there to get their kicks on something and make noise.

Can younger urban musicians play old-time music with the same kind of feeling...

I've been asked that question a whole lot and I wouldn't dare give you a definite answer. I don't really know. Let me ask you a question. How could you know what a live oak tree smelled like when you cut it in two with a saw unless you'd done it? You may extract some feeling of being in the woods if somebody'd give you an absolute description of the sounds and smells and sights of it, but you couldn't really know.

Do you teach at all?

No, I don't have the patience....

What do you have to say to all those people who want to study with you and can't?

Yes, sir, a very simple thing. If you're already playing the guitar, play what you *feel*, not what you hear somebody else play. Once you get started enough, you can innovate on your own.... Do your own thing.

Selecting a Guitar

Few guitarists begin on a Dobro or a twelve-string guitar. Says Stan Werbin of Elderly Instruments in East Lansing, Michigan: "Often twelve-string guitars are difficult to deal with—harder to tune, tougher on the fingers. The beginner gets discouraged and gives up playing (especially if the guitar hasn't been set up well). We recommend a twelve-string only as a person's second guitar, that is, they should own a six-string one too, because a twelve-string is just not as versatile." Each of these instruments requires a special way of being played, or involves special problems that a beginner would do best to avoid for a while. Start on a regular six-string guitar and later on, if you wish, learn to play one of these other instruments.

Your choice of a first guitar makes a lot of difference in how you come along in learning to play it. For some people any guitar is equally easy—or difficult—to play. But other beginners need all the help they can get, and for these people two kinds of instruments are recommended: a classic guitar, or a small or medium-sized steel-string flattop guitar—*not* a jumbo or a dreadnought. A classic guitar is small and easy to hold and has a roomy fingerboard; the nylon strings are especially good for people with tender fingers. A small or medium-sized flattop guitar lacks the volume of a larger guitar, but the more intimate sound may be what you want; volume is not that important during the learning period. Many people find such a guitar is much easier to move around on and to hold than a dreadnought.

PLAYABILITY

Tuning up. Have someone tune the guitar, or tune it yourself. Tune the *sixth* string to an E below middle C, using a tuning device or a piano. Now depress the string at the fifth fret (between the fourth and fifth frets), play the note, and match this pitch of the *fifth* string to this pitch—A. Depress the fifth string at the fifth fret, play the note, and match the pitch of the *fourth* string to this pitch—D. Depress the fourth string at the fifth fret, play the note, and match the pitch of the *third* string to this pitch—G. Depress the third string at the *fourth* fret, play the note, and match the pitch of the *second* string to this pitch—B. Depress the second string at the fifth fret, play the note, and match the pitch of the *first* string to this pitch—E again. You may have to readjust the two Es, and once you play a few chords you may have to fine tune a little more.

Machine Heads. When you tuned the guitar, were the tuners easy to turn? And now that you are in tune,

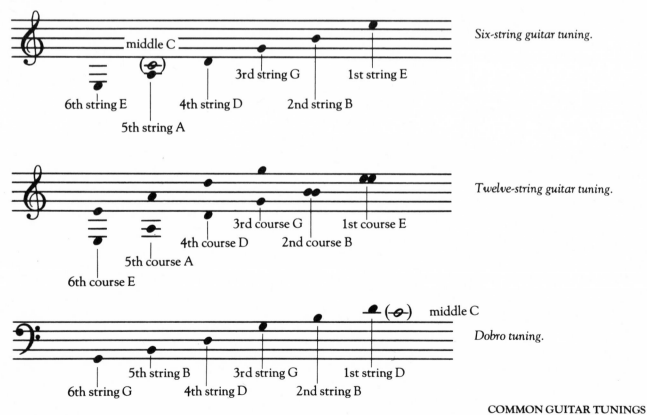

Six-string guitar tuning.

middle C

6th string E   5th string A   4th string D   3rd string G   2nd string B   1st string E

Twelve-string guitar tuning.

6th course E   5th course A   4th course D   3rd course G   2nd course B   1st course E

Dobro tuning.

middle C

6th string G   5th string B   4th string D   3rd string G   2nd string B   1st string D does the instrument stay in tune, or do the tuners slip? Keep in mind that both brand-new strings and a brand-new guitar may need a period of adjustment until they will *stay* in tune. Old strings may neither get in tune nor stay in tune.

The Neck. The neck is the most vulnerable and critical part of a guitar; a guitar with a warped neck may be totally unplayable. Sight down the fingerboard and make sure it is straight. Then make sure the fingerboard has a slight frontward curvature by pressing the first string at the first and the twelfth or fourteenth frets (wherever the neck joins the body) and measuring the clearance (with your eye) over the sixth or seventh fret (the halfway point)—it should be no more than 1/32 of an inch. Do the same on the sixth string; slightly more clearance is okay.

On a classic guitar the curvature should be built into the fingerboard, but on a steel-string guitar the curvature is maintained by a delicate balance between the pull of the strings and the counter-pull of a truss rod. Twelve-string guitars sometimes have two truss rods. Sometimes the curvature has to be—and can be—adjusted by adjusting the rod, *if* the rod is adjustable.

Most guitars and nearly all Dobros do have an adjustable neck; only the very cheapest and some very expensive guitars have a nonadjustable neck. The best advice is to simply avoid buying a guitar with a warped neck; but if the neck can be easily adjusted and the guitar is otherwise worth buying, go ahead and take it home. Keep in mind that adjusting the tension rod cures only some ailments.

Also pay attention to the feel of the neck. Classic, some twelve-fret-neck six-string flattop guitars, and twelve-string guitars have a wider fingerboard than the typical steel-string guitar. Some guitars have big, clunky necks; others have slim, fast necks.

Action. If anything is discouraging about playing guitar it is strings that cut grooves in your fingertips and cause pain, so check the action carefully. Action is set at the factory or by the builder and varies a great deal between brands and models, but even the best companies cannot please everyone. Flatpickers prefer higher action than fingerpickers, for example, and beginners need the lowest action of all. Inexpensive guitars invariably have the most problems with action; many need adjustment.

Average string height above the fourteenth fret is about 4/32 of an inch for the sixth string and 3/32 of an inch for the first string, for a flattop guitar. Rather than approach the guitar with a ruler, approach it with your fingers and play something, anything—just press the strings, if that's all you can do—to see if the strings are easy or hard to press. Pay the most attention to the parts of the fingerboard just above the nut and nearest the bridge, where the strings are highest. Trying some different guitars will give you an idea of differences in action, and will help you understand what is easy and what is hard. You can check the action at nut more scientifically, however. Press each string, one at a time, between the second and the third frets and make sure the clearance above the first fret is no more than the thickness of a business card.

Intonation. First, make sure the bridge is in the right place. Lightly touch the sixth string over the twelfth fret with one finger on your left hand and with your other hand pluck the string until you hear the harmonic. This is a bit tricky, but after a few tries you should succeed. Depress the string all the way to the fret and play that note. The two pitches should be identical. Perform the same test on the first string. Although guitar bridges are almost always glued to the top, they can be repositioned by an experienced repairperson or else the saddle can be worked on.

Now check the fret positions. They are almost always correct, but extremely cheap guitars and some handmade instruments may have problems. Obviously when a fret is in the wrong place, the instrument will play out of tune. Work your way up the fingerboard, a note at a time, on each string. Toward the top the increased tension on the strings may cause the pitches to go sharp, especially if the action is too high. Determining whether the frets are in the right place may be hard for a novice.

Frets. The frets should be smooth, high, rounded, and flush with the edges of the fingerboard.

Number of Frets to Body. Classic guitars and some flattop guitars have twelve frets on the neck before it joins the body; other guitars usually have fourteen frets. The longer neck makes the frets closer to the bridge more accessible.

Scale Length. Since scale length affects playability and sound, find out how long it is. Here are some standards:

Six-String Flattop - 25.4″ (so-called long scale of the Martin D-28)

24.9″ (so-called short scale of the Martin 000-18)

Twelve-String Flattop - 25 5/8″ (scale of Guild guitars)

Dobro - 24.5″

Classic Guitar - 25.5–26.5″

CONDITION AND STUCTURAL INTEGRITY

Tap the top, sides, and back to check for rattling, which may indicate a loose brace or a crack. The sound should be solid. Check the entire instrument for cracks, open seams, defects in the finish and wood, loose binding. On used guitars check the soundboard for excessive warping and make sure the bridge is secure. New or old, a guitar should be structurally sound.

MATERIALS AND HARDWARE

Traditional Steel-String Guitar. The best guitars usually have a solid spruce (and sometimes a solid cedar or koa) top; solid rosewood, maple, koa, or mahogany sides and back; mahogany neck; ebony bridge and fingerboard; ivory or bone nut and saddle (some good companies also use synthetics); and nickel-silver frets. The machine heads are enclosed. Although most guitarists prefer the tonal qualities of rosewood for the sides and back, some musicians like other woods. Some companies use a brass or laminated brass/bone nut, which may affect the tone. And many companies use the excellent machine heads manufactured by Grover or Schaller.

Applause, Matrix, Ovation, and Adamas Steel-String Guitars. These guitars, all manufactured by the same company, utilize some nontraditional materials and must be considered on their own terms. All four lines incorporate the same feature which has become one of the trademarks of this type of guitar: a bowl-shaped back (deep or shallow) made of Lyramold ® or Lyrachord ®, materials similar to fiber glass and nearly identical except for the formation process. The Applause line has an aluminum neck with the frets, fingerboard, and neck cast in one piece. The Matrix is kind of a cross between the Applause and the more expensive Ovation, having a rosewood fingerboard, nickel-silver frets, and aluminum neck core. The Adamas, which is the top of the line, and the Ovation have a hardwood neck and a traditional fingerboard and frets. Soundboard materials vary. The Applause has a laminated spruce top, the Matrix a solid spruce top, the Ovation a solid spruce top, and the Adamas a special top made of "carbon fibers in a sandwich construction with birch veneer as a core material" (according to the brochure); the Adamas top is partially synthetic. Ovation tops are graded A, AA, etc., which refer to the flexibility of the spruce. All of the guitars have a walnut bridge.

It is clear that nontraditionally designed guitars made from a mixture of traditional and nontraditional materials or solely from nontraditional materials have found a sizeable market and numerous converts. Which goes to show there is no one way of doing things.

Dobro. The laminated woods used on this instrument are acceptable because the amount of metal in the top makes a fine piece of solid spruce useless.

Classic Guitars. In brief: the best classic guitars have a solid spruce or cedar top; solid rosewood back, sides, and bridge; mahogany neck; ebony fingerboard; ivory or bone nut and saddle.

Ovation Custom Legend acoustic-electric six-string flattop guitar.

GUITAR DESIGN FEATURES

Consult a guide to guitar repair or construction (see p. 43) for more information on design and construction.

Braces. Braces are needed to offset the pull of the strings on the bridge and top. Builders seek a compromise between strength and responsiveness; that is, thinner braces allow the top to vibrate more freely but do not provide much strength. One compromise on flattop guitars is scalloped bracing, which frees the sound without significantly weakening the instrument. Although many builders assert that scalloped bracing on a big, bass-heavy guitar such as a dreadnought frees the treble range and therefore creates a more balanced sound—and aim for just this effect on their instruments—sometimes (and intentionally) the effect is just the opposite, that is, the sound becomes still more bass heavy. Make sure you understand what the builder is using the scalloping to accomplish and then verify that the results are what you want.

Bridge. On a classic guitar the strings are tied to the bridge, while on most steel-string guitars the strings are held in place with bridge pins. Some inexpensive guitars have an adjustable bridge; some very cheap guitars (and almost all archtop guitars) have a tailpiece to which the strings are attached. Although metal in the bridge deadens the tone, a beginner may find the ability to adjust the action convenient.

Cutaway. Some guitars have a cutaway body that makes the upper frets more accessible. This is usually an optional feature that costs more.

Machine Heads. Classic guitars commonly have the heads mounted in two groups of three, while flattop guitars have them mounted individually. But flattop guitars with a slotted headstock and some very cheap guitars have the heads in groups of three. Many twelve-string guitars have the heads in groups of six.

Neck (Truss) Rod. On most flattop guitars, the neck rod(s) is adjustable at the peghead, but on some guitars the rod(s) is adjustable through the sound-hole. Proponents of the latter design argue that the rod can be longer (and therefore offer greater strength), that there's no unsightly truss-rod cover on the peghead, and that players inclined to tamper unnecessarily or frequently with the rod (the truss rod is easily broken) will be discouraged from so doing.

Saddle. On most guitars, the saddle is slanted with the treble end closer to the neck to improve intonation; some saddles are compensated (see Glossary).

Top bracing systems.

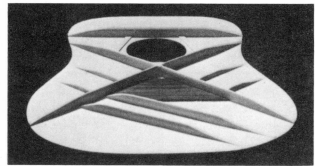

X bracing on Martin D-28.

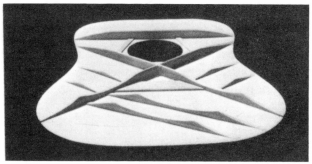

Scalloped bracing on Martin HD-28.

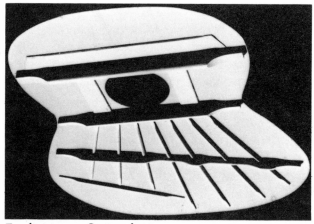

Fan bracing on Gurian classic.

DOBRO DESIGN FEATURES

Headstock. Dobros are built with either a solid or a slotted headstock. The slotted head is more traditional, cheaper, and more convenient for playing lap style: the tuning machines are easier to get at.

Resonator. Most Dobros made today come with one of two types of resonator. Cone resonators are almost always used on metal-bodied instruments and tend to make the sound twangier than that of instruments with a Dobro resonator, which sustains the sound more. Cone resonators, in turn, are made in several sizes. The Duolian® has a 9½-inch cone and is used mainly for playing bottleneck blues, while the other metal-bodied instruments have a 10½-inch cone. The smaller cone produces a more banjo-like and twangy sound with a faster decay than the larger cone. The Duolian® has a funkier sound, and the instrument is modeled after the old National that was so popular with blues guitarists.

BINDING, PURFLING, INLAYS, MARQUETRY

Perhaps the most famous purfling design is the much imitated herringbone pattern found on the original Martin D-28 herringbone and on the current Martin HD-28. Abalone is sometimes used on very expensive instruments. Sometimes the soundhole of a guitar is purfled or inlaid with marquetry. Other decoration includes inlay on the back as well as on the peghead, a carved heel, engraving on the pickguard, mother-of-pearl (m.o.p., or pearl) dots in the bridge pins, and gold plating on the machine heads. We're here speaking mostly of flattop guitars. On a steel-string guitar, position markers are often inlaid on the fingerboard; sometimes these are simple dots, sometimes intricate designs that may be more ornamental than functional. Classic guitars usually have plain fingerboards, though a few dots may be placed on the side of the fingerboard; in general, classic guitars are far plainer looking than their steel-string counterparts. Binding should protect the edges as well as please the eye. Since a good portion of the price of many expensive guitars reflects the amount of ornamentation, make sure the workmanship and quality are first rate.

AFTER YOU FORK OUT YOUR MONEY

After you play your guitar for a few weeks or months, certain changes may occur in the instrument. The string tension pulling upward on the neck may increase the neck relief and change the action.

Herringbone purfling, Martin HD-28.

The sound will probably begin to change too, especially on a guitar with a solid top. The wood dries out, the instrument experiences climatic changes (it may have been built in a temperature- and humidity-controlled shop and now it's in Dallas in August), and the instrument adapts to being played. A repairperson will help you make the necessary adjustments. Eventually a guitar becomes played-in, seasoned; if you're lucky and it's a good guitar and you also treat it well, you could wind up with a prize specimen.

Money Matters

New guitars sell from under $100 to more than $3000. The largest selection falls in the $200–500 bracket. Used guitars sell from under $100 to more than $5000, with a wide selection of quality instruments in the $400–1000 bracket.

Six-String Flattop Guitar

First Guitar: Under $250. Buy a guitar with a solid top, which is possible only if you obtain a discount or acquire a used instrument. If you must buy a new guitar at list price, try to spend no more than $200 for an instrument with a laminated top.

$250–400. Buy a Guild or a guitar with all solid wood; again, a discounted or used instrument will be necessary. Failing to obtain the preceding, buy a guitar with a solid top.

$400–600. Buy either a Guild or an all-solid-wood guitar. A lot of the imported guitars in this bracket simply get fancier-looking without really improving their fundamental quality.

$600–1200. This instrument should either have all solid woods or be a Guild (some Guilds have a laminated back). Guitars built by individuals and small shops are often not discounted, so Guilds and Martins may be better buys. *Tone* ought to be a major part of your considerations. Most instruments built by luthiers or large manufacturers just entering the field after about $700 tend to be basic, unornamented.

Over $1200. Perhaps all that can be said about these instruments is that they ought to please you a lot in all ways: tone, playability, cosmetics, materials, etc.

Twelve String Guitar

Twelve-string guitars run somewhat higher in price than their six-string counterparts. Those with a solid top start about $30 higher, those with all solid wood about $200 higher. Size is not the main reason for the cost differential, since most twelve-strings are not much larger than similarly shaped six-string models. You should be paying for heavier bracing, a stronger neck, and the other features necessary to build a stronger instrument that still sounds good.

Under $400. Although there are some quite inexpensive instruments, do not be stingy. You are probably buying the twelve-string as a second guitar,

Cutaway flattop: Greven single Florentine, model FX Deluxe.

National Triolian (ca. 1928), with wood body.

and you may not be able to go out a year later to buy a better model. If you are on a low budget, get the best instrument you can afford; by all means look for a good deal. Buy a guitar with a solid top.

$400–700. In the list-price category, this price bracket has a pitifully small selection. Look for a discount on a guitar of a higher list price. Herein the more serious player can find quite a good instrument for not too much money, whether it is a first or second twelve-string.

$700–1100. At list price there are some high-quality instruments in this bracket, and at a discount there are also some companies' top-of-the-line models. Get an instrument with all solid wood.

$1100 and above. Most instruments are built by individuals or in small shops. Some luthiers build one model in progressively fancier versions.

Resophonic Guitar

The choice is between a Dobro and an instrument made by individual builders or in small shops. Again, the plainnest models are the best buys.

Classic Guitar

Don't buy an expensive classic guitar if you plan to buy a steel-string guitar eventually. Decent instruments can be obtained for under $250; a solid top is desirable but not really essential.

Kits, Plans, Lutherie Schools, Materials

Thomas A. Bednark, Box 13, Centerville, MA 02632. Guitar kits and plans.

Elderly Instruments, P.O. Box 1795, East Lansing, MI 48823. Instrument plans.

Guild of American Luthiers, 8222 S. Park Ave., Tacoma, WA 98408. Information on various aspects of lutherie; list of lutherie schools.

Gurian Guitars, Box 595, West Swanzey, NH 03469. Materials.

CF Martin, Nazareth, PA 18064. Guitar kit.

Accessories

Slide. A slide is used to play slide/bottleneck-style on either a resophonic guitar or a regular flattop guitar. Some folks make their own.

Glass
Ceramic } $1.00–2.50
Metal

Replacement Parts: Six-String Flattop Guitar

Bridge Pins
Ebony with Mother-of-Pearl Inlay (six pins)—$5.10*
Ebony (6)—$2.40*
Plastic (black) (12)—$0.72*

End Pins
Ebony (1)—$0.50
Martin End Pin and Bridge Pin Set (black)—$2.75

Machine Heads
Grover Rotomatic (solid headstock) (chrome plated)—About $37
Schaller (solid headstock) (chrome plated)—$42

Guitar Brands, Builders, and Manufacturers

Adamas See Ovation. Top-of-the-line guitar.

∾

Alvaraz and **Alvarez-Yairi** (St. Louis Music Supply Co., 1400 Ferguson, St. Louis, MO 63133). An imported line with a fairly good reputation. Available through dealers.

∾

Applause (C. Bruno & Son, 20 Old Windsor Rd., Bloomfield, CT 06002). The Applause is an inexpensive version of the Ovation. See Ovation.

∾

Aria and **Aria Pro II** (Music Distributors, Inc., 3400 Darby, Charlotte, NC 28216). Another reputable imported line of guitars.

Adamas acoustic-electric flattop guitar.

Applause flattop guitar.

Bozo six-string cutaway guitar.

Bozo (Bozo Musical Strings, 2726 University Ave., San Diego, CA 92104). Bozo Podunavac, who has been building guitars for thirty-one years, is one of the most innovative luthiers around. His instruments are very good. Available from Bozo.

❦

Carlos (C. Bruno & Son, 20 Old Windsor Rd., Bloomfield, CT 06002). An inexpensive line of guitars. Sold through dealers.

Bozo double cutaway twelve-string guitar.

Dobro (Original Musical Instrument Co., 18108 Redondo Circle, Huntington Beach, CA 92648). Dobros have been built for over fifty years and are still extremely good instruments. The price guide includes only some of OMI's many models. Write for a brochure ($1). Sold through dealers.

❦

Fender (Fender Musical Instruments, 1300 Valencia, Fullerton, CA 92631). Famous for its electric basses, electric guitars, and amplifiers, Fender now has a line of acoustic guitars built overseas that compare favorably to other imports. Sold through dealers.

❦

Franklin (Guitars Friend, Rt. 1, Box 200, Sandpoint, ID 83864). Franklin, a small company, has been building guitars since 1975. The "OM is styled after the fingerpicker's favorite, the revolutionary 1930 Martin OM," says their brochure. Order from Guitars Friend. Lifetime warranty.

Franklin Jumbo (left) and OM (right) models.

Gallagher (J. W. Gallagher & Son, Wartrace, TN 37183). These excellent, no-nonsense guitars are built in limited quantity (135–150 each year), and have good resonance, clarity, and projection. Available through some dealers and from Gallagher. Lifetime warranty.

∽

Gibson c/o Norlin Music, 7373 N. Cicero Ave., Lincolnwood, IL 60646). Gibson is one of the pioneers in the industry, and certain old Gibson guitars are valuable or make interesting collectors' items. New Gibsons are available through dealers.

Givens (Box 642, Sandpoint, ID 83864). R. L. Givens and his small staff have a good reputation as guitar makers. Order direct.

∽

Gréven (Box 289, Rt. 3, Nashville, IN 47448). Ever since 1964 John Gréven has been making fine guitars. He works mostly on a custom basis. Available through some dealers and direct; direct orders take four to twelve months to fill. Lifetime warranty.

Gréven peghead inlay.

Guild (225 West Grand St., P.O. Box 203, Elizabeth, NJ 07207). Founded in 1952, Guild has established itself as a reliable company dedicated to producing high-quality instruments at reasonable prices. Guild guitars are very popular and an excellent value, and the twelve-string guitars are considered the finest built by a large company; they set the standard in the industry. Available through dealers.

Guild G-312 twelve-string guitar. Note dreadnought body.

Gurian Size 3 guitar.

Gurian (Box 595, West Swanzey, NH 03469). Michael Gurian is one of the more innovative guitar manufacturers, and his instruments have a good reputation. Five people work at Gurian Guitars, building twelve instruments a week. The guitars have low action, are easy to play, and are particularly good for fingerpicking. Available through dealers. Lifetime warranty (for steel-string guitars).

∽

Hoffman (2219 E. Franklin Ave., Minneapolis, MN 55404). Charles Hoffman has a fine reputation.

∽

Ibanez (Elger Distributors, P.O. Box 469, 1716 Winchester Rd., Ben Salem, PA 19020). Ibanez is an imported line with a good reputation. Available through dealers.

∽

R. Q. Jones (P.O. Box 143, Wanette, OK 74878). Jones, who has been building resophonic guitars since 1974, says that his instruments appeal "to the professional or more advanced musician." Order direct.

∽

Krimmel (Wallstreet, Salina Star Route, Boulder, CO 80302). Max Krimmel has a good reputation as a luthier. Order direct.

∽

Bernard Lehmann (34 Elton St., Rochester, NY 14607). Lehmann has been building guitars since 1971, works alone, and finishes about six each year. One of his main concerns is harmony of design. Order direct; delivery takes six months. Lifetime warranty.

∽

LoPrinzi (LoPrinzi Guitars, 16 Model Ave., Hopewell, NJ 08525).

∽

Madeira (Guild Guitars, 225 W. Grand St., P.O. Box 203, Elizabeth, NJ 07207). Madeira is Guild's (imported) entry into the budget-guitar field. Although there is a good selection, the line does not contain guitars with cosmetic differences. Sold through dealers.

Martin oo-45 Grand Concert.

Martin (CF Martin Organisation, Nazareth, PA 18064). Martin, which has been a family-run operation since its founding in 1833, has grown but remains dedicated to quality and tradition. Martin's dreadnought guitar, introduced about fifty years ago, is the most copied flattop guitar in the world, and Martin guitars are the standard of the steel-string-guitar industry. Available through dealers, often heavily discounted. Most of Martin's smaller guitars must be special-ordered; write for information or ask your dealer. Five-year warranty. Martin also has a Custom Shop to do special work.

Matrix. See Ovation. An entry between the Applause and the Ovation.

Mossman (2101 E. 9 St., Winfield, KS 67156). Stuart Mossman has a fine reputation. His instruments use a special "I-beam" bracing; supposedly this has the same effect as scalloped bracing in opening up the treble range, but it is claimed to be stronger. Available from Mossman.

Neptune Rising (P.O. Box 834, New Glarus, WI 52574). Write Dennis O'Brien for information.

Neptune Rising custom guitar.

Ovation (Ovation Instruments, Inc., Blue Hill Ave. Ext., Bloomfield, CT 06002). Ovation is one of the most innovative instrument manufacturers of the century. There is still a great deal of prejudice against these instruments by traditional luthiers and by dealers and players, but these guitars are well made, popular, and here to stay. Their acoustic-electrics are highly acclaimed. Ovation guitars (and the other lines, such as Adamas) have a balanced sound that some find boring, "too balanced." Ovations are good for recording as well as for traveling (they're easily replaced, unlike handmade instruments). Sold through dealers.

Petillo (1206 Herbert Ave., Ocean, NJ 07712). Phillip Petillo is another highly regarded luthier.

Santa Cruz Guitar Company model FTC with flat top, arched back, and single Venetian cutaway.

Santa Cruz Guitar Company (328 Ingalls Ave., Santa Cruz, CA 95060). Founded in 1976, this small company now builds forty to forty-eight guitars per year. "At the present," Richard Hoover, one of the two partners, says, "two-thirds of our instruments are built according to custom specifications." The FTC model is "designed . . . to meet the standards of acoustic jazz guitarists. The H model is patterned after the Gibson Nick Lucas Special and is recommended "for fingerpickers and lead players who like the sweet sound of small guitars but need more volume." Available through dealers and from SCGC; direct orders take four to eight months to fill. One-year warranty.

Sho-Bro (Shot Jackson's Guitar and Service Center, 416 Broadway, Nashville, TN 37203). The Sho-Bro is a custom-built resophonic guitar. You have a choice of woods and number of strings. Shot Jackson says, "We don't use the circle sound ring in there; we use a sound post upon a smaller, thinner sound ring of hard maple, which gives better sustaining quality and makes the notes seem to be a little larger."

Shot Jackson playing Sho-Bro, with his wife, Donna Darlene.

Sigma (CF Martin Organization, Nazareth, PA 18064). Sigmas are essentially budget-priced guitars built in the Orient to the specifications of Martin. Good quality for the money. Available through dealers.

Somogyi (3052 Telegraph Ave., Berkeley, CA 94705). Irwin Somogyi has a very good reputation as a luthier.

Takamine (C. Bruno & Son, 20 Old Windsor Rd., Bloomfield, CT 06002). Takamines, which are manufactured in the Orient, have a reputation for being, along with Yamaha, among the best inexpensive guitars. You probably can't go wrong with one of these. Sold through dealers.

Taylor (7936 Lester Ave., Lemon Grove, CA 92045). Taylor produces instruments ranging from midrange to very high prices. A three-man operation, it builds about three hundred instruments a year. Kurt Lasteg, one of the partners, says the 500s are for "someone looking for a great-quality guitar for the money"; 700s are a "good bluegrass guitar. Traditional sound"; 800s are for "the player who can hear the difference"; 900s are for "people who want a bright sound or a choice collector's-item-type guitar." Available from dealers or from Taylor.

Washburn (Fretted Industries, 1415 Waukegan Rd., Northbrook, IL 60202). These imported instruments sport the old Washburn name (same name, different manufacturer). There's a wide selection of these low- to medium-priced guitars. Available through dealers.

Yamaha (Yamaha International Corp., Box 6600, Buena Park, CA 90622). Yamaha, a Japanese-based company founded in 1887, is a highly regarded manufacturer of guitars. Yamahas are known for their consistent quality, sound, and sturdiness. Some of the older instruments, from the 1960s, are sought after today. Yamaha's inexpensive instruments are highly recommended. Available through dealers.

Discography

STEEL-STRING GUITAR: SIX- AND TWELVE-STRING FLATTOP, ARCHTOP, NATIONAL

Atkins, Chet, and Doc Watson. *Chet Atkins/Doc Watson: Reflections* (RCA AHL1-3701).

Barbeque Bob. *Chocolate to the Bone* (Mamlish 3808). Twelve-string guitarist.

Basho, Robbie. *Art of the Acoustic Steel-String Guitar: 6 & 12.* (Windhan Hill). Basho is an interesting player who might be grouped with Fahey and Kottke—although all three have different styles.

Blind Blake. *Bootleg Rum Dum Blues* (Biograph 12003) and *Search Warrant Blues* (Biograph 12023). Funky fingerstyle player. Other albums also available on Biograph.

Broonzy, Big Bill. *Do That Guitar Rag* (Yazoo 1035), *1935-42* (Biograph C-15), and *Young Big Bill Broonzy* (Yazoo 1011). One of the greats.

Cotten, Elizabeth (Libba). *Negro Folk Songs and Tunes* (Folkways 3526) and *Shake Sugaree* (Folkways 31003). Important, influential musician. *Country Girls* (Origin Jazz Library 6).

Crary, Dan. *Lady's Fancy* (Rounder 0099) and *Bluegrass Guitar* (American Heritage 27). Incredible flatpicker.

Fahey, John. *Blind Joe Death* (Takoma 7002) and *Death Chants, Breakdowns, and Military Waltzes* (Takoma 7003). Highly inventive modern fingerpicking guitarist.

Hurt, Mississippi John. *In 1928* (Yazoo 1065), *Volume 1 of a Legacy* (Piedmont 1068), and *Worried Blues* (Piedmont 13161). A thoroughly enjoyable musician. Fingerstyle. Many more albums available on various labels.

Johnson, Blind Willie. *Blind Willie Johnson (1927-1930)* (Folkways RF-10) and *Blind Willie Johnson; Blues* (Folkways 3585). Gospel blues. One of the most inspired musicians who has ever recorded.

Johnson, Lonnie. *Mr. Johnson's Blues* (Mamlish 3807). Jazz and blues great.

Johnson, Robert. *King of the Delta Blues Singers*, Vols. 1 & 2 (Columbia CL-1654 & C-30034). Quirky, inspired, forceful. An amazing, influential bluesman without peer.

Kottke, Leo. *6 and 12 String Guitar* (Takoma 7024). Especially fine and popular player specializing in twelve-string work.

Lang, Eddie, with Carl Kress and Lonnie Johnson. *Jazz Guitar Virtuoso* (Yazoo 1059); with Joe Venuti, *Stringing the Blues* (CBS 2-CSP JC2L-24). Jazz great; usually played roundhole archtop guitar.

Ledbetter, Huddie (Leadbelly). *Last Sessions*, Vol. 2 (Folkways 294AB/CD) and *Easy Rider; Leadbelly Legacy*, Vol. 4 (Folkways 2034). A singer and twelve-string guitarist of unrivaled power. Many other albums are available.

McTell, Blind Willie. *The Early Years: 1927-1933* (Yazoo 1005). Twelve-string bluesman.

Memphis Minnie. *Memphis Minnie 1934-42* (Blues Classics 1); with Kansas Joe, *Memphis Minnie 2* (Blues Classics 13).

Reinhardt, Django, with the Quintet of the Hot Club of France. *Django '35-39* (GNP 9019) and *Django 1935* (GNP 9023). A true jazz immortal—inventive, influential, technically brilliant, and colorful—and a pleasure to listen to.

Tampa Red. *Bottleneck Guitar* (Yazoo 1039) and *Guitar Wizard* (Blues Classics 25). Blues player who used a National.

Watson, Doc. *Doc Watson* (Vanguard 79152), *Doc Watson and Son* (Vanguard 79170), and *The Essential Doc Watson* (Vanguard 45/46). Six- and twelve-string guitar; flatpicking and fingerpicking; also some banjo and harmonica. Clean, musical, dazzling playing; simple, unadorned singing.

White, Bukka. *Sky Songs*, Vols. 1 & 2 (Arhoolie 1019 & 1020) and *Sic 'Em Dogs on Me* (Herwin 201). Bluesman who played a National.

White, Clarence, with the Kentucky Colonels. *The Kentucky Colonels 1965–1967* (Rounder 0070). Seminal flatpicker with an excellent bluegrass band. White also played with the Byrds.

OTHER GUITAR RECORDINGS

Babe, Smoky. *Hot Blues* (Arhoolie 2019). Twelve-string player.

Barenberg, Russ. *Cowboy Calypso* (Rounder 0111). Excellent flatpicker.

Bottleneck Blues (Testament 2216).

Christian, Charlie. *Solo Flight* (2-Columbia CG-30779). Early jazz pioneer who played electric guitar.

Fuller, Blind Boy. *Truckin' My Blues Away* (Yazoo 1060). Excellent blues-rag fingerpicker.

Fuller, Jesse. *Frisco Bound* (Arhoolie 2009). Twelve-string musician.

Mendoza, Lydia. *La Gloria de Texas* (Arhoolie 3102). Mendoza plays Texas-Mexican music on a twelve-string guitar. This is one of three Arhoolie discs featuring La Mendoza.

Rice, Tony. *Tony Rice* (Rounder 0085). The final link in the Crary-Barenberg-Rice triumvirate of great modern guitarists.

Spence, Joseph. *Folk Guitar* (Folkways 3844) and *Bahaman Guitarist* (Arhoolie 1061).

Tharpe, Sister Rosetta. *Best of Sister Rosetta Tharpe* (2-Savoy). The great gospel singer also plays good guitar.

Van Ronk, Dave. *In the Tradition* (Prestige 7800) and *Dave van Ronk Folksinger* (Prestige 7527). One of the first revivalist bluesmen of the early sixties, as pleasing as ever.

Williams, Big Joe. *Big Joe Williams and Nine-String Guitar* (Folkways 3820). Williams plays a converted twelve-string.

Other Blues Musicians: Reverend Gary Davis, Stefan Grossman, Son House, Blind Lemon Jefferson, Mance Lipscomb, Mississippi Fred McDowell, Lightnin' Hopkins, and Charlie Patton (and many, many more too numerous to list here).

More bluegrass guitar can be heard on many of the records listed in Appendix A.

DOBRO, HAWAIIAN, AND STEEL GUITAR

Auldridge, Mike. *Dobro* (Takoma 7033) and *Mike Auldridge* (Flying Fish 029). Excellent musician. See also recordings of the Seldom Scene.

Brother Oswald, Bashful. *Bashful Brother Oswald* (Star 192/1192) and *Brother Oswald* (Rounder 0013). One of the best Dobro players, who has been with Roy Acuff for years.

Graves, Buck ("Uncle Josh"). *Something Different* (Puritan 5001) and *Bucktime* (Puritan 5005). Another great Dobro player, who has recorded with Flatt and Scruggs.

Hula Blues (Rounder 1012). Hawaiian lap guitar.

Smeck, Roy. *Wizard of the Strings* (Blue Goose 2027).

Taylor, Tut. *Friar Tut (1971)* (Rounder 0011). A fine Dobro player.

That Dobro Sound's Going Round (Star 340/1340).

Other: Kalama's Quartet/Early Hawaiian Guitar Classics (Folklyric 9022), *The Gabby Pahinui Hawaiian Band* (PAN 3023), and *Steel Guitar Classics* (Old Timey 113).

More Dobro can be heard on many of the bluegrass recordings listed in Appendix A.

Bibliography: Chords, Theory, Instruction, Songs, Styles

GUITAR CHORDS

The first three books are all extensive compilations.

Arnold, Jay. *7488 Chords.* Hansen, 1979.

Bay, Bill. *Mel Bay's Deluxe Encyclopedia of Guitar Chords.*

Pearse, John. *The Guitarist's Picture Chord Encyclopedia.* AMSCO, 1977.

Pickow, Peter. *Guitar Case Chord Book.* Acorn, 1977. Useful, convenient.

THEORY

Greene, Ted. *Chord Chemistry.* Dale Zdenek Publications, 1971.

Silverman, Jerry. *A Folksinger's Guide to Note Reading and Music Theory: A Manual for the Folk Guitarist.* Oak, 1972.

GUITAR INSTRUCTION, SONGS, STYLES

Bailey, Mike. *Mel Bay's Flat Pickin' Guitar Songbook.* Mel Bay, 1980. Tablature and music. Intermediate level.

Barenberg, Russ. *Clarence White/Guitar*. Oak, 1978. Tablature and music. Music and style of the legendary Clarence White.

Barenberg, Russ. *How to Play Bluegrass Guitar*. Acorn, 1977. Tablature and music. Beginning level. This one is designed to be used with a teacher and is slightly harder to use by yourself than the following book by Barenberg.

Barenberg, Russ. *Teach Yourself Bluegrass Guitar*. AMSCO, 1978. Tablature. See previous entry.

The Blues Song Book. Chappell Music. No-nonsense arrangements for piano or guitar, including tunes by Jimmy Reed, Muddy Waters, and Willie Dixon.

Charters, Samuel. *Robert Johnson*. Oak, 1973. Music and story of the great bluesman.

Crary, Deacon Dan. *Flat-Picking Guitar Technique*. Musicprint, 1974. Tablature and music. Intermediate level.

Flint, Tommy. *Country Blues Guitar*. Mel Bay, 1974. Tablature and music. Travis picking; not really what you think of when you think of country blues.

Flint, Tommy. *Mel Bay's Anthology of Fingerstyle Guitar*. Mel Bay, 1978. Tablature and music. Intermediate to advanced levels.

Griffin, Neil and Steve. *Mel Bay's Deluxe Bluegrass/Flat-Pickin' Guitar Method*. Mel Bay, 1979. Tablature and music. Beginning level. Half the book consists of exercises. Once the tunes begin, there is no commentary. One wishes the authors would introduce the reader to styles and licks of living, practicing musicians.

Grossman, Stefan. *The Country Blues Guitar*. Oak, 1970. Tablature and music. Good sourcebook but hard to follow unless you read music (and even then it's not easy) and buy the accompanying tape or record. The same can be said of the following two Grossman books.

Grossman, Stefan. *Delta Blues Guitar*. Oak, 1969. Tablature and music. Music of players such as Robert Johnson and Charlie Patton.

Grossman, Stefan. *Ragtime Blues Guitarists*. Oak, 1970. Tablature and music. Includes music of Blind Blake, Big Bill Broonzy, Blind Lemon Jefferson.

Grossman, Stefan. *Stefan Grossman's Book of Guitar Tunings*. AMSCO, 1972. A useful book of tunings and tunes; includes discography.

Lieberson, Richard. *Old Time Fiddle Tunes for Guitar*. AMSCO, 1974.

Mann, Woody. *Six Black Blues Guitarists*. Oak, 1973. Tablature and music. Includes Rev. Gary Davis, Memphis Minnie, and Blind Blake.

Miller, John. *Finger Picking Gershwin*. AMSCO, 1980. Tablature and music. Fifteen arrangements for the accomplished guitarist.

Perlman, Ken. *Fingerpicking Fiddle Tunes: Traditional Dance Music Arranged for Finger Style Guitar*. Chappell, 1978. Tablature and music. Intermediate level.

Perlman, Ken. *Finger Style Guitar*. Spectrum/Prentice-Hall, 1980. A good, solid book.

Robinson, Marcel. *Fingerpicking Bach*. AMSCO, 1981. Tablature and music. Twelve arrangements for the accomplished player.

Roth, Arlen. *How to Play Blues Guitar*. Acorn, 1976. Tablature and music. Beginning level.

Roth, Arlen. *Slide Guitar*. Oak, 1975. Tablature and music. Blues and country. Very good book. Includes soundsheet.

Schoenberg, Eric. *Finger Picking Lennon & McCartney*. AMSCO, 1981. Tablature and music. Sixteen arrangements for the accomplished musician. Cassette available.

Silverman, Jerry. *Folksinger's Guitar Guide*. Oak, 1962. Tablature and music. Beginning level. A popular but poorly organized book. Record available.

Silverman, Jerry. *Folksinger's Guitar Guide*. Vol. 2, Oak, 1964. Tablature and music. Intermediate level. See previous entry for comments. Record available.

Seeger, Pete, and Julius. *The 12 String Guitar as Played by Leadbelly*. Oak, 1965. Tablature and music. Record available.

Traum, Happy. *Bluegrass Guitar*. Oak, 1974. Tablature and music. Intermediate level. Quite good. soundsheet included.

Traum, Happy. *The Blues Bag*. Consolidated Music, 1965. Tablature and music. Beginning level.

Traum, Happy. *Finger-Picking Styles for Guitar*. Oak, 1980. Tablature and music. Beginning to intermediate levels.

Traum, Happy. *Guitar Styles of Brownie McGhee*. Oak, 1971. Tablature and music.

Traum, Happy. *Happy Traum's Basic Guitar Lessons*, Vols. 1–4. Acorn, 1976. Music as well as some tablature. Good series for the beginner.

Travis, Merle, and Tommy Flint. *The Merle Travis Guitar Style*. Mel Bay, 1974. Tablature and music. Travis is a superb and influential player.

DOBRO INSTRUCTION, TUNES

Eidson, Ken, and Tom Swatzell. *Mel Bay's Country Dobro Styles*. Mel Bay, 1974. Tablature and music.

Beginning level.

Phillips, Stacy. *The Dobro Book.* Oak, 1977. Tablature. Soundsheet included. Suitable for beginners.

Toth, Stephen F. *Dobro Techniques for Bluegrass and Country Music,* Vol. 1. Colonial Press, 1975. Tablature.

GUITAR INSTRUCTION TAPES

Homespun Tapes, Box 694, Woodstock, NY 12498. A series of cassette lessons, with tablature. Most series consist of six tapes. Available are *Bluegrass Dobro, Bottleneck/Slide Guitar, Ragtime Guitar, Country Blues Guitar, Guitar for Beginners, Country Guitar Styles, Advanced Flatpick Guitar, Flatpick Country Guitar,* and *Fingerpicking Series.* Teachers include Russ Barenberg, Arlen Roth, Stacy Phillips, Merle Watson, and Happy Traum.

Stefan Grossman's Guitar Workshop, P.O. Box 804, Cooper Station, New York, NY 10276. Three items of interest to the guitarist: 1) Cassette or reel-to-reel tapes to accompany Grossman's books, some of which are listed in the previous section; 2) taped guitar lessons for blues, fingerstyle jazz, fingerpicked fiddle tunes, ragtime, and country flatpicking, taught by Grossman, Duck Baker, John Renbourn, Eric Thompson, and others; 3) tablature for cuts on Kicking Mule Records. Most of the lessons are for the intermediate to advanced player.

INSTRUCTION RECORDS

Seeger, Pete. *The Folksinger's Guitar Guide* (Folkways CRB-1/8354). Goes with Silverman book, Vol. 1.

Seeger, Pete. *The 12 String Guitar as Played by Leadbelly* (Folkways (2) CRB-8 or 8371). CRB-8 includes the book of the same name; 8371 does not.

Silverman, Jerry. *Folksinger's Guitar Guide,* Vol. 2 (Folkways CRB-5/8356). Goes with book of same name.

Bibliography: Guitars, Guitar Music, Guitarists, Other

Bellow, Alexander. *The Illustrated History of the Guitar.* Colombo, 1970. The color plates are an outstanding feature.

Broonzy, William, and Yannick Bruynoghe. *Big Bill Blues.* London: Cassell, 1955; revised edition,

Oak, 1964. An as-told-to autobiography of the great bluesman.

Charters, Samuel. *The Bluesmen.* Oak, 1967. Music, biography, history. Musicians discussed include Charlie Patton, Robert Johnson, Blind Lemon Jefferson, and Bukka White.

Charters, Samuel. *Sweet as the Showers of Rain: The Bluesmen,* Vol. 2. Oak, 1977. Biography, history, some music. Included are Memphis Minnie, Blind Willie McTell, and Blind Blake.

Cook, Bruce. *Listen to the Blues.* Scribner's, 1973. Blues and blues people. Recommended.

Editors of *Guitar Player Magazine. The Guitar Player Book.* Grove Press/Guitar Player Magazine, 1979. Interviews with guitarists; articles on wood, repair, strings, etc. Noninterview material is spread a bit thin but is useful nonetheless.

Evans, Tom and Mary Anne. *Guitars: Music, History, Construction and Players: From the Renaissance to Rock.* Paddington, 1977. An ambitious book that attempts to be comprehensive but winds up with too much information and an insipid style. Still, useful.

Grunfeld, Frederic V. *The Art and Times of the Guitar: An Illustrated History of Guitars and Guitarists.* Macmillan, 1969. A good book that unfortunately devotes little attention to steel-string guitars or nonclassical musicians.

Longworth, Mike. *Martin Guitars: A History.* Colonial Press, 1975. History, photos, serial numbers, specifications, etc., all dealing with Martin guitars, and of great interest to the Martin-guitar afficionado and anyone interested in the origins and development of this great company.

Traum, Happy. *Folk Guitar as a Profession.* Guitar Player Books, 1977.

Bibliography: Repair, Construction

The staff of *Guitar Player Magazine. Guitar Repair Manual.* Oak, 1972. Very basic; anyone serious about repair will need another book.

Evans, Tom and Mary Anne. *Guitars: Music, History, Construction and Players.* Paddington, 1977. Contains several extensive sections on construction.

Kamimoto, Hideo. *Complete Guitar Repair.* Oak, 1975. Although some of the explanations could be more clear and concise, this is the only book that is both affordable and fairly complete.

Sloane, Irving. *Classic Guitar Construction.* Dutton,

1961. Excellent, and useful even for anyone interested in nonclassic-guitar construction.

Sloane, Irving. *Steel-String Guitar Construction.* Dutton, 1975. Good historical section; lucid.

Teeter, Don. *The Acoustic Guitar: Adjustment, Care, Maintenance, and Repair.* University of Oklahoma Press. Vol. 1, 1975; Vol. 2, 1981. These are the best books on guitar repair. Aside from being extremely well illustrated and detailed, they are a sheer pleasure to read. Their audience is the serious craftsman. Combine these books with Sloane's book on classic guitar and you will have a good foundation for the business of lutherie and repair.

Young, David Russell. *The Steel String Guitar: Construction and Repair.* Chilton Books, 1975. A very good book that is well illustrated.

Wheeler, Tom. *The Guitar Book: A Handbook for Electric and Acoustic Guitar.* Harper and Row, 1978. A couple of sections of interest. See p. 000 for evaluation.

Magazines

Frets, P.O. Box 28836, San Diego, CA 92128. $18/year (monthly). Interviews, record and book reviews, articles on repair, instrument evaluations, news of new products. Columns by Dan Crary (guitar), Mike Auldridge (Dobro), and other specialists. Recommended.

Guitar Player, P.O. Box 28836, San Diego, CA 92128. $17.95/year (monthly). Interviews, columns by Jerry Silverman and Stefan Grossman (of interest to the acoustic guitarist), reviews, articles, new products—in a slick format. Emphasis on electric guitar, but good coverage of acoustic guitar too.

Guitar Review, 409 E. 50 St., New York, NY 10022. $16/year (triquarterly). An attractive and intelligent periodical of interest primarily to the classical guitarist.

Guitar World, 79 Madison Ave., New York, NY 10016. $18/twelve issues (bimonthly). Wide range of features and interviews, record reviews, instructional material, new products. Of some interest to the acoustic guitarist.

International Musician and Recording World, 1500 Broadway, New York, NY 10036. $18/year (monthly). Though little in this magazine is of specific relevance to the acoustic guitarist interested in folk, old-timey, and bluegrass music, Stephen Delft's instrument evaluations are excellent. He

manages to be persuasive and authoritative without hurting feelings or beating around the bush.

Journal of Guitar Acoustics, Box 781, Michigan Center, MI 49254. Send large, self-addressed stamped envelope for free information.

Living Blues, 2615 N. Wilton Ave., Chicago, IL 60614. $6/four issues (quarterly). News, photos, record reviews, interviews, articles, all about the blues. A serious publication in a professional but nonslick format. Covers blues and blues musicians in depth without being academic.

Resophonic Echoes, Beverly King, RR1, Box 320, Madill, OK 73446. $5.25 or $6.90/year (monthly). A newsletter for players of resophonic guitars.

Festivals

National Flat-Picking and Fingerpicking Championships, Winfield, Kansas. September. Write: Box 245, Winfield, KS 67156. This is the granddaddy of festivals for the picker.

See Appendix E for festivals of interest to the bluegrass and old-timey musician.

BLUES

Beale Street Music Festival, Memphis, Tennessee. May. Write: 12 S. Main St., #107, Memphis, TN 38103.

ChicagoFest, Chicago, Illinois. July/August. Write: ChicagoFest, Navy Pier, 600 E. Grand, Chicago, IL 60611.

Delta Blues Festival, Greenville, Mississippi. September. Write: MACE, 815 Main St., Greenville, MS 38701.

New Orleans Jazz and Heritage Festival, New Orleans, Louisiana. April. Write: Festival, Box 2530, New Orleans, LA 70176.

Oregon Blues Festival, Eugene, Oregon. October. Write: Ray Varner, 1240 E. 29 Place, Eugene, OR 94703.

Sacramento Blues Festival, Sacramento, California. September. Write: 3809 Garfield, Carmichael, CA 95608.

San Francisco Blues Festival, San Francisco, California. September. Write: 573 Hill St., San Francisco, CA 94119.

Western Regional Folk Festival, San Francisco, California. October. Write: Golden Gate National Recreation Area, Ft. Mason, San Francisco, CA.

CHAPTER 4
THE BANJO

Of the four main instruments in a bluegrass band, three either derive from, or double as, classical instruments. The guitar developed from the classic guitar, the arched-top mandolin from the round-backed mandolin used by classical musicians; the fiddle is the same instrument as the violin. Although the banjo has been used to play classical music, it did not develop from a classical instrument. True, the other instruments originally came from folk instruments (all instruments were originally folk instruments at some time in their history), but the banjo is the only one with no classical intermediary, having developed directly from its African ancestor. The banjo is the only instrument used in American music—folk, country, blues, or jazz—that is one hundred percent "folk" in its ancestry and development.

The banjo somewhat resembles a tambourine with a neck and strings, producing its characteristic sound through the interaction of wood, metal, and a drum head (although some instruments have neither metal nor a drum head). Early American banjos appear to have been made of whatever materials were handy—animal skin, scraps of metal and wood, gourds. A tradition also developed of decorating the banjo. But while early instruments might have been adorned with beads or bric-a-brac, modern instruments are engraved, carved, and gold-plated—a strange fate for the African instrument we have transformed into the emblem of bluegrass.

Another especially fascinating aspect of the banjo's construction and development is its technical "sophistication" compared with other instruments. The violin, mandolin, and guitar, for example, are built primarily of wood, often almost entirely by hand, and are held together primarily by glue. The banjo, on the other hand, usually has a plastic head and metal parts, and is more bolted together than glued. While the banjo is not exactly space age in its construction, it is in a sense more modern than, say, the violin, which is built pretty much the same way it was four hundred years ago. It is perhaps ironic that this most folklike of instruments should also be our most "technologically advanced."

Various kinds of banjos are used today: the five-string *resonator* (*bluegrass*) banjo, used mostly for bluegrass; the five-string *open-back* (*old-time, frailing*)* banjo, used mostly for old-time music; the four-string *tenor* banjo, used for Irish music and dixieland; the four-string *plectrum* banjo, used for dixieland jazz; the five-string, *long-neck* banjo, used for some folk music; the *fretless* banjo, used for some old-time music; the *banjo-mandolin* or *banjolin*, an eight-string cross between a banjo and a mandolin used for some Irish, folk, and ragtime music; and the *uke-banjo* (or *banjo-uke*) and *guitar-banjo* (or *banjo-guitar*), both rather obviously hybrids.

*Often the only difference between a bluegrass and a frailing banjo is the presence or absence of the resonator.

Bluegrass and frailing banjos are often tuned GDGBD; tenors are tuned in fifths, CGBD; plectrums are tuned like the four main strings of a five-string banjo, DGBD or CGBD, sometimes DGBE; the banjolin is tuned like a mandolin, GDAE, and so forth. Many more tunings are used, however, especially by open-back banjo players. Bluegrass banjos are picked with two fingerpicks and a thumbpick (fingers up, thumb down); frailing banjos are stroked downward (there are various styles: frailing, stroke style, clawhammer, drop thumb; sometimes they mean the same thing, sometimes not); tenors and plectrums are played with a plectrum (pick). Tenors are good for playing rhythm and single notes (like flatpicking a guitar), while plectrums make better chord instruments. The other banjos are picked or frailed or strummed in various ways. (Plectrums are beyond the domain of this book, as are the hybrids. Some further information on tenors is included later in this chapter.)

Bluegrass and frailing banjos are built to match their uses. The standard bluegrass banjo is heavy and has a large proportion of metal to wood in the body. This helps produce the loud, cutting sound that fits in perfectly with the sound of the dreadnought guitar and F-5 mandolin typically used in bluegrass. The result? The characteristic bluegrass blend.

The frailing banjo predates the bluegrass banjo and generally has a smaller proportion of metal to wood, producing a quieter, mellower, less metallic sound that fits in with the entirely different character of old-time music.

You can still get fretless banjos for playing old-time music. These banjos have their own special sound and feel. Some people like the slightly additional range of a long-neck banjo, but these banjos are relatively rare today.

Mandolin-banjo: Gibson MB-4 (ca. 1924).

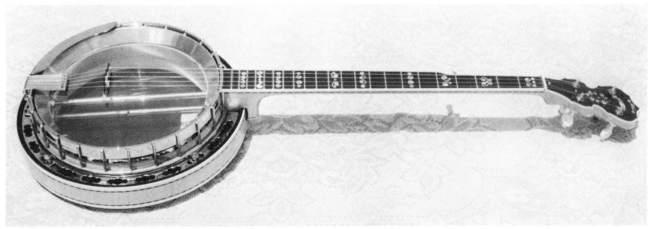

Bluegrass banjo: Deering Calico. Note transparent head.

Woodtop banjo, by L. O. Stapleton.

Plectrum banjo: Gibson PB-5 Mastertone Deluxe (1928).

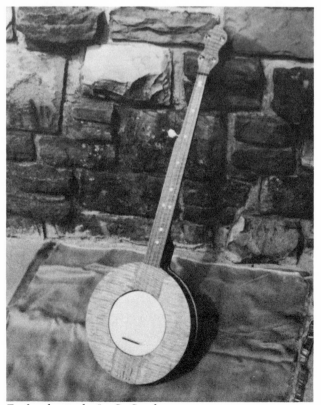

Fretless banjo, by L. O. Stapleton.

Interviews with Art Rosenbaum and Tony Trischka

Both Art Rosenbaum and Tony Trischka were raised in New York City and got an early taste of folk music through recordings of Pete Seeger and the Almanac Singers. Both went on to play banjo, make records, write books, and perform. But the similarities end there. Art lives in Alabama and rubs shoulders with young musicians playing old-time music and with "real" old-time players. He is somewhat of a musicologist and folklorist and does not support himself by playing music. Tony lives in New York City and moves in a circle of accomplished young urban musicians whose roots are in bluegrass but whose leanings are toward experimentation, eclecticism, and jazz. Tony supports himself by playing, teaching, writing, and recording.

INTERVIEW WITH ART ROSENBAUM

What attracted you to old-time music when most players seem attracted to bluegrass?

Well, I guess that dates me, because when I first heard old-time music, there wasn't much bluegrass to be heard. That would have been in the fifties. . . . Bluegrass had been around, but I liked the diversity and the *sound* in old-time music. Bluegrass is built on a few patterns that reoccur, but old-time music has idiosyncratic combinations of musicians and musical ideas that reflect certain places at certain times.

Is there a reason for that diversity?

As recently as this year, we met a guy, W. Guy Bruce, in the North Georgia Mountains. He's eighty-five years old and he plays the banjo without reference to any recorded music at all. And he's only one example, that's the thing. Bluegrass, great as it is, comes out of a professional music based on radio and records. Old-time music, even though there were records out fifty years ago, is still a people's music that people make for their own enjoy-

ment, or their community's, without reference to the larger music "scene," or how you "make it," or how you become a professional, or anything like that. That's another reason I'm interested in old-time music—I gravitated toward the music I like to play. It was just by accident that I got some prominence as a player, or a recording artist, or a teacher. It's just an outlet; it's not my main occupation.

You teach art?

I'm a painter. I teach at the University of Georgia. It's incidental, but in that sense I do relate to the function the music seems to play in the lives of the people I've learned from. They were very avid and passionate musicians, but for the most part they weren't full-time or professional musicians. Mainly they were playing for their own outlet, for their family or community.

Is that because of the differences in rural and city living? Country folk are more isolated than city folk, who come into contact with more musicians and outlets

for performing, are tempted in that direction.

Probably some time ago that was true, but nowadays modern media reach everywhere and they can find ways to get on T.V. or radio—it's just a question of where their musical values lie. And there are urban musicians who might just want to play for the fun of it, for their own enjoyment, and might not want to make compromises in order to make it. There just seem to be some characteristics of traditional music that put it apart from commercial music. Traditional music doesn't have to be rural.

You mentioned W. Guy Bruce, who just discovered there are other banjo players, or professional banjo players—but maybe he's atypical.

He's from another time, but it testifies to the persistence and vigor of traditional music. It's only when the question arises, you know, "Are you going to play in Washington or another festival?" that this guy says, "Well, am I really good enough, am I as good as these pickers I see on T.V.? You know, I'm just an old-time banjo picker." But then he realizes that he's an artist when people appreciate him; he says, "Yeah, I really got the feeling, I get into it, I pick my special way, and I know a version that no one else does, people have recognized my art when I play here and there." And so every artist has, you know, a kind of ego. Maybe it's a question of what comes first—whether the need to express yourself comes first, or whether the desire to do what will satisfy a market or a public comes first—that makes the difference. If somebody gets paid for their music or finds an audience it doesn't mean they've sold out.

Is old-time music developing?

It's complicated, because first you have to define old-time music. Old-time music was always changing. We think of people like Charlie Poole and the North Carolina Ramblers as old-time music, but they were influenced by jazz, and pop music of the 'teens and twenties. There was more archaic music being played in the Southeast, where Charlie Poole was recording, than he recorded. So the label "old-time music" stuck to the pre-bluegrass, string-band stuff, and that was the progressive music of its day, although it was rooted in various traditions. And then you get to the contemporary grooves. You get the Red Clay Ramblers, who are, I guess, more creative and re-creative than the New Lost City Ramblers, who are reproducing all original performances—maybe it's just a case of musicians feeling more free to make their own statement once they've assimilated the rudiments of the idiom. I think that's important, that you don't have a casual, promiscuous acquaintance with a kind of musical idiom and then start ripping it off for your own statement. But then if you're really into something you get into it more deeply, and when you are you can modify it, change it. Some of the old-time songs that were sung fifty or sixty years ago in the South are really powerful and don't seem dated at all. That's why I like to sing and play them. You know, like the numbers I learned from Pete Steele, or from the Eller Brothers, who are still working in North Georgia. I realize it's music that had its height at an earler time, but it still has a message. That brings the most freedom to me, in my music, but there are other musicians who like to innovate, and mix different styles, and develop—and I think that's great.

Is interest in old-time music widespread or regional?

It would be hard to generalize for the whole country. It's been a sort of minority interest, never something for the mainstream. In the sixties there was a lot of interest, but it's generally been assumed that was because of the big folk boom, with people like Dylan and Baez, and that made room for interest in some of the sources of their music, of their sound.

Right here, in Athens, Georgia, there's a very small following for the authentic music of the region on the university campus. And there are plenty of really fine regional musicians.

There's more old-time music in Ithaca, New York, than around here. I don't know whether it's too familiar, or people are just trying to be more sophisticated, but it's a specialized interest. There's nothing wrong with that. Some people are interested in string quartets, and some people are interested in Appalachian music. It's hard to say where the big interest is; I just try to keep a small portion of the interest alive.

Are people overseas interested in American old-time music?

Usually, you pull out the audience that has cultivated an interest. I was touring in France with Stefan Grossman, Happy Traum, and Duck Baker four or five years ago. In a couple of places—they tended to be the more provincial places—our music, since it was American, and exotic in that way, was viewed by the younger people who went to the event as if it were kind of mainstream pop music. They got as big a kick out of it as if we were a bunch of pop stars, or big stars—I guess Stefan Grossman would be in that category in Europe. And I found that sort of interesting because I think of my music as music that has a regional appeal.

INTERVIEW WITH TONY TRISCHKA

How did it all begin?

My parents were into the Weavers, and the Almanac Singers, but it was really the Kingston Trio that got me turned on to it—the banjo break in "MTA." I was playing guitar at the time, but that really turned my head around. And then I started looking for other kinds of music that featured the banjo and found out about bluegrass. I think a Scruggs record was the first bluegrass record I heard.

Then what?

I started when I was about 14, in 1963, and in those days there were just starting to be some new sounds heard after a long period during the fifties when there weren't any radically new sounds. A guy named Bill Keith was coming up with a new style, and the person I was taking lessons from had a sort of modern orientation, although he knew Scruggs style. He taught me the traditional styles the way he knew them . . . and he also taught me the more modern styles, like Bill Keith and Don Reno. So right from the start I was getting a more modern orientation, which seems to be the case with Northern banjo players.

Was bluegrass different back then for you?

I did all my intense bluegrass listening back in the sixties, and bluegrass was a little more intense back then. The Stanley Brothers were still around, Bill Monroe was at one of his peaks around 1966, and the music had a lot more sound and depth than it does now. I was able to be influenced by that, whereas now a lot of it seems removed from the initial depth of the music.

Was there a major influence besides Bill Keith?

I was incredibly involved with Bill Monroe back in '64 to '67, a four-year period when he was God to me. The band of that period had a deep influence on my own music. It wasn't even so much the notes they were playing. They had this feeling; it was this supercharged atmosphere they would create on stage—Monroe is a superman musically. I was back stage at the Opry in Nashville four or five years ago, and I walked into this small dressing room, and the Blue Grass Boys were getting tuned up to go on stage. As I walked in, the guitar player was singing the lead for a tune and I shut the door behind me and sat for about twenty seconds. Then Monroe came in on the chorus, and suddenly the room was too small to take the sound—it was so powerful. He's got this incredible musical power, and when he's on, it's beyond words and description.

Inspiration . . .

Exactly. That's what it was back then, on a very high level, and the whole band was tuned to him—Peter Rowan, Richard Greene, and Lamar Greer. They were all very distinctive voices on their own. As far as I could tell, they revered Monroe and came to his music with a lot of respect, and came at it from a Northern standpoint. But they'd really learned their lessons well. In the past a lot of the bands were under Monroe's tutelage and he would teach them what to do. But this band—even though I'm sure they learned an awful lot from him—they also gave him a lot of input back and challenged him. . . . It put bluegrass deep in my heart, and it will always be there for that reason, and because of that band.

And yet you went a different direction.

I found that my own direction led to a more modern viewpoint. I kept developing my style, which was more far out than most people were playing.

Can you describe your style?

It's hard to define one's own style exactly. I haven't had much game plan for developing my style; it's just come out the way it's come out.

What has been your contribution to blue-grass banjo?

Let's say five-string as opposed to bluegrass banjo, because some people take the bluegrass style and embroider it a little bit but stay within the style—people like J. D. Crowe and Allen Shelton—whereas I think my role has been taking it beyond strictly bluegrass. I'm not inventing a new style *per se*. I'm using a little Scruggs style, the melodic style, and the single-string style—and I'm using them to my own

twisted ends. I've taken all these techniques and put them to my own uses, coming up with a more pattern-style playing. It's a different conception rhythmically. I get a lot more into syncopation than a lot of people do and also into playing three notes at a time—playing full chords over and over again, different chords. It's a much more exciting, percussive style to me. I guess I could say that I take a lot of chances, and I couldn't say I always pull them off, but I guess more often than not I do. And it's fun because I come up with things that are unexpected. That's one reason it's hard for me to describe my style, because it comes from a deeper place inside. Without getting heavy about it, it's just not on the tip of my tongue or on the tips of my fingers. It comes from somewhere inside me that I'm not always in touch with—it just comes out and surprises me.

Has your style changed over the years?

I've cut out on the stylistic excesses. As the years have gone by I've explored new territory and also gone back and shored up my tradi-tional influences, learned more about what Scruggs was doing.

What else do you do that's different from other banjo players?

One thing is playing out of different keys without a capo. A whole lot can be done in that realm that hasn't been done yet. Most banjo players play in G, C, or D—once in a while in F—and then capo up to get other keys. For example, if you want to play, say, in the key of B flat, most people would capo at the third fret and play at the G position. But I worked out a fiddle tune in the key of B flat without a capo—playing on the first and second frets and open positions, where most people don't have those extra notes available. You get to play out of the character of the key. B flat has a much different sound from G. Part of it is that the open strings provide a different function in the key, and you get a different sound. By playing in the key of B flat you get more of the real property of B flat. Plus, you can get tired playing out of G position all the time.

Why don't banjo players play without a capo more often?

They're scared. Well, I shouldn't say they're scared—Alan Munde has done that—but a lot of good players haven't thought about it. That's the thing about bluegrass. I'm tempted to say it's a stagnant form, like a museum piece. It is what it is, and one hundred years from now it's not going to have changed much or it's not going to be bluegrass any more. Earl Scruggs back in 1945 just never conceived of doing these things without a capo, although he's done more than most, playing out of F, which most people don't. But people over the years have not done that because they didn't have the knowledge or the inclination or were just caught up in these old habits. Only fairly recently have people started playing without a capo and it's getting more and more common. It's something I've tried to trailblaze to a certain

extent; it helps you to get away from all the old licks. If you can get away from the standard licks, which are usually played out of G, by not using a capo, then you can come up with a whole other set of licks.

You're forced to do something else?

Exactly. It's a good way to expand your knowledge on the instrument.

Where are you headed musically?

Just last week I took my first lesson with a jazz improvisation teacher named John Carlini, so hopefully that's going to have some effect on my playing, learning all the modes, all the scales—in other words, getting a body of knowledge handed to me that I've been unfamiliar with up until now. If I could start adapting some of this information I could make a quantum leap forward. Until now, I've had one year of lessons, and from there on, although I have listened to other people and been influenced here and there, for the most part it has been a slow, gradual development on my own. Especially in the last ten years, my music has been mostly what I've come up with on my own.

Are you talking about playing straight jazz tunes?

You can't take bluegrass too far out because then it's not bluegrass, so what I'm talking about is being more jazz oriented. Initially I will probably play all the standard jazz tunes, learn how to improvise off them, and then take it somewhere else from there. I think I have a pretty well defined compositional style, and I'm pretty used to doing that, so I hope I can soon be composing my own tunes utilizing more jazz technique.

Ideally I'd like to apply some of this knowledge of jazz and work more arranged material, more composed, lengthier pieces. Instead of a banjo playing with a straight chord backup, have banjo with composed backup. Actually, we're already doing this a little with our band. We just worked up a tune that I wrote called "Elbow Room," and in the background our bass player wrote a four-part composed thing for two guitars, mandolin, and bass.

Do you improvise a lot right now?

Yeah, but not on my own tunes or on fiddle tunes. I play fiddle tunes and my own tunes almost note for note every time. To me, fiddle tunes are like classical music, and they're already pared down to the essence.

What are you doing with the Tony Trischka Band?

We didn't have any preconceived notions when it started, but it's turning into a bluegrass-oriented, country-rock-jazz-swing band. In other words, we're trying to cover a lot of bases—not intentionally, but we just find certain songs that appeal to us and happen to fall into these categories. We're trying to do something new within the medium and at the same time not to get so far out that we alienate people. We're all getting to express our musical desires or esthetics and at the same time be commercially palatable. It's not like Dawg music [David Grisman's inventive synthesis of bluegrass, swing, rock, and other musics] or newgrass—it's based on other styles. It's different but not radically different.

I understand that you're learning some clawhammer banjo.

Some. Old-time music has a lot more bounce than bluegrass—it really has that dance quality to it. I'm trying to put that bounce into our band now. It's something people can relate to more, if a band has a certain dance sound, even if you're not actually playing a dance.

Does the banjo have limitations?

The banjo has an obnoxious tone, let's face it (laughter). It's very raspy—it's a noisy instrument. But it depends on what you're doing. For straight-ahead bluegrass its sound is exactly what you want....Of all the instruments in a bluegrass band, the banjo is the most offensive and also the one that identifies something immediately as bluegrass. But you can also get a very nice tone out of the banjo if you play further from the bridge. The range is somewhat limiting too....But I really think you can play anything.

Selecting a Five-String Banjo

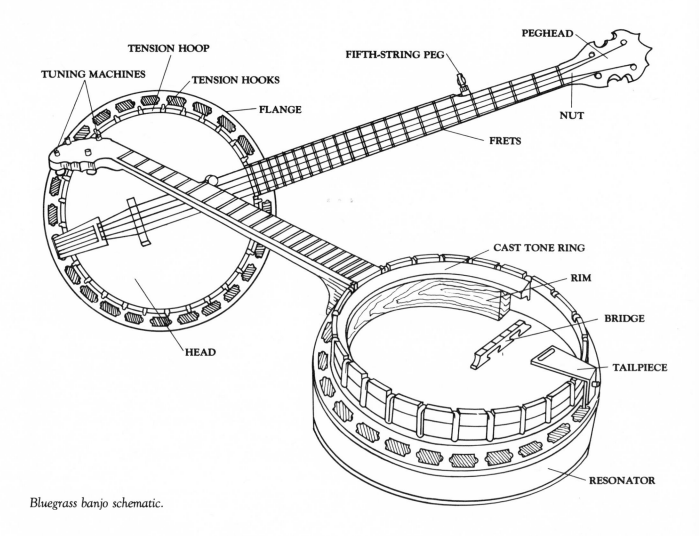

Bluegrass banjo schematic.

The most important consideration for a beginner in selecting a banjo is playability. A beginner should avoid a long-neck banjo; the neck is tiresome to play without a capo, and it goes out of kilter easily. Besides, the long-neck banjo is usually played *with* a capo, essentially making it into a regular twenty-two-fret banjo. The fretless banjo has a special sound and feel but is best left for the time when a regular open-back banjo seems too civilized. That leaves you a choice of two banjos: bluegrass or frailing.

Regardless of your musical interests—or if you are still not sure of them—get either a bluegrass or a frailing banjo, since tonal differences in really inexpensive instruments (if that's what you get) are not significant. Inexpensive bluegrass banjos are easier to find than inexpensive open-back banjos,

however, so circumstance may leave no alternative. Some banjos can be easily converted from resonator to open-back status and vice versa; having a banjo with this adaptability is a worthwhile consideration. Says Art Rosenbaum: "I've seen quite a few authentic players play with some kind of resonator banjo, although openbacked banjos do have a more agreeable sound for old-time music. It's a very personal kind of thing." When you start playing with other musicians, however, you may find the open-back getting drowned out in a bluegrass group and the bluegrass banjo drowning out the other instruments in an old-timey group.

Of course, if you are investing over three or four hundred dollars, you may as well get the banjo of your choice.

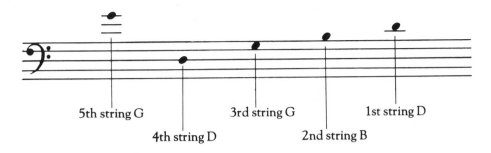

5th string G

4th string D

3rd string G

2nd string B

1st string D

Banjo G tuning.

PLAYABILITY

Tuning. If you cannot find someone to tune your banjo for you, try tuning it yourself. Start with the fourth (and thickest) string, and tune it to D below middle C, using a piano or a tuning device such as a pitchpipe or tuning fork. Then press the fourth string at the fifth fret (between the fourth and fifth frets, just below the fifth fret) and match the pitch of the third string to this G. Press the third string at the fourth fret and match the pitch of the second string to this B. Press the second string at the third fret and match the pitch of the first string to this D (an octave below the other D). And finally, press the first string at the fifth fret and match the pitch of the fifth (and short) string to the G (an octave below the other G). Play all the strings at once with a strum; you should hear a G chord, a nice, harmonious sound. (You can also tune each string to a reference pitch.)

The pegs or tuning machines should turn easily and should not slip. Pay very close attention to the fifth-string peg, which may not work easily on cheap banjos.

Tuning Pegs. Most banjos costing over about $250 have planetary pegs on the four main strings and a special geared tuner on the fifth string. Guitar tuners, found on many inexpensive banjos, are quite good—in fact, very good for the beginner because they're easy to fine tune. Older instruments and cheap banjos may have mechanical friction pegs, which can work quite well or can be so poor they don't work at all. And some banjos have wooden pegs, similar to those of a violin; avoid these unless you are an experienced musician. If you buy a banjo with friction pegs and they're slipping, have your local repairperson install mechanical frictionpegs, guitar machines, or planetary tuners and replace the fifth-string peg with a good geared peg.

Guitar Machines (set of six)—From $5
Stewart-MacDonald Friction Pegs (four)—$10.60
Schaller Planets (four)—$23
Stewart-MacDonald Planets (four)—$44
Schaller Geared Fifth (nickel plated)—$5.25
Stewart-MacDonald Fifth-String Planet
(nickel plated)—$13.25

Tuning pegs. From left to right: Grover fifth-string peg, Stew-Mac fifth-string friction peg, four Stew-Mac friction pegs.

Rim Size. On new banjos the standard outside rim diameter is almost always 11 inches, but on old banjos the diameter varies considerably between the various models and makes. The greatest difficulty with a banjo of nonstandard rim size is replacing its parts.

Bridge. Most common is a 5/8-inch-high, maple-ebony, three-footed bridge. Cheap banjos often have a rosewood bridge, which many repairpersons recommend replacing with the maple-ebony kind ($2-3). Expensive banjos may be equipped with a compensated bridge (Shubb compensated bridge: $6).

Tension Hooks. These hold the head to the rim, distribute the tension on the head, and thus affect the tone. Too few hooks, and the head may break or won't tighten enough to produce a crisp sound. Quality banjos have twenty-four hooks, but twenty is acceptable. Some cheap banjos and some expensive old ones have thirty hooks, which may be good for those particular banjos but is not necessarily better than twenty-four.

Neck. Aside from the head, the most vulnerable part of a banjo is the neck. Make sure it is straight by sighting down the fingerboard as if you were looking down the barrel of a rifle. Then make sure the fingerboard has a slight frontward curvature by pressing the first string at the first and twenty-second frets and checking the clearance above the seventh fret—it should be no more than 1/32 of an inch. Unless the neck is badly warped, the curvature is usually correctable if the banjo has an adjustable truss rod, the adjustable end of which is found beneath a thin plastic plate on the peghead or at the

Checking neck relief.

1925 Gibson TB-3 (tenor banjo) body with style TB-4 resonator; five-string neck made by Gruhn Guitars.

base of the neck. Some cheap and some expensive banjos have a nonadjustable neck, however. If you must buy a banjo with a nonadjustable neck, make sure the warranty is adequate. Buy a banjo with a defective neck only when you are sure the problem can be corrected and is worth correcting.

Check the feel of the neck. Cheap banjos may have a thick, unwieldy neck. One extremely inexpensive instrument has a neck whose crude paint job is not especially conducive to fast playing up and down the neck. Make sure also that the neck is not so thin that your fingers get crowded.

Action. Some experienced bluegrass musicians like high action, which means a clearance of about 1/4 of an inch at the twenty-second fret; 1/8 of an inch is considered low action. Most old-timey players like high action, and the range is on the high end—usually between 3/16 and 1/4 of an inch. When the banjo has a coordinator rod (rim rod, rim stick), and the neck isn't warped, the action can easily be adjusted; a repairperson can adjust the neck angle in other ways too. Also check the action at the nut. Press the fourth string between the second and third frets; the string should clear the first fret by the thickness of a business card. Check the other strings the same way.

Intonation. Make sure the bridge is correctly placed (see p. 58). If possible, adjust the bridge position, so that you can check the accuracy of the fret positions. To do the latter, work your way up the scale, one note at a time, on each string. Toward the top and at the very bottom—especially when the action is too high—the pitch may be high because of the string tension. Most new instruments are correctly fretted, but be careful with either custom or cheap banjos.

Frets. Make sure the frets are smooth, high, rounded, and flush with the edges of the fingerboard. Make sure they are the same height too, or the strings may buzz. Check for fret height and string buzz the same way you check fret position.

Scale Length. The standard banjo scale is between 26 and 27 inches.

CONDITION AND STRUCTURAL INTEGRITY

For the banjo to sound and work its best, it must be solidly assembled. No rattles, no wobbly neck, no loose hooks. Rattles are less important than the loss of vibrations between ill-fitting parts. Also, inspect the instrument for split pegs, loose hooks, split wood, and signs of haphazard workmanship such as a sloppy finish.

MATERIALS

The most expensive new bluegrass banjos have a hard-maple rim; a heavy cast-brass or cast-bronze tone ring or a spun-brass and steel tone ring; a maple, walnut, mahogany, or rosewood neck; an ivory or bone nut; an ebony or ebonite (synthetic) fingerboard; a maple-ebony bridge; nickel-silver frets; and nickel-, chrome-, or gold-plated steel or brass flange, hooks, brackets, tailpiece, hoop, and other external hardware; and a resonator whose wood matches that of the neck.

CONSTRUCTION: RIM AND TONE RING

The most important parts of the banjo are the rim and tone ring; usually they are considered a unit. This is illustrated by the frequent practice of taking old four-string banjos, removing the four-string neck, and substituting a five-string neck (newly built in most cases). No one cares too much about the neck; they care about the *pot*—everything *but* the neck. (This procedure is aptly called "cannibalization.")

Tone rings and rims

Bluegrass. Earl Scruggs, the man whose playing is virtually synonymous with the style and sound of bluegrass banjo, played a Gibson Mastertone banjo during his most influential years, and so most bluegrass players have played either Gibsons or something that sounded pretty close. So persuasive is the preference for the so-called prewar sound that most manufacturers—including Gibson itself—try either to duplicate the old Gibson down to the content of the alloy in the tone ring or to equal or surpass the Gibson sound in their own way. And so close are the variations on the prewar Gibson that their designs are loosely referred to as *Mastertone construction.* This type of construction is typified by a heavy cast-metal tone ring tightly fitted to a thick wood rim. The variations in brands of Gibson-style tonal systems are in weight, thickness, alloy, shell construction, and tone-ring design.

Since premium-quality old Gibsons are expensive and rare, manufacturers have their work cut out for them, and most seem content to stick to the proven formula. Unfortunately, it is impossible to compete with the effects of time on a musical instrument and with the even more powerful effects of mystique. As many people point out, if Earl Scruggs had played a different banjo, or if a different banjo player had come to exemplify the bluegrass banjo sound, everything might be very, very different. (Some say that Scruggs would sound the same regardless of the instrument he played.)

The other major kind of pot design is the *itegral rim,* so called because the rim and tone ring are integrated into a one-piece rim made of cast steel or aluminum, spun aluminum, or plastic. No wood is used. This design can produce a respectable sound, but it is not the sound preferred by professional bluegrass musicians. Integral rims make inexpensive banjos possible. Some very inexpensive banjos mold the entire pot in one piece, excluding the resonator (although even that has been tried).

Other tonal systems pop up here and there. There's a wood rim and simple tone hoop, which are more common on open-back banjos and occasionally used on inexpensive bluegrass instuments. And there's the Ome system, described at length in the directory of builders and manufacturers at the end of this chapter.

Tone rings, whether Mastertone-style or not, also are made with two further refinements: archtop (raised head) or flathead. The flathead, with more resonating space on top, has a darker, plunkier sound than the archtop, which limits the resonating area of the head.

The best wood rims are from 1/2 to 7/8 of an inch (usually 3/4 of an inch), laminated hard maple; the fewer layers of wood, the better. Sometimes the laminate is "wrap"—three to fourteen thin layers wrapped into a circle; some rims employ a block laminate.

The best tone rings are cast brass or bronze and are quite heavy. The composition of the alloy affects the tone. Often the words *brass* and *bronze* seem to be used interchangeably, and some manufacturers say "sandcast" brass or "bell" metal ("bell brass," "bell bronze"). Don't worry about these terms unless you are planning to build banjos yourself; these terms are used loosely and often erroneously. Archtop tone rings sometimes have forty holes. Although a heavy ring produces the tone bluegrass players like, excessive weight can muddy or overamplify the sound. Most important of all is a snug fit between the rim and the ring.

Integral rims also have differences. For example, too light or flimsy a rim may produce a weak, hollow sound.

Vega Whyte Laydie #2 five-string open-back banjo.

Frailing. Although "frailers by and large like the Vega sound," says Ed Sulfinger of Bucks County Folk Music Shop in New Britain, Pennsylvania, no single old-time sound is all-pervasive in the way that there is one dominant bluegrass sound. Categories of tonal systems include a wood rim with no metal, a metal rim without wood (integral), a wood rim with a thin metal shell, a wood rim with a tone ring, and a wood rim fitted with a metal hoop. Regardless of the design, the result, at least on older instruments, is similar: a sound influenced more by wood than by metal. Less weight also means less volume. The rule in buying an open-back banjo is on the order of, "If you like the banjo, buy it," rather than, "If it doesn't sound like a Gibson, it's not worth buying." Players have famous-name instruments like Vegas, Bacons, and Orpheums, or they have instruments with no names at all.

Old open-back banjos tend to have thinner rims than bluegrass banjos—3/8 to 5/8 of an inch (leaning toward the smaller number)—while newer instruments often have thicker rims. The outside rim diameter on new instruments is fairly standard—11 inches—but on old instruments 10 1/2 inches, 10 5/8 inches, or 10 15/16 inches is common.

Old-timey banjo players usually go more by sound

and funkiness than anything. Volume is important in some bands, however, and so some players prefer instruments with tone rings or that are very loud.

CONSTRUCTION: TENSION HOOP, FLANGE/BRACKETS, TAILPIECE

Tension Hoop. The tension hoop holds the head to the pot and is usually tightened from the bottom. Some companies offer the option of top tension. Hoops are either grooved or notched to receive the hooks.

Flange/Brackets. The tension hooks are attached to either a flange or a bracket shoe or shoes. Resonator banjos have flanges (also called resonator flanges), sometimes in addition to bracket shoes, while openbacks usually have bracket shoes; the flange also holds the resonator on and is decorative. Sometimes the flange is sectional; you can remove the sections and have an "open back" banjo. Cast-flange designs are made in either one or two pieces; the tube-and-plate flange is a popular two-piece design. The weight of the flange affects the sound, and some players prefer certain types of flanges to others.

Tailpiece. The tailpiece holds the strings at the back end of the banjo and, when adjustable, can significantly affect tone. The tailpiece should be solid and adjustable, although some tailpieces on old open-back instruments cannot be adjusted. For a beginner, length is unimportant.

Tailpieces are tension, finger-type tension, or nontension. Tension tailpieces can be raised and lowered by adjusting one or more screws; by varying the stress on the bridge, one consequently varies the tone, volume, and sustaining quality of the banjo. With a finger-style tailpiece each string can be individually adjusted to a different tension. The nontension tailpiece just holds the strings at a constant, low tension.

There is little choice on inexpensive banjos. You usually get a copy of a clamshell or Waverly tension tailpiece; these are often light, may bend or rattle, but are usually quite acceptable and may appear in higher-quality versions on expensive instruments. Finger-style tailpieces appear on low-moderate to expensive instruments and sport names like "bear claw," "eagle claw," and "puma claw"; some people believe these are "more show than go," but they are still popular. Some of the better tailpieces are the Kershner and Presto—actually, "Kershner-style" or "Presto-style," since they're copies of old originals. Tailpieces are relatively inexpensive, so you can

always experiment.

Buck Puma Claw (nickel plated)—$26
Buck Clamshell (chrome plated)—$10
Kershner style (nickel plated)—$27.95
Presto (nickel plated)—about $14
Waverly (nickel plated)—$18.50

CONSTRUCTION: NECK AND RESONATOR

Neck. Banjo necks are often multi-laminated vertically for additional strength and for beauty.

Resonator. The resonator increases the volume of the banjo by helping to project the sound; it works the same way as the bowl at the Hollywood Bowl, for example. The wood is laminated, and better resonators have fewer laminations (six is about average). The type of wood affects the tone; generally, the hardest woods produce the brightest tone.

POSITION INLAYS AND COSMETICS

Most banjos have position inlays. When the inlays get fancy—a vine, for example—using them becomes more difficult. If you are paying top dollar for looks, make sure the cosmetic work is worth the money.

Selecting a Tenor Banjo for Playing Irish Music

Select a tenor banjo in pretty much the same way you would select a five-string banjo, keeping in mind the differences in the instruments and the fact that Mastertone construction is not crucial to getting a desirable sound for Irish music. The most prized old tenor banjo is the Bacon and Day Silver Bell.

Hot-Rodding

The banjo has been called "the hot rod of musical instruments" because it lends itself so well to tinkering and custom design. You can, for instance, experiment with different brands of heads, whereas a guitar player cannot change soundboards so easily. You can experiment with different tailpieces, even necks and tone rings.

There are two kinds of experimenting: improving appearance and trying to improve quality of sound and playability. The first kind is entirely up to you; if you want to get your hardware gold plated, that's fine. If you want to inlay some designs into the fingerboard, that's okay too. But be careful with the second kind, because each banjo, cheap or expensive, has its limitations. You cannot transform a $150 banjo into a $1500 model. By the time you get through with it you may have a different banjo than you began with—and maybe should have bought that $1500 banjo instead. Likewise, fooling too much with that $1500 banjo may make it prettier, but chances are you aren't going to make any major improvements.

Setting Up a Banjo

Playing a banjo that isn't set up is like riding a bicycle with a flat tire, unadjusted brakes, and a seat that is too high. Setting up a banjo isn't especially difficult, but try to get the dealer to do it for you the first time. You may need to set up an instrument you are considering.

Positioning the Bridge. Press the first string at the twelfth fret and pluck the string; then lightly touch the string over the twelfth fret and pluck the string again; this note is the harmonic. When the bridge is correctly placed, the two tones will be exactly the same. If the fretted note is higher than the harmonic, move the bridge (hold each side between the thumb and index finger and slide it very slowly) slightly toward the tailpiece; if the fretted note is lower in pitch, move the bridge away from the tailpiece. Repeat the testing process until the two notes agree. Then repeat the procedure on the fourth string. Expect the bridge to wind up at a slight angle, with the treble side closer to the neck.

Adjusting the Neck Relief. Turn the end of the truss rod—using a deep-socket wrench (sometimes a different tool is needed)—clockwise to decrease relief, or counterclockwise to increase relief. Turn the nut one-eighth to one-quarter turn at a time and be very careful, because snapping the thin steel rod means major surgery on the neck. Test the relief by measuring the clearance above the seventh fret when the strings are pressed at the first and twenty-second frets.

Adjusting the Action. Low action is 1/8 of an inch; high action, 1/4 of an inch (some clawhammer players may go even higher). Adjusting the action really means adjusting the neck angle—the higher the neck, the higher the action. To adjust the neck angle you have to adjust the bottom coordinator rod. Most bluegrass banjos have two such rods, but some have only a lower one; in place of the top rod, which holds the neck to the pot, is a bolt. Frailing banjos may have other systems. Sometimes you can just substitute a higher or lower bridge.

To raise the action, first loosen the nut on the upper rod. Then loosen the outer nut and tighten the inner nut (on the bottom rod); to lower the action, loosen the inner nut and tighten the outer nut. Hold the rod still by inserting a nail or allen wrench into the hole in the rod. *Be extremely careful not to strip the nuts,* and turn the nut no more than one or two turns at a time before checking the action.

Adjusting the Tailpiece. For bluegrass and a loud, bright sound, tighten the tailpiece so that it is low, exerting high stress on the bridge. Old-timey players prefer less volume and a darker sound, so they may loosen the tailpiece; some players like just enough tension to hold the bridge in place (and may thus use a nonadjustable tailpiece).

Tightening the Head. For bluegrass, the head should be very tight; it should sink only slightly

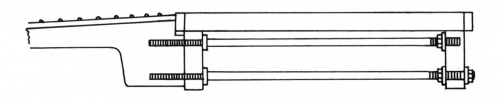

Coordinator rod setup for adjusting the neck angle and hence the action.

under moderate finger pressure. Clawhammer players prefer a looser head, so that the sound is not too bright. To tighten the head, first tighten four tension hooks in opposite corners; then tighten the other hooks finger tight, going in one direction around the head. (You can also tighten opposite hooks, going in a circle until all are finger tight.) Now use the bracket wrench to tighten each hook a quarter-turn at a time. Check the tightness of the head by each hook after each revolution and make sure that when you are finished the head is evenly tight. Look across the head and make sure the tension hoop is equally visible all the way around. The aim is to tighten the head and evenly distribute the tension.

HEADS

Plastic heads, which most players use, are available in several sizes and textures. An unfrosted (unsprayed, uncoated) head, either clear or transparent, produces a thinner, crisper tone than a frosted head, but most players use a head that is frosted on the outside. The crown—the raised portion of the head—comes in three heights—low, medium, and high. Fitting the head may be tricky, since the height you need depends on the specifications of the banjo and there is no precise rule on which size goes on which banjo. Measure the head already on your banjo when it's time to change it and match the old head with the new one. Some players use calfskin, which is good for an old-time sound but at the complete mercy of the elements as well as a chore to change; a synthetic called Fiberskyn works well for old-time music.

Heads:
Stewart-MacDonald Five-Star (11 inch)—$13.25
Weather King (10 to 12 1/8 inches)—about $12
Weather King Fiberskyn—about $12
Calfskin—about $20

ACCESSORIES

Armrest. An armrest elevates your arm and also protects the banjo head. Many banjos come equipped with an armrest, but many are not.
Stewart-MacDonald Five-Star (nickel plated)—$16.25

D Tuners. Also called Keith, Keith-type, or Keith-Scruggs pegs or tuners, these contraptions enable you to quickly and accurately retune the banjo into a different key by locking the strings within limits so that they tighten or loosen only so far. They're not

cheap; they're also not really necessary until you're pretty good.
Keith Pegs (two) (stainless steel)—$112.50
Saga D Tuners (two)—$65.00

Money Matters

THE POLITICS OF PRICE

New bluegrass banjos sell for from less than $100 to almost $5000; the range for open-back banjos is somewhat narrower. Prices for tenor banjos generally are the same as for bluegrass banjos, except that fewer inexpensive models are available. Bluegrass banjos divide into two main categories: under $500, with an integral rim; over $500, with a cast tone ring. Banjos in the first category are almost always used by beginning and intermediate players. Open-back instruments divide up less neatly, since there's a wider range of preferences, but less expensive instruments usually look plainer and are more simply constructed than more expensive instruments.

In each category, most companies tend to build *one basic instrument* that is available in increasingly fancier-looking, increasingly expensive versions; meaningful improvements are sometimes made but are often minimal. Companies with more than one line of banjos do this within each line.

Integral rim: a company may sell a very plain banjo for $150; a nicer-looking, perhaps slightly improved banjo for $250; and a still nicer-looking, probably not-any-more-improved banjo for $400. All these banjos may sound exactly the same; meaningful improvements may be in the tuning pegs or tailpiece, but a good deal of the increased price goes for cosmetics.

Cast tone ring: many companies make *only* cosmetic changes in their models. For example, the Liberty that retails for $1400 sounds and feels the same (or is supposed to) as the Liberty that retails for $4400. Both instruments have the same hardware (tone ring, rim, tuning machines, tailpiece, etc.), but the expensive one has carved wood, engraved metal, gold plating, etc.

On expensive banjos this practice is not deceptive, since manufacturers and individual builders make it quite clear what they are doing. Sometimes, indeed, they even brag that "all our banjos sound equally good." But on inexpensive instruments cosmetic differences are misleading and a waste of your money. Furthermore, the important differences are often

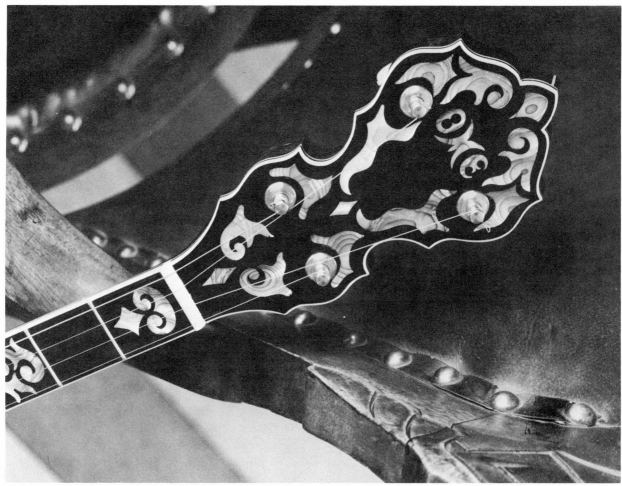

Peghead, Ome banjo.

hard to discern. It may be to your advantage, if you want a slightly better inexpensive banjo, to buy a better fifth-string peg, for example, or an adjustable tailpiece, and install it yourself or have it installed for you.

BANJO BUDGETS

First Bluegrass Banjo: Under $200. Decent, playable new banjos begin around $120. For those who want to spend the least, $200 ought to be your limit.

First Open-Back Banjo: Under $300. Decent banjos, with some choice of tonal systems.

Bluegrass Banjo: $200-500. Unless you buy a banjo with a cast tone ring, which should be your first choice, stay *low* in this bracket. The $850 banjo you can get at a discount for $500 may be as good a banjo as you ever need. With the discounts available, there seems little reason to move up the ladder incrementally.

Open-Back Banjo: $200-500. There are fewer choices, but the advice is similar to that for bluegrass banjos: stay low or buy a really good banjo.

Bluegrass or Open-Back Banjo: $525-700. Banjos selling at list price may keep you happy quite a while; banjos discounted to this bracket may be all the banjo a lot of folks'll ever need. Bluegrass banjos ought to have a cast tone ring.

Bluegrass or Open-Back Banjo: $700-1400. At list price, all the banjo many people will ever need; at discount, all the banjo most people will ever need.

Bluegrass or Open-Back Banjo: Over $1400. You are paying for cosmetics, special options, brand name, "customizing" or a custom banjo, the occasional banjo whose base price is high, or a valuable used banjo—or paying too much.

Tenor Banjo. Prices are generally the same for new tenors as for bluegrass banjos; with few exceptions too, the banjos are the same except for the neck. A few inexpensive tenors are manufactured, mostly in the Orient. Because of relatively low demand for tenor banjos, *used* instruments are probably a better buy than new ones. You can probably find one for under $300 if you stay away from the famous instruments. Some of these inexpensive instruments may have unusual or less-than-desirable features like a very wide rim, but such a banjo may suit your purposes just fine.

Resonator inlay on Stelling Scrimshaw.

Kits

Building a banjo kit is an excellent way to learn about the banjo as an instrument and also to get more quality for your money: a kit becomes an instrument worth about twice its price. The two major kit manufacturers, Stewart-MacDonald and Saga, offer a complete line of instruments from integral-rim bluegrass and frailing banjos to instruments with a cast tone ring or a wood rim and tone hoop suitable for old-time music; Stew-Mac also sells a tenor-banjo kit. The kits of both manufacturers are similar; the

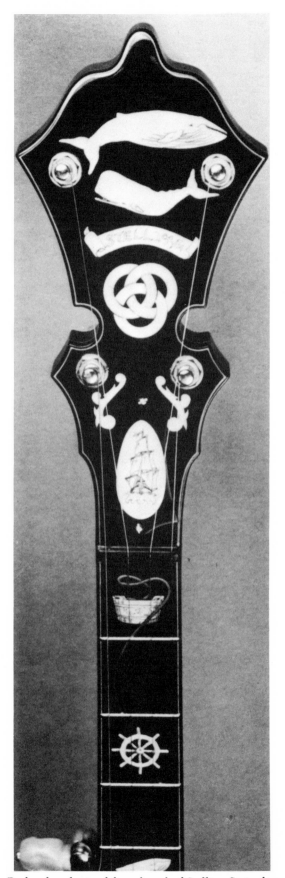

Peghead and top of fingerboard of Stelling Scrimshaw.

Sagas are slightly less expensive, the Stewart-MacDonalds are of higher quality. Two other companies—Hughes and Here, Inc.—also make kits.

Stewart-MacDonald Diamond Eagle banjo kit.

Banjo Brands, Builders, and Manufacturers

Alvarez (St. Louis Music Supply Co., 1400 Ferguson, St. Louis, MO 63133). A respectable Japanese brand. Sold through dealers.

Aria Pro II (Music Distributors, Inc., 3400 Darby, Charlotte, NC 28216). Another well-known Japanese make. Sold through dealers.

Bacon. A long-deceased company whose banjos are worth investigating if you come across one.

Berger (Berger's Guitar Shop, 30 W. 4 St., Apopka, FL 32703). Paul Berger builds open-back banjos and may be hard to contact.

Carlos (C. Bruno & Son, 20 Old Windsor Rd., Bloomfield, CT 06002). Beginners' instruments imported by a well-known firm. Sold through dealers.

Chacey-Built (Rt. 1, Amesville, OH 45711). Ron Chacey has been building instruments since 1961, works alone, and completes six to eight banjos each year. He also engraves metal parts for other builders

and is highly regarded."Only the finest and most elaborate models are being produced," he says. "These are all individually designed, decorative works of art, and every banjo is an endeavor to surpass the previous one....The materials...are absolutely superior. The decorative possibilities are unlimited." Available directly from Chacey; delivery takes three to six months.

Creed (Rt. 3, Box 231A, Galax, VA 24333). Kyle Creed is a well-known musician who also builds open-back banjos.

Deering (3615B Costa Bella St., Lemon Grove, CA 92045). Greg Deering has been building banjos since 1971 and started the Deering Banjo Co. in 1976. His company has eight employees and produces seven hundred to one thousand banjos per year. Deering's aim has been to make quality banjos at affordable prices, and he has succeeded admirably. He pays a lot

Bacon & Day Silver Bell #1 tenor banjo.

Some of Ron Chacey's work.

of attention to the necks of his instruments, especially on the inexpensive models. He describes the sound of his instruments: "Basic—bright and crisp," "Intermediate—more punch than the Basic," "Deluxe—very sweet, well rounded, but still plenty of crispness and punch," "Maple Blossom—very bright, solid, crisp," and "Calico—same as Maple Blossom when made of maple, sweeter when made of walnut." Available through dealers and also via direct contact.

Ellis (7208 Cooper Lane, Austin, TX 78745). Custom bluegrass banjos. Order from Tom Ellis. Lifetime warranty.

Fender (Fender Musical Instruments, 1300 E. Valencia, Fullerton, CA 92631). Fender, justly famous for its electric guitars and basses, imports two banjos, which are good buys. Available through dealers.

Inlaywork on Greg Deering Limited Edition banjo.

Ellis banjo.

Chicago (Fred Gretsch Enterprises, 715 Grays Highway, Ridgeland, SC 29936). The brochure claims it is "the lowest priced banjo in the world." The instruments are modeled after the popular old Harmony banjos. They may need considerable setting up. Sold through dealers.

❀

Gibson (c/o Norlin Music, 7373 N. Cicero Ave., Lincolnwood, IL 60646). For some, Gibson is the only name in banjos and prewar Gibsons are the *crème de la crème.* The new instruments are good, but for less money you can acquire an equally good if not better banjo without the famous brand name. Tenors available. Sold through dealers.

❀

Glenn (Rt. 1, Box 327, Sugar Grove, NC 28679). Leonard and Clifford Glenn make a fretless banjo and have quite a reputation as traditional craftsmen. Write for information. Delivery takes one to eight weeks.

Gold Star (Saga Musical Instruments, P.O. Box 2841, South San Francisco, CA 94080). The Gold Star, which many believe to be the most successful and reasonably priced copy of a prewar Mastertone, is popular and widely distributed through dealers.

❀

Great Lakes. Out of business, but their banjos are worth keeping a lookout for.

❀

Here, Inc. (29 S.E. Main St., Minneapolis, MN 55414).

❀

Hughes (Hughes Dulcimer Company, 8665 W. 13th Ave., Denver, CO 80215). Hughes has been making banjos for nine years. According to a spokesman, "although many beginners use this instrument, it is also popular among experienced players because its simple style and unfinicky nature make it possible to take it anywhere. The sound of the wood top is typical of old-time banjos, but with a slightly quieter nature." The kit takes eight to fifteen hours to assemble. Available through dealers and from Hughes.

❀

Ibanez (Elger Distributors, P.O. Box 469, Ben Salem, PA 19020). As of early 1981 these excellent imported Gibson copies were no longer being produced. Some dealers may have them in stock, however.

❀

Iida (C. Bruno & Son, 20 Old Windsor Rd., Bloomfield, CT 06002). Iida's inexpensive instruments are fairly popular, but the whole line has far too many different models with insignificant variations. Tenors. Available from dealers.

❀

Imperial (2527 S.W. 59 St., Oklahoma City, OK 73119). Founded in 1971, Imperial has three employees and produces two hundred instruments a year. Ty Piper, the head of the operation, aims to replicate the best prewar sound—somewhere between plunky and piercing—"full—rich—well-balanced—a little bass heavy—loud." Their market: anyone with money who is past the beginners' stage. Available through dealers or from Imperial; direct orders take two months to fill.

STYLE IV

Imperial Chaparral.

Kirk (408 Winchester Rd., Huntsville, AL 35811). M. K. Kirk builds open-back banjos.

Ledford (125 Sunset Heights, Winchester, KY 40391). Homer Ledford builds open-back banjos.

Liberty (2472 Main St., Bridgeport, CT 06606). Liberty Banjo Co., a major supplier of banjo hardware, was founded in 1966 and began making its own banjos in 1976. Liberty aims for a prewar-Gibson sound and markets for the serious player. "When he is all through with the imports and is truly looking for a quality instrument," says Paul Morrissey, "we fill the bill." Ornately carved relief on the expensive instruments gives a distinctive look. Available through dealers or from Liberty.

Morgan (Morgan Springs, Rt. 3, Box 147-1, Dayton, TN 37321). Tom Morgan has been building instruments since 1961 and offers a custom banjo, either open back or resonator, ranging from "about $750 for a very plain open back" to "as high as $1800 for a fancy bluegrass model."

Ode (sometimes **Baldwin-Ode**) (Kustom/Gretsch, 908 W. Chestnut, Chanute, KS 66720). Five thousand Ode banjos are manufactured each year. Says Stan Werbin of Elderly Instruments in East Lansing, Michigan: "I'm very often asked how an Ode might compare with a Gibson or an Ome . . . and my tendency is to think the Ode is not as loud . . . but might have a sweeter tone—I'm not sure that's the proper word for it either, because that really doesn't describe what a bluegrass player wants. And yet bluegrass banjo players want Ode banjos. They're top quality . . . right up there, certainly. . . ." Ode makes tenors too. Available through dealers.

Ome (4575 N. Broadway, Boulder, CO 80302). Ome, which completes two hundred banjos each year, has a reputation for excellence and innovation due in great part to founder, Chuck Ogsbury, who also started Ode and who invented the integral-rim banjo, the one-piece cast pot design now used on one of Deering's banjos, his own Gibson variation, and a non-Gibson tone ring design. Ome banjos have either a cast tone ring a la Gibson or a two-piece, spun brass and rolled steel tone ring. The latter has a fuller, more balanced sound with good sustain and a less cutting tone; Ogsbury does not aim for the loudest banjo ever built. Although the spun-brass system is most popular with tenor players, bluegrass players use them too. One musician has said the spun-brass system has more depth, more lows, and more resonance than the cast-ring designs, that it

Liberty Cotillion. Note carved relief.

Ome banjos.

blends well with guitar, and that it's a "musical instrument first, a banjo second." Available through dealers or from the manufacturer.

Orpheum. Long out of business, but their five-string open-back banjos are still around and worth hunting for.

Paramount. Out of business, but good tenors and plectrums.

Raimi (4028 Woodland Park North, Seattle, WA 98103). A builder of good, inexpensive open-back banjos. Available through dealers or directly from Richard Raimi.

Saga (Saga Musical Instruments, P.O. Box 2841, South San Francisco, CA 94080). Imported instruments. Saga kits and assembled banjos are good buys. Sold through dealers.

Arthur E. Smith. A recently defunct manufacturer

of fine-quality open-back banjos. New ones can still be found at some dealers.

.

Norman Lee Smith (Park Plaza #7, River and Ski Mountain Roads, Gatlinburg, TN 37738). Builder of fretless banjos with either a calfskin or spruce head.

Stapleton (Hillbilly Dulcimer Shop, 201 Midland Ave., Springdale, AR 72764). L. O. Stapleton tends toward one-of-a-kind instruments.

Stelling (8815 Kenwood Dr., Spring Valley, CA 92077). Stelling Banjo Works was established in 1973. Called the "Mack truck of the bluegrass banjo" by some, Stellings have a reputation for excellence, good volume, and cutting power. Geoff Stelling is one of the few innovators in the banjo business. His wedge-fit design for fitting the ring to the rim is a superb way of insuring a snug fit, and he has patented his designs for a compensated nut and a special tailpiece. Perhaps his only flaw is trying too hard to compete with Gibson. Tenor banjos too. Available through dealers or directly from Stelling.

S. S. Stewart. Long defunct, this famous company's open-back instruments are worth trying to find.

Stewart-MacDonald (Box 900, Athens, OH 45701). According to a company spokesman, Stew-Mac is "the largest domestic manufacturer of banjo components." The Style 3 open-back kit is a good way to get an affordable open-back banjo with a wood rim, and you can later add a resonator and tone ring. Most of the work is assembling and finishing. Stewart-MacDonald is a responsible, responsive, professional company. Tenors available. Order through dealers and from the manufacturer.

Sunhearth (RD 1, Box 74, Roaring Springs, PA 16673). Manufacturer of fretless banjos.

Vega. Vega banjos are among the most valuable instruments on the market, even though the original company no longer exists. Make sure you check the dates on any instrument to be sure it's an authentic Vega, since other companies have manufactured—and may still be manufacturing—instruments under the Vega name.

Warner (Warner String Works, 10 Eichelberger St., Hanover, PA 17331). Chris Warner, who has been building banjos by himself since 1971, says his bluegrass banjos are patterned after the prewar Gibson Mastertone. Prices range from $800 to $2500, and instruments are all built on a custom basis. Order directly from Warner; delivery takes one to two months. Lifetime warranty.

Washburn (Fretted Industries, 1415 Waukegan Rd., Northbrook, IL 60062). Washburn is an imported line of banjos made to the specifications of Fretted Industries, which now owns the old Washburn name. These instruments are worth investigating. Available through dealers.

Wildwood (445 T. St., Arcata, CA 95521). Says Mark Platin of Wildwood Banjo Co.: "We're selling to a market that probably would have bought old-time vintage instruments and paid a lot more money and probably would have been slightly dissatisfied . . . because an instrument forty or fifty years old would have shown wear." Admitting that "the standard bearers in old-timey music are the Whyte Laydie and Tu-ba-phone," Platin makes versions of both instruments. The Whyte Laydie variation uses a solid brass hoop on top of a scalloped tone ring; the Tu-ba-phone-style system is a brass hoop welded to a hollow, square brass tube (the "tubaphone"). Both ring systems perch on top of a wood rim. Wildwood also sells resonators for these banjos as well as a bluegrass banjo. Available through dealers.

Discography

CLASSICAL, RAGTIME, OTHER

Ball, William J. *A Banjo Galaxy: The Classic Banjo of William J. Ball* (Rounder 3005). Very enjoyable.

Camp, A. L. *A. L. Camp Plays the Banjo* (Folkways 3525).

Lillywhite, Derek. *Banjo Reminiscences* (Rounder 0095).

Ossman, Vess, and Fred Van Eps. *Kings of the Ragtime Banjo* (Yazoo 1044).

Peabody, Eddie. *16 Great Banjo Hits* (MCA AB-4010). Plectrum.

Reser, Harry. *Banjo Crackerjax (1922-30)* and *Banjos Back to Back* (Reser Record Co.). Reser is considered the greatest tenor player of all time.

Others: Perry Bechtel, Skip Duvall, and Lee Floyd.

OLD TIME

Banjo Pickin' Girl (Women in Early Country Music, Vol. 1) (Rounder 1029).

Boggs, Dock. *Dock Boggs, Vols. 1 & 2* (2-Folkways 2351/2392).

Clawhammer Banjo (County 701). With Kyle Creed, Wade Ward, Fred Cockerham, and George Stoneman.

Folk Banjo Styles (Elektra 7217 O.P.).

Jarrell, Tommy. *Come and Go with Me* (County 748).

Macon, Uncle Dave. *Early Recordings* (County 521).

Melodic Clawhammer Banjo (Kicking Mule 209). More modern style.

Old-Time Banjo in America (Kicking Mule 204).

Poole, Charlie. *Charlie Poole and the North Carolina Ramblers* (County 505).

Rosenbaum, Art. *The Art of the Mountain Banjo* (Kicking Mule 203) and *Five-String Banjo* (Kicking Mule 208).

BLUEGRASS

Crowe, J. D. *J. D. Crowe and the New South* (Rounder 0044).

Grier, Lamar, with Bill Monroe. *Bluegrass Time* (MCA 116).

Jenkins, Snuffy. *Crazy Water Barndance* (Rounder 0059), *33 Years* (Rounder 0055), and *Carolina Bluegrass* (Arhoolie 5011). First important modern three-finger picker, and thus an important link between old-time and bluegrass styles.

Keith, Bill. *Something Auld, Something Newgrass, Something Borrowed, Something Bluegrass* (Rounder 0084).

Munde, Alan. *Banjo Sandwich* (Ridge Runner 0001) and *The Banjo Kid Picks Again* (Ridge Runner 0022).

Scruggs, Earl. *Foggy Mountain Banjo* (Columbia 10043), *The Golden Era* (Rounder SS05), and *Blue Ridge Cabin Home* (County CCS-102).

Shelton, Allen, with Jim and Jesse. *Bluegrass Special* (Columbia CSP 12641).

Trischka, Tony. *Banjoland* (Rounder 0087) and *Bluegrass Light* (Rounder 0048).

Others: Sonny Osborne (of the Osborne Brothers), Don Reno, Ralph Stanley, and Bobby Thompson.

See Appendix A for more recordings featuring bluegrass and old-time banjo.

IRISH

De Dannan (Polydor 2904005).
The Johnston's Sampler (Trailer 16).
Stokton's Wing (Tara 2004).

Bibliography: Instruction, Songs, Styles, Chords

TEACHING AND TABLATURE

Tony Trischka: When someone comes for a lesson I'll have the tab for them—usually—but I'll just play it for them and we'll do it by ear, and I'll ask them to play back from memory—that's the way I learned. The very first banjo lesson I had, I learned two tunes the way Eric Weissberg played them and in that one lesson all the secrets of Scruggs style opened to me: so this is how you do it! I give them tab to take home...but as I'm teaching I have them use their ears.

Art Rosenbaum: I think tablature does have some pitfalls, because you can play things that you don't really hear. You go from eye to fingers without really going through the heart...and it is essentially a music you feel and assimilate.

Tony Trischka: Bela Fleck did in five years what it took me fifteen years to do. When I was learning, bluegrass banjo had gone only so far...and now there's infinitely more material available; people can go a lot further and faster. I think tablature has a lot to do with it.

Erbsen, Wayne. *A Manual on How to Play the 5-String Banjo for the Complete Ignoramus.* Pembroke Music, 1977. Tablature and music. Beginning level. This is really a book on clawhammer banjo. A bit skimpy but fairly good. Soundsheet included.

Erbsen, Wayne. *Starting Bluegrass Banjo from Scratch.* Pembroke Music, 1978. Tablature. Beginning level. This book is quite nicely done. Soundsheet included.

Griffin, Neil. *Mel Bay's Deluxe Bluegrass Method.* Mel Bay, 1974. Tablature and music. Beginning level. Contains lots of useful exercises. No attempt is made to connect the material with the world of bluegrass and its performers.

Knopf, Bill. *Hot Licks and Fiddle Tunes for the Bluegrass Banjo Player.* Chappell Music, 1976.

Knopf, Bill. *The Theory of Chord Construction for 5-String and Plectrum Banjo.*

Krassen, Miles. *Clawhammer Banjo.* Oak, 1974. Tablature. Beginning level. Includes soundsheet.

Muller, Eric, and Barbara Koehler. *Frailing the Five String Banjo.* Mel Bay, 1973. Tablature.

Perlman, Ken. *Melodic Clawhammer Banjo.* Oak, 1979. Tablature. Intermediate level. Fine book.

Rosenbaum, Art. *Old-Time Mountain Banjo.* Oak, 1968. Tablature and music. Intermediate level. Various playing styles: clawhammer, picking, frailing, etc.

Sandberg, Larry. *The Original Banjo Case Chord Book.* Acorn, 1978. Useful and handy.

Scruggs, Earl. *Earl Scruggs and the 5-String Banjo.* Pier International, 1968. Tablature and music. Intermediate level. Historical data on Scruggs, styles; how to play Scruggs style; tunes; how to build a banjo. Useful, interesting book. Record available.

Seeger, Peggy. *The Five String Banjo: American Folk Styles.* Hargail, 1960. Music.

Seeger, Pete. *How to Play the Five String Banjo.* Self-published, 1962; distributed by Oak. Tablature and music. A good introduction to various playing styles.

Slater, Alec. *Mel Bay's Clawhammer Solos on Modal Music in the Irish Tradition.* Mel Bay, 1979. Tablature. Intermediate level. Hard to read, but one of the better Mel Bay books.

Smeck, Roy. *3 in 1 Tenor Banjo Book.* Robbins Music, 1967.

Streeter, Harold. *Beginners' Bluegrass 5-String Banjo.* Le Walt (P.O. Box 1865, Sedona, AZ 86336), 1976. Tablature. Lots of explanations and instructions make this a useful method for slow learners. Cassettes available.

Streeter, Harold. *5-String Banjo Improvisations for 3-Finger Picking.* Le Walt, 1974. Tablature. Intermediate level. Music theory and special arrangements. Cassettes available.

Sullivan, Anthony. *Sullys Irish Banjo Book.* Manchester, England: Halshaw Music, 1979. A good tenor-banjo method with more than fifty tunes.

Trischka, Tony. *Banjo Songbook*. Oak, 1977. Tablature. For the intermediate or ambitious beginning player. Explanations of different bluegrass styles, instruction, interviews, tunes. Excellent.

Trischka, Tony. *Bill Keith/Banjo*. Oak, 1978. An exploration of the style of banjo innovator Bill Keith.

Trischka, Tony. *Melodic Banjo*. Oak, 1976. Tablature. Excellent, once you have mastered the basics. Includes soundsheet.

Weissman, Dick. Five String Banjo: For Beginners Only. Vol. 1. Big 3, 1979. Tablature and music.

Weissman, Dick. *Five String Banjo: For Beginners Only*. Vol. 2. Robbins music, 1974. Tablature and music. Covers frailing and bluegrass styles.

Weissman, Dick. *Five String Banjo: For Beginners Only*. Vol. 3. U.A. Music Publishing Group. 1977. Tablature and music. Covers classical, bluegrass, blues, and some nontraditional music. All three volumes are well put together and cover a good range of styles. These are good books for someone who wants to progress slowly and not settle on one kind of music just yet. Cassettes available.

Weissman, Dick (arranger), and Dan Fox (ed.). *Schirmer's Easy Five String Banjo Book*. Schirmer, 1978. "Folk" songs collected or written by Oscar Brand, Leadbelly, Alan Lomax, John Jacob Niles, Jesse Fuller, Pete Seeger, and others.

Wernick, Peter. *Bluegrass Banjo*. Oak, 1974. Tablature. Unless you learn very slowly, this is the best book for the beginner.

INSTRUCTION TAPES

Homespun Tapes, Box 694, Woodstock, N.Y. 12498. Three series of banjo lessons (six cassettes apiece), taught by Happy Traum, Bill Keith, and Tony Trischka.

INSTRUCTION RECORDS

Muller, Eric. *Frailing the 5-String Banjo*. (Sunny Mountain 1001). This record goes with the Muller book.

Seeger, Pete. *How to Play the 5-String Banjo* (Folkways CRB-2/8303). Two records that go with the Pete Seeger book.

Bibliography: Repair, Construction, Maintenance

Banjo Maintenance Manual. Deering Banjo Co.,

1981. Designed for the owner of a Deering banjo, but useful regardless of the brand of banjo you have.

Sandberg, Larry. *Complete Banjo Repair*. Oak, 1979. Although not complete enough to get you started in the repair busines, this book is nevertheless recommended as an excellent source of information on the banjo.

Scruggs, Earl. *Earl Scruggs and the 5-String Banjo*. Pier International, 1968. Contains section on building a banjo.

Sloane, Irving. *Making Musical Instruments*. Dutton. 1978. Sloane is a lucid writer, but the banjo chapter is not as good as it could have been.

The Stelling Banjo Field Service Manual. Stelling Banjo Works, 1979. Designed for Stelling owners but useful for all. Similar format to the Deering booklet but shorter and pithier.

Wiggington, B. Eliot. *Foxfire 3*. Anchor/Doubleday, 1975. Reprinted from *Foxfire*, Vol, 8, No. 3 (Fall 1974). Contains a long section on fretless banjos.

Bibliography: Banjoists

Reno, Don. *The Musical History of Don Reno: His Life, His Songs*. Riverdale, MD: Don Reno Productions, 1975. Reno is an important, distinctive, innovative player.

Magazines

Banjo Newsletter, Box 1830, Annapolis, MD 21404. $12/year (monthly). The banjo player's bible: news, classifieds, ads, instruction, inteviews, articles, reviews, columns by players like Sonny Osborne. Stronger on bluegrass than on old-time music. Highly recommended.

F.I.G.A. News, 2344 S. Oakley, Chicago, IL 60608. Write for information.

Frets, P.O. Box 28836, San Diego, CA 92128. $18/year (monthly). Interviews, instrument evaluations, technical talk, column by Alan Munde, banjo lore. Of greatest interest to bluegrass players. Recommended.

International Banjo, P.O. Box 328, Kissimmee, FL 32741. $15/year (semimonthly). Covers all kinds of banjo players and music. A relatively new magazine.

Festivals

See Chapter 6 and Appendix E for listings of festivals.

CHAPTER 5

THE MANDOLIN

Like many instruments used in traditional American music, the mandolin is undergoing a renaissance. Musicians are moving into fresh new territory and in doing so redefining the limits of the instrument.

The mandolin has been played for several hundred years and has been used to play both classical and popular music. Both Vivaldi and Beethoven composed for the mandolin, yet the traditional bowlback instrument is often called a Neapolitan mandolin, indicating its relationship to the popular music of Naples. Mandolin orchestra sprang up in the early part of the century in the United States; Dave Apollon, a great mandolinist, played vaudeville; and then Bill Monroe, the father of bluegrass, brought the mandolin to a wider audience. But in spite of Apollon, Monroe, and other innovative and virtuoso mandolinists, the instrument has always taken a back seat to the fiddle, banjo, and guitar in American folk and popular music.

Now all that is changing, through the efforts especially of David Grisman, whose "Dawg" music, a blend of bluegrass, jazz, rock, and other musical elements, has been growing in popularity. Grisman has made the mandolin the featured instrument in his recent groups; in fact, he usually uses two mandolins. And he has worked especially hard to overcome some of the chording problems, one of the major limitations of the instrument. Andy Statman, a former Grisman protégé, is playing progressive jazz and exotic ethnic blends, and Barry Mitterhoff, formerly with the bluegrass band Bottle Hill, is now moving between the worlds of classical music and progressive bluegrass, showing that mandolinists can play just about anything. The mandolin is also being used to play Irish music.

Why has the mandolin become a convenient vehicle for such diverse music? For one thing, the mandolin has a tradition in various kinds of music. For another, although it has certain limitations,

The Los Angeles Mandolin Orchestra (1981).

rather than stifling players, these limitations have actually encouraged them to experiment. And finally, the more talented and musically educated players have simply begun to realize the inherent limitations of bluegrass and have begun to explore classical and ethnic music as well as jazz, three vast reservoirs with long and complex traditions. Room for innovation still exists in bluegrass, but many bluegrass-oriented musicians believe that excessive deviation from the essence of bluegrass produces a music that isn't bluegrass. Either you play bluegrass or else you may as well drop the bluegrass tag and call your music something else. And when you've done that, you've given yourself a ticket to the future.

Like the violin, the mandolin is tuned in fifths, GDAE, but unlike the violin, which has four strings, the mandolin has four *pairs* of strings. The mandolin has frets and is always played with a pick, while the violin is played primarily with a bow and only sometimes plucked for effect.

A-style mandolin with f holes, by Stiver.

F-5-style mandolin, by Givens.

Mandolins come in three common styles: round-back or bowlback, A style, and F style (sometimes called Florentine). A- and F- style instruments have round, oval or f holes, depending on the manufacturer or era.* Although the A and F models are sometimes called *flatbacks*, most actually have arched backs. The bowlback is the oldest of the types and is built a little like a lute, while the so-called flatback, a later development credited to Orville Gibson, is constructed more like a violin.

Roundback mandolins are used mainly in mandolin orchestras playing classical music and are not especially favored by folk musicians because they aren't as loud as the other instruments; also, they're cumbersome. Some people (notably Kenny Hall) do use them, however, for playing old-time music.

Bluegrass and jazz musicians prefer F-5 instruments—Florentine shape with f holes—because they are louder than roundbacks and usually louder and more cutting than A models. However, an A model with f holes will probably be closer in sound to an F-5 than to an A model with an oval hole. F-5 mandolins are also flashier-looking than the others and are traditionally used for bluegrass because Bill

*"A" and "F" are actually model numbers for old Gibson mandolins but have become generic terms used by most manufacturers and individual builders. The F-5, for example, refers to a specific Gibson, but copies are also called F-5s.

Monroe uses one (although he has used other instruments too); many musicians just have to own such an instrument. Musicians playing Irish or old-time music prefer the more mellow, somewhat quieter A model. In the context of their respective kinds of music, each type of instrument is quite appropriate: the sound of the A model fits in well with that of the open-back banjos usually used in old-time music, and the more cutting sound of the F-5 fits in with the much louder banjos and with the generally louder instrumentation in bluegrass. Bob Givens, a mandolin builder, states the case:

The two mandolins just sound completely different. It seems to be just personal preference as to the sound somebody likes. The sound of an F cuts through. You can hear it very clearly when an A and an F are played together. An A model has a fuller, rounder sound. When you're playing really high notes, you can hear how the power of the F comes through. It has a more percussive sound when you hit it with a flatpick.

Nevertheless, there are exceptions. Andy Statman and Red Rector both use an A mandolin for bluegrass.

It should be noted that members of mandolin orchestras use any of the three types of mandolins.

Musicians playing Irish music sometimes use a mandola, which is tuned a fifth below a mandolin.

INTERVIEW WITH ANDY STATMAN

Andy Statman is a serious musician. His grasp of music history, his understanding of the creative process, and his expertise in music as diverse as jazz, bluegrass, klezmer, and baroque is impressive. Although Andy has played with lots of musicians and continues to do so, there's something of the lone explorer in him as he moves out over new territory, assimilating and conquering. One senses this separateness in his first solo album, *Flatbush Waltz*.

"Bluegrass is the first music I seriously studied, but I listened to a lot before I played bluegrass. I was into Broadway show music a lot. We had some old Yiddish 78s, and I listened to them a lot. When I was around six, I was into early rock 'n' roll. I listened to Mozart and Beethoven. . . . And then I got completely freaked out on Gilbert and Sullivan. But bluegrass was the first focus that lasted.

"I really wanted to play the banjo, so I started taking lessons, but around the time I was fourteen or fifteen I decided I was really attracted to the mandolin. There were one or two mandolin solos—there's a record called *Mountain Music Bluegrass Style*, and Earl Taylor played a version of "White House Blues" and took a great solo. And on a Flatt and Scruggs record, someone takes a mandolin break, maybe Curley Seckler—a very simple break—and I fell in love with the sound of the instrument. A lot of other good banjo players were in New York at the time, and since I wanted to play in a band anyway, I decided to take up mandolin.

"When I was fifteen I'd been playing and listening to bluegrass—I was a fanatic—for several years already. I took some lessons with David Grisman, and his method was basically teach yourself. David had access to the entire recorded and also live-show catalog of bluegrass, so he let me tape everything he had. I would go home and slow down the tapes and

figure out the stuff, and when I couldn't figure out something I went back to him. In the course of two years I took about six lessons. I learned basically every mandolin solo by Bill Monroe, Frank Wakefield, Bobby Osborne, and others that was recorded between 1939 and 1967. I learned how to play all these styles, plus I started learning what fiddle players were doing. I would spend an hour trying to figure out whether Bill Monroe would do two tremolo strokes on a note or three. I had become musically and technically on top of all the developments of the mandolin up to that point—I'd studied everything that had been done and I could do everything that had been done. . . . I was a fanatic.

"What led me out of bluegrass was going through bluegrass. I had come through it around 1966. By that time I'd realized that the only thing for me to do further would be to go down South and join a bluegrass band. And I realized that culturally these guys are just on a whole other trip than I am. Musically I'd begun developing a style, and I was also beginning to find bluegrass very, very limiting, and I started listening to jazz. I needed outside influences to take bluegrass further, either within that style or else I needed to totally abandon that style and go somewhere else. I got more and more into jazz and into ethnic music, which led me back to Jewish music.

"I began listening to Indian music, Tibetan music, Balkan music. By the early seventies I was studying different kinds of ethnic music—Greek, Jewish, Turkish. I began playing free jazz on the saxophone; I was playing in rhythm-and-blues bands.

"I don't feel at this point that any one style in particular will satisfy what I want, so what I choose to do is play and study a variety of styles and fuse them into something of my own creation. . . . I'm open to everything."

Selecting a Mandolin

Regardless of the kind of music you like, price is going to determine the kind of mandolin you buy, since the cheapest new F-style instrument lists for about $700. You can begin on an A model or even on a roundback. Jethro Burns, for example, began on a roundback, then "when I got to be about ten years old, my father went out and bought me a real fine old Gibson mandolin. . . . It was an 'A' model with a round soundhole. I played that for many years, but all of a sudden I got involved in playing with other musicians, and it wasn't loud enough."[1] He then acquired an F-5 mandolin.

PLAYABILITY

Tuning. Have someone tune the instrument or tune it yourself. Start with the second set of strings and tune both strings to the A above middle C, using a piano or tuning device. Then press the third string* just below the seventh fret and match this pitch to the A. Then press the fourth string just below the seventh fret and match this pitch to the D. And finally, press the second string just below the seventh fret and match the pitch of the first string to the note (E) on the A string. You may need to do some readjusting when you're through. The machine heads should turn easily and not slip.

Neck. The neck is a critical part of the mandolin; with few exceptions, when everything about the neck checks out and the rest of the instrument is in decent condition, the mandolin will be playable. To

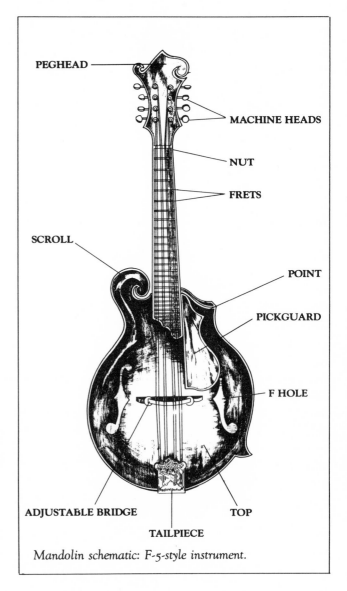

Mandolin schematic: F-5-style instrument.

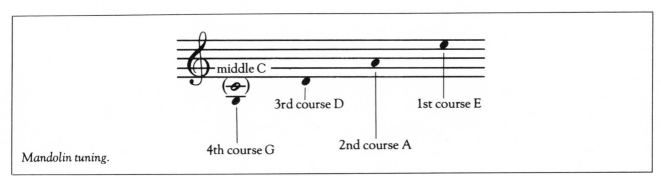

Mandolin tuning.

counteract the upward pull of the strings, older instruments tended to have thick necks, but newer instruments have thinner, steel-reinforced necks.

Make sure the neck isn't warped by sighting down the fingerboard from the top as if you were looking down a rifle barrel. Consider an instrument with a badly deformed neck no further. Now make sure the fingerboard has a very slight frontward curvature.

*To simplify matters we're calling the third set the third string, the second set the second string, and so forth.

Press the fourth string at the first fret and also at the twelfth fret (or at the last fret where the neck joins the body) and look for a small amount of clearance over the seventh fret—no more than 1/32 of an inch. Do the same thing on the first string; here the clearance can be slightly less.

An incorrectly relieved fingerboard can usually be fixed if the neck has an adjustable truss rod. Since "usually" is not "always," make sure the instrument can be adjusted or is adjusted when you buy it. Buy a mandolin without an adjustable neck only if the fingerboard is properly curved and the instrument has a good warranty. A good repairperson can fix just about anything, but some repairs can be expensive.

Also make sure the neck feels comfortable. A thick neck may be hard to hold, though some players don't mind and even like them. Experiment with different instruments to see how they feel.

Action. Many mandolin players like high action, but a beginner has to worry about sensitive fingers. Since most mandolins have adjustable bridges—you can adjust the action yourself—action is something to worry about only when the bridge is nonadjustable. Press the strings at the top of the fingerboard, nearest the bridge, where they are highest; they should be easy to depress. Trying different instruments will show you the difference between easy and hard. Also check the action at the nut. Press the strings, one at a time, between the second and third frets. They should clear the first fret by about the thickness of a business card.

Intonation. First, make sure the bridge is correctly positioned. Lightly touch the fourth string over the twelfth fret with one finger of your left hand and then with the other hand pluck the string until the harmonic sounds. Then depress the string all the way to the fret and play that note. The two pitches should be identical. Perform the same test on the first string. When the notes are different, the bridge is in the wrong place: too close to the peg head when the fretted note is high, too close to the tailpiece when the fretted note is low. Since a mandolin bridge is usually freestanding (not glued to the top), it's simply a matter of fiddling with the bridge until the harmonic and the fretted pitch match. Ask the dealer to do this if you are a novice or ask the dealer's permission if you are not. Positioning the bridge is important; otherwise, you cannot check the accuracy of the fret positions.

Now check the frets by working your way up the scale, a note at a time, on each string. Toward the top, the pitches tend to go sharp because of the string tension, especially if the bridge is too high. Frets are usually correct, but can be off even on custom instruments. A misplaced fret makes playing in tune impossible. Since the scale length of a mandolin is approximately half that of the guitar or banjo, a small but noticeable discrepancy will be twice as noticeable on the mandolin.

Frets. Make sure the frets are smooth, high, rounded, and flush with the edges of the fingerboard. Make sure they all look even too, or you may get string buzz. Check for buzzing by playing your way up the fingerboard, a note at a time, the same way you checked fret positions.

Number of Frets to Body. Mandolins have ten to fifteen frets on the neck before it joins the body. A longer neck makes the higher notes somewhat more accessible.

Scale Length. Scale length affects playability and tone. Most scale lengths are 13 7/8 inches, that of the Gibson F-5.

CONDITION AND STRUCTURAL INTEGRITY

Repairman Marc Horowitz warns, "Above all, if you're buying an inexpensive instrument, you're looking for structural integrity. You don't want the thing to fold up on you in six months." Unless you're an expert, of course, predicting mandolin collapse is difficult, if not impossible, unless the signs are loud and clear. Protect yourself by purchasing an instrument with a reinforced neck, either made by a well-known builder or manufacturer or bought from a responsible dealer, with a good warranty. Be especially careful with old bowlbacks; many have caved-in tops and badly warped necks due to basically shoddy construction and poor-quality materials.

Make sure the instrument feels solid. Tap the top and back; there should be no rattles, no loose braces. Inspect the entire instrument for cracks. Make sure the seams and the joint where the neck joins the body are tight.

MATERIALS

Traditionally, the finest mandolins have a solid (curly) maple back, neck and sides; ebony fingerboard and bridge; solid spruce top; ivory, mother-of-pearl, or bone nut; and nickel-silver frets. Good but less expensive instruments may substitute mahogany or rosewood for maple, rosewood for ebony. Some very good instruments use koa, walnut, and other

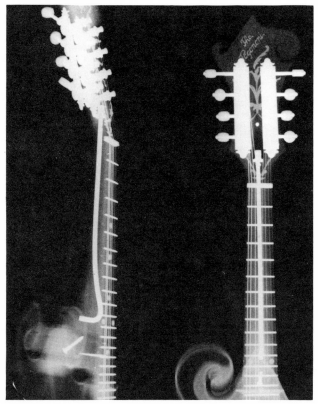

Neck X-ray, Paganoni F-5-style mandolin. Note truss rod running through neck.

Gibson F-4 mandolin: Florentine body, oval sound hole.

fine hardwoods. The least expensive instruments use laminated woods and may even have brass frets.

DESIGN FEATURES

Body. Most mandolins built today are copies of, or modeled after, old Gibson instruments. Few builders or manufacturers deviate from the successful Gibson formula, and when they do, the changes are small, if often noticeable.

A-style mandolins in the Gibson manner—or Gibson mandolins—usually have an arched, carved top and back; the top is graduated, that is, tapers in thickness toward the sides. But some mandolins—for example, the Flatiron (also modeled after an early Gibson design)—have a flat top and back. The Martin has a raised top.

F-style mandolins always have a scroll. They usually have f holes these days but in the past were also built with a round or oval sound hole. They always have an arched, carved top and back. F models are distinguished by the scroll and points—the sharp protuberances on the body.

On arched-top mandolins the top and back are carved, either totally by hand or (as is more likely) in part—the rough work is done on a machine and the vital work done by hand. The best instruments have a "tap tuned" top and back and tone bars, meaning the pitch of the wood is adjusted—"tuned"—by tapping it.

Bridge. Because the intonation problems inherent in fretted instruments are more pronounced on the mandolin, a compensated bridge, which many instruments are equipped with, is a useful feature.

PICKGUARD AND INLAYS

A pickguard is optional. For the beginner, simple fingerboard inlays are more helpful in locating notes than are complex designs.

Money Matters

Because so many mandolins are re-creations of Gibsons, past a point the differences between various brands are subjective. The peghead shapes vary, as do the inlays; the sound of one instrument appeals to one person but not another; construction methods vary somewhat; prices differ.

FIRST MANDOLIN: UNDER $300

Try to buy a mandolin with at least a solid-wood top, or even with all solid woods, but this needn't be a prime consideration. This instrument will be an A style either of the arched-top variety or of the flattop variety like the Flatiron. Buy a kit or even a used roundback if you are on a tight budget.

MANDOLIN: UNDER $700

Buy a new F model (imported usually), a new A model (domestic), or used style A Gibson. Instruments in this and higher price brackets ought to be made of solid woods.

MANDOLIN: UNDER $2500

Buy a new American-made A or F model or a valuable used instrument. With the exception of prized old Gibson and the new Gibson (which now sells for $3500), instruments in this bracket should be the best money can buy.

MANDOLA

Budget-conscious musicians should look for used mandolas as a possible alternative to the "less expensive" new instruments. Demand for old mandolas is low, so prices are not astronomical; and demand for new instruments is low, so no cheap instruments are built.

Flatiron mandolins.

Kits, Plans, Materials

Buck Musical Instrument Products, 40 Sand Rd., New Britain, PA 18901. Materials

Elderly Instruments, P.O. Box 1795, E. Lansing, MI 48823. Plans and some materials.

Gurian Guitars, Box 595, W. Swanzey, NH 03469. Materials—everything you need to build a mandolin . . . except plans.

Here, Inc., 29 S.E. Main St., Minneapolis, MN 55414. Kits.

Tom Morgan, Rt. 3, Box 147-1, Dayton, TN 37321. F-5 plans.

Stewart-MacDonald, Box 900, Athens, OH 45701. Kit and hardware.

Mandolin Brands, Builders, and Manufacturers

Aria Pro II (Music Distributors, Inc., 3400 Darby Ave., Charlotte, NC 28216). Aria mandolins are imported and comparable in quality to Washburns and Kentuckys. Sold through dealers.

Capritaurus (P.O Box 153, Felton, CA 95018). Capritaurus, which has been building mandolins since 1976, has a good reputation. Available through dealers. Expect a two-month delay when ordering from the manufacturer. Custom models available directly from the firm. One-year warranty.

Ellis (7203 Cooper Lane, Austin, TX 78745). Tom Ellis has been building fine mandolins since 1978; he has one assistant. "Each one is an individual creation, and much time is given to discussion, the instrument, the player's wants, style of playing, etc." The $2100 price "can be less depending on such factors as no stain, no inlay, and so on." Order direct; six-month wait on delivery.

Flatiron (Backporch Productions, 321 E. Main, Boseman, MT 59715). These instruments, styled after the Gibson Army-Navy model sold through Army and Navy PXs during World War I, are an excellent value. What the manufacturer saves by building a mandolin with a flat top and back is put

Capritaurus mandolin.

into good-quality materials. Available both directly through Flatiron and through dealers. Lifetime warranty.

Gibson (c/o Norlin Music, 7373 N. Cicero Ave., Lincolnwood, IL 60646). Certain old Gibsons are among the most prized instruments sold today. Presently Gibson manufactures the F-5L, a copy of the valuable old Lloyd Loar model, but it's expensive and may be hard to obtain. The used F-5 instruments are sometimes difficult to find at a dealer's, but according to Stan Werbin of Elderly Instruments, "the last fellow I knew who *seriously* looked found three or four for sale around the country. They're around if you have the money and are not concerned

Gilchrist mandolin.

with how clean they are (or, for that matter, how they sound)." Although new Gibsons have a good reputation, many less expensive instruments built by individual builders are as good if not better. Sold through dealers.

Gilchrist (Gruhn Guitars, 410 Broadway, Nashville, TN 37203). Stephen Gilchrist, an Australian builder, reportedly builds a very good mandolin and mandola. Options include a curved or flat fingerboard, large or small frets. Specify size and shape of neck and the kind of tone you like. Order from Gruhn.

Givens (Box 642, Sandpoint, ID 83864). Since 1966, R. L. Givens has been building high-quality instruments. He and his assistants produce about fifteen F models each year and seventy-five A models. Givens states: "I started with a Lloyd Loar I took apart in 1966. But when I put one together with the same dimensions it didn't sound the same. I don't think that Loar F-5s sound the same today as they did in 1927. And new F-5 copies today will not sound the same as original F-5s. So I changed my designs

over the years to experiment with the sound.... I make my mandolins to sound the way I like them to sound. I try to put them together as well as I can, but I have seen some Loars that are absolute perfection. And that's hard to beat." Available from Givens and through some dealers; expect a three-month wait when ordering from the builder himself.

Here, Inc. (29 S.E. Main St., Minneapolis, MN 55414). A well-known manufacturer.

Horner (Rt. 1, Box 170-A, Rockwood, TN 37854). Working alone since 1955, Charles Horner builds six to twelve instruments each year. He says his mandolins have "a deep, woody tone with good carrying power." Most of his instruments are sold to good amateur musicians, but Jesse McReynolds (of Jim and Jesse) owns some Horners too (along with instruments built by other builders listed in these pages). Available from Horner.

Ibanez (Elger Distributors, P.O. Box 469, Ben Salem, PA 19020). As of April 1981, Ibanez does not make mandolins; however, they may begin opera-

Here, Inc., mandolin.

tions again. Either way, look for these instruments, because they have an excellent reputation for commercial mandolins. Imports.

Kentucky (Saga Musical Instruments, P.O. Box 2841, South San Francisco, CA 94080). These imported mandolins are comparable in quality to Washburns and cost somewhat less. Kentucky has just extended its line, too, so there are many models to choose from. Available through dealers.

Lehmann (34 Elton St., Rochester, NY 14607). Berhard Lehmann, who has been building mandolins by himself since 1971, builds handsome, reasonably priced instruments. Available directly from the builder; delivery takes six months. Lifetime warranty.

Martin (CF Martin Organisation, Nazareth, PA 18064). Martin, of course, needs little introduction: it is the premier manufacturer of steel-string guitars in the world. Stan Werbin says, "We sell *lots* of used mandolins to folk musicians." Martin also makes new mandolins on special order.

Monteleone (41 Degnon Blvd., Bay Shore, NY 11706). John Monteleone, who has been widely praised for his quality and creativity, explains his philosophy: "The F-5 (Gibson) is an instrument that Gibson should be responsible for and not me. It's fine that people want to copy it, but I do not feel it is a product totally of my own creation." He has stopped making his own F-5 copy and is now building an instrument "inspired by the F-5." He likes "to have

an instrument that sounds very rich, but with each note having a somewhat bell-like quality and an even-sounding, smooth response. A lot of times the bass seems to get lost—something seems to get lost. And part of the challenge is to get the total spectrum of response to happen." Available from Monteleone or through some dealers; expect a six-month delay when ordering from the builder himself.

Morgan (Rt. 3, Box 147-1, Dayton, TN 37321). Tom Morgan, who has been building instruments since 1966, says his mandolins "invariable go to only the most discerning people. We don't strive for a 'slick' instrument...so our finish is hand-rubbed instead of buffed." Order directly from Morgan; delivery takes one and one-half years.

Nugget (P.O. Box 712, Nederland, CO 80466). Says Mike Kemnitzer, a builder since 1972, "I strive to make as close a reproduction as possible to what you could buy in the 1920s (excluding inlay).... Complete satisfaction is guaranteed." Contact Nugget directly; delivery takes six months. Lifetime warranty.

Paganoni and Sons (13418 Gordon Drive, Manassas, VA 22110). John Paganoni has been in business since 1971 and is a respected luthier. Order direct; delivery takes six to twelve months.

Stelling (Stelling Banjo Works, 8815 Kenwood Dr., Spring Valley, CA 92077). Geoff Stelling, known mostly for his quality banjos, has been building mandolins since 1979. They are a variation of the A

Peghead, Nugget mandolin.

model but not copied from Gibson. Available through dealers or directly from Stelling; delivery time is one to three months. Two-year warranty.

Stewart-MacDonald (Box 900, Athens, OH 45701). Stew-Mac has an outstanding reputation as a manufacturer of instrument kits, hardware, and accessories. On the mandolin kit, the top is almost fully carved; all you need do is fine-sand, finish, and assemble the instrument.

Stiver (1129 Florida Ave., Akron OH 44314). Ever since 1969, Louis Stiver has been building only mandolins. He works alone, trying "to make every mandolin one I would want for myself." He completes about twenty-four instruments each year. Stiver will sell to you direct if you live in Akron; otherwise order from Elderly Instruments in East Lansing, Michigan.

Warner (Warner String Works, 109 Eichelberger St., Hanover, PA 17331). Chris Warner has been in business since 1971 and works alone. His mandolins are "custom design" and the sound is "Gibson

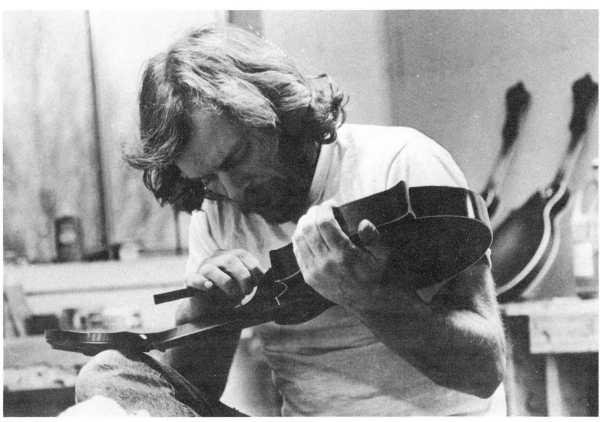

R. L. Givens.

prewar." Available from Warner; expect a one- to two-month wait. Lifetime warranty.

❦

Washburn (Fretted Industries, 1415 Waukegan Rd., Northbrook, IL 60062). These imported instruments compare favorably with other good imports. Widely distributed. Limited lifetime warranty.

❦

Wynn (Rt. 2, Box 106-69, Ozark, MO 65721). In business since 1966, John Wynn has two assistants and builds ten to twelve mandolins per year. He aims for a "bass-heavy sound unless the customer wants a treble sound." His customers include mostly bluegrass musicians and also old-time, country, and jazz musicians. Order direct. Lifetime warranty.

Discography

Apollon, Dave. *Mandolin Virtuoso—Dave Apollon* (Yazoo 1006).

The Blue Sky Boys. *Sunny Side of Life* (Rounder 1006).

Bottle Hill. *Light Our Way along the Highway* (Biograph 6009). With mandolinist Barry Mitterhoff.

Burns, Jethro. *Jethro Burns* (Flying Fish 042).

Bush, Sam, with Alan Munde and Wayne Stewart. *Poor Richard's Almanac* (Ridge Runner 0002). Bush is a newgrass specialist.

Bill Monroe.

Duffey, John, with the Country Gentlemen. *Country Gentlemen*, Vol 1. (Folkways 2409). Duffey is now with the Seldom Scene.

Grisman, David. *The David Grisman Rounder Album* (Rounder 0069), *Hot Dawg* (Horizon 731), and *Quintet '80* (Warner 3469).

Hall, Kenny. *Kenny Hall* (Philo 1008) and *Kenny Hall and the Sweets Mill String Band*, Vols. 1 & 2 (Bay 727 & 103).

Leibovitz, Abraham. *Mostly Bach, Mandolin 2* (two albums with this same name), and *Mandolin Recital* (Hed-Arzi; order from Elderly Instruments, P.O. Box 1795, E. Lansing, MI 48823). Classical virtuoso.

Los Angeles Mandolin Orchestra (order from Mariam Townsley, 163 N. Formosa Ave., Los Angeles, CA 90036).

The Louvin Brothers. *Songs That Tell a Story* (Rounder 1030).

McReynolds, Jesse, with Jim and Jesse. *Bluegrass Special* (Columbia CSP-12641) and *Mandolin Workshop* (Hilltop 202). One of the all-time great players and groups.

Goichberg, Sol. *Vivaldi: Concerto in C; Concerto in G for Two Mandolins* (Odyssey 32160138). A great classical player.

Martin, Bogan, and Armstrong. *The Barnyard Dance* (Rounder 2003). Black string band, together since 1931.

Monroe, Bill. *Bluegrass Instrumentals* (MCA 104E) and *High, Lonesome Sound* (MCA 110E); with Charlie Monroe, *Feast Here Tonight* (2-Bluebird AXM2-5510).

Moore, Tiny. *Tiny Moore* (Kaleidoscope F-12); with Jethro Burns, *Tiny Moore and Jethro Burns: Back to Back* (Kaleidoscope 9).

Old-Time Southern Dance Music: String Bands (2-Old Timey 100/1).

Rachell, Yank. *Mandolin Blues* (Delmark 606).

Ragtime: The Country. Mandolin, Fiddles, and Guitars (Folkways RBF 18).

Statman, Andy. *Flatbush Waltz* (Rounder 0116). *The Virtuoso Classical Mandolin* (Everest 3244).

Others: Jimmy Gaudreau, Doyle Lawson, Mike Marshall, Davi Martini, Boddy Osborne, Red Rector, Ricky Skaggs, Jerry Stuart, Hershel Sizemore, Frank Wakefield, and Buck White.

Some of these players can be heard on recordings listed in Appendix A.

IRISH MUSIC

Instruments on these albums include mandolin and

Irish bouzouki, an instrument resembling a mandola.

Brady, Paul. *Welcome Here, Kind Stranger* (Mulligan 024).

Gavin, Frankie *Frankie Gavin* (Shanachie 29008).

Irvine, Andy. *Rainy Sundays... Windy Dreams...* (Tara 3002); with Paul Brady, *Andy Irvine and Paul Brady* (Mulligan 008).

Moloney, Mick. *Strings Attached* (Green Linnet 1027).

Planxty. *After the Break* (Tara 3001).

Pumpkin Head (Mulligan 001).

Bibliography: Instruction, Theory, Tunes

Before you can create your own style you have to be rooted in a number of styles. The reason I can go really far out is because I'm very well grounded in a number of traditional forms.
—Andy Statman

Allen, Charles. *Pocket Dictionary of Mandolin Chords*. Kenyon.

Burns, Jethro, and Ken Eidson. *Jethro Burns: Mandolin Player*. Mel Bay, 1976. Tablature and music. Intermediate to advanced levels. The mandolin according to Mr. Burns. Tape available.

Hayth, Gene, and Ken Eidson. *Old Time Mandolin solos*. Mel Bay, 1979. Tablature and music. Minimal basics, then fiddle tunes.

Holmes, Michael I. *Mandolin Instruction: Old Time, Country and Fiddle Tunes*. Folkways CRB 16 (two records and book) or CRB 16b (book only). Tablature. Quite good for the beginner.

Johnson, Sara and Maynard. *Backporch Flatpicking for Mandolin and Guitar*. Saginaw River Music. Tablature and music. Good.

Kaufman, Alan. *Beginning Old-Time Fiddle*. Oak, 1977. Music.

Knopf, Bill. *The Theory of Chord Construction for Mandolin*. (Order from Ryckman & Beck Music Publishing Co., McNab Industrial Plaza, 1300C W. McNab Rd., Fort Lauderdale, Fl 33309).

O'Neill, Francis. *O'Neill's Music of Ireland: Eighteen Hundred and Fifty Melodies*. Daniel Michael Collins, 1963. Music. The classic collection of tunes.

One Thousand Fiddle Tunes. M. M. Cole, 1967. Music.

Statman, Andy. *Jesse McReynolds/Mandolin*. Oak, 1979. Tablature. Intermediate to advanced levels. A very good book.

Statman, Andy. *Teach Yourself Bluegrass Mandolin*. AMSCO, 1978. Tablature.

Tottle, Jack. *Bluegrass Mandolin*. Oak, 1975. Tablature and music. A fine book.

Valle, Ray. *Mel Bay's Deluxe Bluegrass Mandolin Method*. Mel Bay, 1974.

Bibliography: Mandolinists, Construction

Rooney, James. *Bossmen: Bill Monroe and Muddy Waters*. Dial Press, 1971.

Siminoff, Roger. *How to Build a Bluegrass Mandolin*. Order from *Frets* (see below for address). Complete plans and instructions on building an F-5 mandolin.

Magazines

F.I.G.A. News, 2344 S. Oakley Ave., Chicago, IL 60608.

Frets, P.O. Box 28836, San Diego, CA 92128. $18/year (monthly). Column by David Grisman. Articles, instrument evaluations, interviews, shoptalk, record reviews. Good mandolin coverage.

Mandolin and Guitar, 1600 Billman Lane, Silver Spring, MD 20902. $9/year (bimonthly). Tunes, instruction, reviews, interviews.

Mandolin World News, Box 2225, San Rafael, CA 94902. $7/year (quarterly). Covers bluegrass, jazz, classical, etc. Interviews, shoptalk, instruments, record and book reviews. Recommended.

Festivals

See chapters on guitar and violin and Appendix E. Wherever there's bluegrass, there's going to be something of interest to mandolin players and enthusiasts.

CHAPTER 6
🍂 THE VIOLIN 🍂

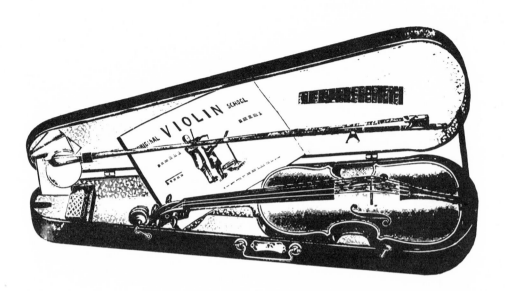

The violin is an instrument of special, extraordinarily wide appeal. Although some classical musicians tend to regard the violin as their own special property, the violin has been adopted by musicians of every persuasion for as long as it has been played. And each culture or cultural group that has taken to the violin has in turn made it its own. To an outsider the violin seems an Irish invention when used to play jigs and reels, an American invention when used to play fiddle tunes and jazz, an Indian invention when used to play ragas, a French invention in the hands of a Stephane Grappelli, a Russian invention in the hands of any of the great Russian violinists. The violin makes friends, good friends, wherever it travels.

How to explain the violin's appeal? The violin is an expressive instrument (it is usually played while held against the vocal cords) capable of great variation in dynamics, coloration, articulation, and tone, as well as of spellbinding virtuoso effects. The violin can make you weep or make you want to dance, the way no other instrument can. Maybe the violin has some magic force embodied in its shape and sound that is released whenever the strings are rubbed by the bow. "Maybe," as fiddler Byron Berline says,

> it's just an instrument that's always been around, that's been used, and there's more tunes that people are familiar with on the fiddle, that they relate to. Even back in the days of the pioneers, they always used the fiddle—somethin' that got the people dancin', made them feel good. You can get your emotions out a little more in a fiddle.

There are different kinds of guitars, mandolins, and banjos, but there is just one violin. Minor (though often significant) variations in dimensions aside, all violins are the same shape and size, and are virtually the same as they were in sixteenth-century Italy. Although builders have sought to improve the instrument, the greatest violins built by Antonio

Stradivari and Giuseppe Guarneri in the seventeenth and eighteenth centuries have never been surpassed. The instruments built by Stradivari during his golden period (the pinnacle was around 1714) have served as models for violins built since.

How does the violin differ from the fiddle? Although the two instruments are usually set up differently, with fiddlers preferring steel strings and a flatter bridge, they're the same instrument, named according to the context they're played in. The "violin" is used in classical music, jazz, gypsy music, popular music, even rock; the "fiddle" is used in country music, bluegrass, and Irish and old-time music. Although classical violinists are sometimes called fiddlers (and fiddlers, violinists) the word *fiddle* usually has folk and country connotations. (Technique differs according to the type of music played, too.)

Violin, front view. Made by David Gusset, San Francisco. Received gold medal for workmanship at 1980 New York International Competition and Exhibition for Violin- and Bowmakers.

Interviews with Kenny Kosek and Liz Slade

Kenny Kosek, 30 years old, grew up in the Bronx, and after making the rounds of music festivals, wound up back in New York playing commercials in the studios, doing some album work—mostly for Rounder Records—and rehearsing with several bands, one of which is Deliverance. Kenny doesn't like to label his style, preferring to let the studios do that ("if somebody's calling for a Burger King jingle I play country fiddle"), but when "somebody asks what I'm doing then I explain I play bluegrass and old-time music and Irish music and Cajun music and a little swing and a little experimental acoustic music and rock and new wave."

Liz Slade, who is 24, grew up in the Northeast and is especially attracted to old-time music because of its nonprofessionalism. She goes to conventions, meets old-time fiddlers, and calls square dances. For someone who can hardly wait to get down South in the summer, it seems ironic that she should currently be living in New York City.

INTERVIEW WITH KENNY KOSEK

What are your feelings about city boys and girls playing country music?

Well, I think it's fine. Since there is no such thing as a folk movement any more—the media have seen to that for the last twenty years or so—in this country you'd be hard pressed to find people who have learned from their families or neighbors and not had a TV or a record player to have endless amounts of other inputs. I mean, the standard definition of a hillbilly now is probably somebody in a mobile home with two TVs. So, somebody born, say, in 1965, and growing up in Raleigh or in New York City and learning fiddle now—they're probably learning the same way. They're probably buying the same records and slowing them down or buying the same Oak publications or whatever. The old grandpa-in-the-hills thing is almost like a museum relic.

Can a city person play with the same feeling as a country person?

Oh, sure, I've seen people who got that feeling. They succeeded instrumentally. And that's the point: *instrumentally* they've done it. But vocally, no. Vocally, even if there's no folk-music movement left . . . there still are regional accents. When I was growing up in New York, there was good singing, but it never had the kind of heart like the Stanley Brothers or the old, really emotionally strong music, and that was always the weak point. I've always had lots of fun playing bluegrass in New York, but even more fun playing it down South, running into these old guys and playing with them, because the emotional sense of the music is with the singing.

Doesn't the strongest music come out of the region where it was born?

Yeah, I think that still exists. My voice would be much better suited to singing streetcorner do-wop than to singing bluegrass.

It seems ironic then that so much country music is now being played in cities. Are you part of the "Urban Cowboy" scene?

I'm part of a group of studio musicians that are getting together to try and crack the New York country club scene. You know, people are realizing there's money to be made there, and even people who haven't been into country music before are getting into it.

Do you like playing in these clubs?

I think all musicians are bitter about playing in bars. All of a sudden in the last year there have been five new ones in Manhattan. It's phony cowboys, hats, riding a phony bull, and it's taking the place of disco as a nightlife scene, some kind of fantasy world that people can enter. Disco is a native Brooklyn phenomenon, so it suits New York better. What they're doing is trying to duplicate shitty road houses in Texas. And here people have been playing country music a long time in New York and saying, "Oh, boy, now there's going to be a place where I can play good country music and get a response and play all the time, " but not so. You work in these bars and they want to hear more or less the top 40 of country music; they want to hear the same old shitty, danceable stuff that people will recognize, going for the lowest common mentality. Now you can make fifty dollars a night in New York in a shitty bar instead of having to go to Baltimore or Virginia to play in a shitty bar.

You told me you do a lot of studio work. Is that any better than playing the clubs?

If I had to do a jingle, it was hard to reconcile myself to the fact that they're looking for the lowest-common-denominator fiddle stuff. If I could play something wonderful and brilliant, they wouldn't want to know it—they'd want to hear simple hoedown stuff, because they want to create an immediately successful impression.

In a way that's a kind of creativity, being able to give somebody exactly what they want, no matter how painful it might be to you.

Where is your playing going?

I like the fact that I'm playing different kinds of music. I play some country western, some Irish, and get a lot of strange, different gigs. And the studio is good for that too. I'd like to work on a project that would reach a larger audience. I mean, I've done the thing of throwing together a band for sixteen hours and it was lots of fun and dues paying and great to be making a lot of very personal music and getting a good response—I'd like to do that and have it become commercially successful. If it was ever possible, it would be possible now, because the distinc-tions are eroding between various kinds of closely related music. Lots of people who learned to play bluegrass are learning to play swing. You can go from old-time Appalachian music to bluegrass—that transition should be apparent. But then you can go from bluegrass to country music. And from country western you can get into Western swing, and once you're in Western swing you're halfway to Stephane Grappelli and Jo Venuti. Anyway, the musi-cians I'm working with and I are trying to come up with an alternate string-band sound. Like David Grisman's band—he did that. He took bluegrass instrumentation made up of players who were originally bluegrass musicians who had become kind of enlightened beyond that; he composed for them and got good manage-ment. And wham, it was accessible.

INTERVIEW WITH LIZ SLADE

What attracted you to the fiddle?

For one thing, there's no way you can learn how to play fiddle from a book or from written-down music. There is no tablature for old-time fiddle once you get past a certain point. You have to go around and learn from other people. You have to listen to records, and you have to go to fiddlers' conventions and decide how you want to play and seek out the people who play in the style you're interested in. It's a way of adventuring and meeting people and exploring. One thing else that's nice is that old time music is a part-time music. A lot of people who have been really influential in the music didn't spend their lives studying music and or being musi-cians. It's an accessible music, a very satisfying kind of music for someone who doesn't want to devote their life to it.

What style interests you most?

The Round Peak area of North Carolina and southwestern Virginia. That's a style that has a lot of openness and is very rhythmic. I think Tommy Jarrell is a really wonderful Round Peak fiddler and banjo player.

Have you visited him?

He loves to have young people visit him. The first time I visited him, a friend and I just went to his house—he doesn't have a phone—and said, "Hi, here we are." And he played some tunes for us on his fiddle and we played some tunes for him, and he gave us some advice on how he plays. And he insisted that we stay and have a meal with him. So many of these old people just love to have young people visit, talk with them.

Do you make changes in the tunes you learn?

It varies. First of all, I use a tape recorder a lot. Then I can work on things. There's two pushes. One is the push to be really authentic, and that gets down to a scholarly, ethnomusicological kind of thing. It's really nice, because you're preserving the music. But 1) technically I don't think I could reproduce things exactly, and 2) everyone has their own taste and preferences, and things just change—music changes, folktales change, as they get handed from person to person. I'm not really good at improvising, but some old-time musicians really like to improvise a lot.

So if you taped a song one week and went back the next week, the song might be played differently?

It would probably be a little different. But there are really standard ways to play some tunes. They just change from county to county and from town to town and from person to person. Some people prefer to individualize a song more than others, but I think everybody individualizes a song without even knowing it.

Isn't it true that what we call old-time music is really a music influenced in the past by newer music like jazz and other "nontraditional" influences? Were the real old timers such purists as you encounter today?

Well, a lot of people I know really do see it as a tradition. When I first visited Tommy Jarrell and played a tune with a new kind of lick I had liked and put it, he said, "Well, gal, you have that tune almost right. It's pretty good, but you're playing it wrong." It's true, old-time music has absorbed a lot of influences, and it was called old-time music back in the twenties. Back then it was called old-time music to hark back to the kind of music people's grandfathers were playing back in the eighteen hundreds. There are always going to be people who are collectors and scholars, and then there're people who really do change things around a lot and take the tradition and go on with that.

Where are you in this?

Kind of between the two. Style is something that's really important to me, something I love and don't want to throw away. But I don't feel I have to play a tune exactly the way it was played on the old 78s or play it according to the style or the county where I learned that tune. Right now I'm interested in developing my bowing further and seeing where I can take the kind of bowing I like in terms of getting more bounce, making it more vibrant. I think the bowing's really interesting—the thing that sets a lot of old-time music apart from other kinds of music. To me—and a lot of people would argue with this—the bowing's more important than the notes. Rhythm's also very important to me; I'll probably see myself working on just doing more with rhythm.

Selecting a Violin

For the experienced player, tone is undoubtedly the main consideration in choosing an instrument, but for the beginner, the tone need only be decent. Since evaluating the tone of a violin is nearly impossible unless you play or have someone play for you, it is really essential to bring along a knowledgeable person when looking for an instrument. What the inexperienced person *can* do is evaluate playability, condition, and size, which for the beginner are more important than sound anyway. Those of you who must select a violin on your own should at least know how to make sure it works and fits your proportions.

SIZE

Most violins are full or three-quarter size, but smaller instruments also exist. Unless you are very small or are buying for a child, you probably will need a full-size violin. Full-size instruments are close in size, but a large person would probably take a "large" instrument, a small person a "small" or ladies' size instrument. Here are the measurements of two violins that can be considered to be typical of instruments in the full-size and ladies'-size categories:

	The "Messiah" Stradivarius		"Ladies' Size" Guarnerius (1667)	
Body	14″	(356 mm)	13⅞″	(252 mm)
Upper Bouts	6⅝″	(168 mm)	6¼″	(159 mm)
Middle Bouts	4⁷⁄₁₆″	(113 mm)	4⅜″	(111 mm)
Lower Bouts	8³⁄₁₆″	(208 mm)	7¾″	(197 mm)
Sides	1¼ - 1⁵⁄₃₂″ (29-32 mm)		—	
Fingerboard	10½″ (267 mm)		—	
String (Scale) Length	13″	(330 mm)	13″	(330 mm)

Violins and bows are usually bought separately; that is, a violin ordinarily does not come with a bow.

Note the small differences in dimensions between these two instruments. A large violin at most will be 14½ inches long (at the body); a small ladies' size, 13½ inches long. Half-size instruments are even smaller.

CONDITION

Make sure the violin is complete; missing strings are easy to replace, but a new bridge must be fitted and adjusted. Look inside to make sure there is a soundpost. The soundpost, which should not be glued in place, may be rattling around or even missing; it may have to be set.

Next, evaluate the overall condition of the wood and the finish. Is the finish thickly applied and is the instrument obviously brand new, has the finish been touched up a lot (pretty common), has the finish worn off in places or perhaps even completely off the instrument? Condition greatly affects price, although many classic old violins have little or no finish remaining.

Now check for cracks. Many violins, especially old ones, have cracks. A well-repaired crack is either invisible or clean; a poorly repaired crack may appear a wide, dirty scar. The worst place for a crack is over or under the soundpost or over the bass bar. Well- or easily-repaired cracks are acceptable, but cracks in the scroll, around the pegs, over or under the soundpost, or over the bass bar (which reinforces the top and affects the tone) can be difficult and costly to repair. Sometimes an instrument with a well-repaired crack is an excellent value, since a crack may lower the price of the violin without necessarily hurting the tone or affecting the playability of the violin.

Finally, check the seams to make sure they are tight.

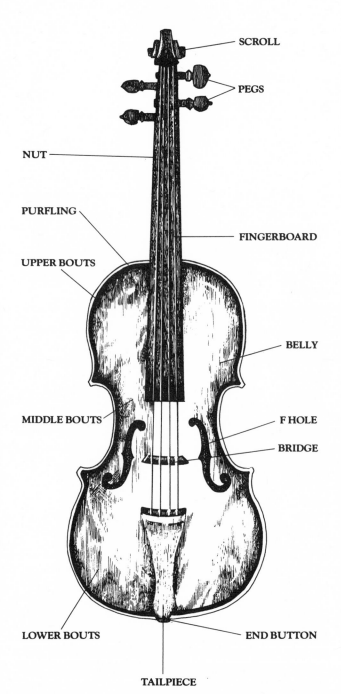

Violin schematic.

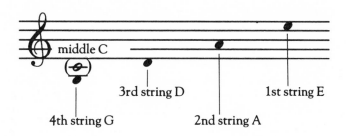

middle C

4th string G   3rd string D   2nd string A   1st string E

Violin tuning.

PLAYABILITY

Tuning. Because the violin has no frets, tuning has to be by ear, using one reference pitch. If you cannot hear the interval of a fifth, you will have to use four reference pitches. Tune the second string to an A440, and then tune the other strings accordingly: from bass to treble, GDAE. *Make sure the soundpost is in place before tuning up.* If the pegs do not work easily and you still buy the violin, have them replaced or refitted by a repairperson. A set of four ebony pegs costs from $7 to $20.

Action. At the nut, the strings should barely clear the fingerboard—by about the thickness of a post-card. At the other end, the strings on the bass side ought to clear the fingerboard by 5-7 millimeters, on the treble side by 2-4 millimeters; for the steel strings many fiddlers use, these measurements will be smaller, because steel strings are harder to play than gut strings: they hold more tension, offer less flexibility.

Neck Projection. Draw a line from the top of the bridge end of the fingerboard to where it would hit the bridge and measure the distance from the belly to that point of contact—that's neck projection. It should be 27-27.5 millimeters. When the neck is too low, the bridge has to be lowered accordingly, with a corresponding effect on sound: with less string tension there is less sound and brilliance. When the neck is too high, the action is too low and you will need a higher bridge to compensate. Both instances are undesirable; the ideal sound comes only with that one very precise measurement. Fortunately, the bridge can be adjusted within limits. In extreme cases, a neck that is too high

or low will have to be reset—usually lifted off the fingerboard. Sometimes what has happened is that the fingerboard collapsed onto the belly.

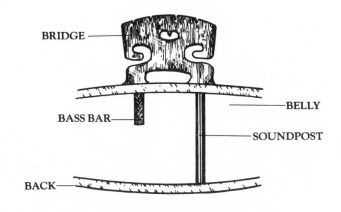

BRIDGE

BASS BAR

BACK

BELLY

SOUNDPOST

Cross-section of violin body.

Bridge. The feet of the bridge must make perfect contact with the belly or the sound will suffer. The bridge should also lean back ever so slightly. When the bridge is too high (or too low), the tone suffers and the action may be too high. You may need to have an expert fit the bridge, although some bridges have adjustable feet that automatically conform to the arch of the belly. These bridges may seriously hurt the sound of the instrument, however.

Soundpost. The soundpost reinforces the top under the treble side of the bridge and also helps to conduct vibrations to the back; it must be in just the right place. Even experienced players and repairpersons have a hard time doing this.

MATERIALS

The best violins have a maple back, sides, scroll, and neck; spruce belly; boxwood, rosewood, or ebony pegs; ebony nut, fingerboard, tailpiece, chinrest, and end button (fittings); and maple bridge. The costliest maple is flamed; the best spruce comes from Europe. A close, narrow grain on the belly is usually preferred, but some good instruments have a wide grain. The back can be one or two pieces; the belly is two pieces. On less expensive but good instruments the fittings may be rosewood or boxwood and the flame pattern is plainer; and on really cheap instruments the fittings may be maple or some other wood dyed black, or possibly even plastic. A plastic chinrest can be very uncomfortable.

Ebony Tailpiece—$5–15
Ebony Chinrest—about $20

PURFLING

Purfling strengthens and decorates the edge of the violin belly, serving much the same purpose as the binding on a guitar. Single purfling consists of a strip of light wood sandwiched between two strips of dark wood (usually stained light wood), and is inlaid around the belly. Maggini violins and Maggini copies have double purfling—two sets of single purfling. Since inlaying real purfling is time-consuming and thus costly, cheap factory instruments often have painted-on "purfling" or just lines scratched in the wood. Real purfling often indicates a handmade violin, but some fine old instruments have painted-on or even no purfling, while some factory instruments have real purfling.

CONSTRUCTION

On the cheapest violins the belly and back may be made of wood that has been stamped to shape under heat and pressure. Although the belly and back of a good instrument may be roughed out by machine, the final work—the fine carving—is done by hand and is a delicate, time-consuming process. Making a violin by hand takes about a month (applying the finish consumes a great deal of that time), but Stradivari built one instrument per week . . . with helpers.

Viola, back view. Made by David Gusset, San Francisco (1981). (Note: The viola is tuned a fifth below the violin and is also slightly larger.)

FINISH

The finish is very important on a violin, for its effects on both the tone and the eye. For a long time people believed—and some still believe—that the key to the greatness of a Stradivarius violin lay in the finish. Theories have been concocted, experiments conducted, analyses of the finish carried out in university laboratories—all to no avail. There are no secret ingredients in Stradivari's finish; he was, quite simply, a genius and an artist in each aspect of his craft.

As Joseph Wechsberg notes in his book *The Glory of the Violin*:

> Visually...the back is very important. Many experts and collectors often look at it first. A handsome piece of maple, its striking pattern brought out by a soft, beautiful, translucent varnish, seems like a great painting. Sometimes the back gave the violin its name, as in the case of the "Dolphin" Stradivari, made in 1714: its two-piece back shows the changing, iridescent colors of the dolphin.[1]

TONE

The great violin makers differed little from each other, but where they did differ, the results are significant. The qualities of copies often reflect the qualities of the originals:

Amati—usually small, sweet tone; sometimes similar to that of a Strad

Stainer—quiet, sweet tone

Stradivarius—the standard

Guarnerius—rich, sonorous, loud, dark, large sound

Maggini—very loud sound

Bluegrass and country musicians sometimes like the Maggini sound (although few if any have originals).

Selecting a Bow

As Alberto Bachmann says in *An Encyclopedia of the Violin:* "It is absolutely essential that the violinist have some knowledge of the construction of this mysterious wand which, externally of incomparable lightness and elegance in appearance, is nevertheless subjected to the hardest usage."[2]

The bow is a simple mechanism that has to work just right to perform well. A screw at the frog end tightens or loosens the horsehair (or nylon), which affects the ease of playing the attack, and the tone. When the fibers of the hair or nylon are covered with rosin, they become sticky and the friction of the bow against the strings produces the tone. A perfectly smooth bow would produce little sound—just a kind of whining. When the horsehair or nylon is too loose, there's no pressure against the strings, and again the sound will be meager. The bow must be flexible so that it will respond to different amounts of wrist pressure. A bow that is too heavy or that is heavy at the top will be unwieldy and hard to control.

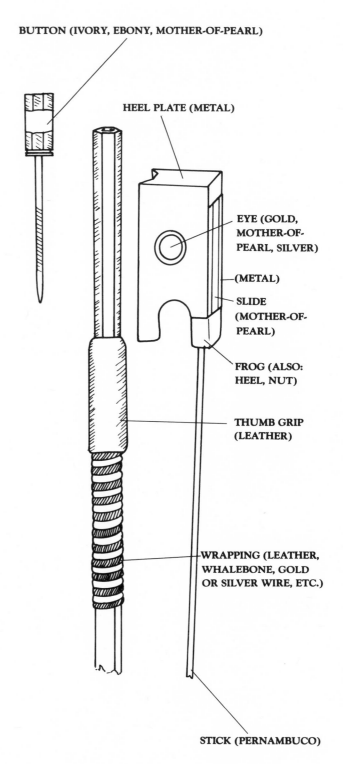

BUTTON (IVORY, EBONY, MOTHER-OF-PEARL)

HEEL PLATE (METAL)

EYE (GOLD, MOTHER-OF-PEARL, SILVER)

(METAL)

SLIDE (MOTHER-OF-PEARL)

FROG (ALSO: HEEL, NUT)

THUMB GRIP (LEATHER)

WRAPPING (LEATHER, WHALEBONE, GOLD OR SILVER WIRE, ETC.)

STICK (PERNAMBUCO)

Violin bow schematic.

When buying a bow, take along the violin you plan to use (and someone to try them together if you can't yet play the instrument). First, check to see that the bow works and that all its parts are there. Especially important is the tip, since the tip protects the bow if it falls; when an ivory tip breaks, for example, it shatters, and in shattering absorbs most of the shock, protecting the rest of the bow. Then make sure the bow is straight (from side to side) when the hairs are loose and slightly curved to the left, if at all, when the hairs are tight. Note the balance and weight of the bow when you play. Next, inspect the bow for cracks: around the frog, where the screw enters the stick, in the stick itself, and in the tip; do not buy a bow with a split tip or a crack unless it has been carefully repaired. Also examine the back of the bow head, especially if the tip is made of metal.

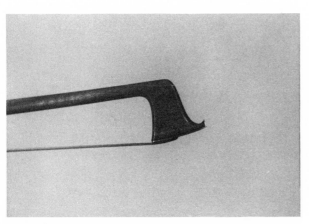

Violin bow tip: made by Reid Kowallis.

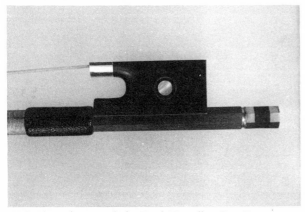

Violin bow frog: made by Reid Kowallis, San Francisco.

MATERIALS

The best bows have an ivory tip, sometimes mother-of-pearl; pernambuco (a variety of brazilwood) stick: ebony frog; and fittings of whalebone, silver, gold, leather, or mother-of-pearl; unbleached white horsehair. Good but less expensive bows may use brazilwood instead of pernambuco, and the less expensive a bow is the less silver, gold, ebony, abalone, and ivory will be used on it. Really cheap bows use a lot of plastic; the stick may be fiberglass and the "hair" nylon. Fiberglass bows may or may not be better than some cheap wood bows, and nylon is good in the tropics; otherwise little can be said for synthetics. Some violinists use black horsehair, which produces a coarser sound than white, wears better, but is less resilient, or even a combination of white and black. The stick is either round or octagonal, and the whole bow averages 29 inches in length, give or take half an inch.

Money Matters

The price of a violin depends on the maker, the condition of the instrument, the figuration of the back, the quality of the materials (regardless of the overall quality of the instrument), the location of the dealer, and, on expensive instruments, the tone. Bow pricing is similar.

Very roughly, violin prices break down as follows:

1. Inexpensive, new, factory made: from about $150 to $1000; usually under $500.

2. Inexpensive, old, factory made: usually under $1000; in good condition averaging $200–500.

3. Inexpensive, new, handmade: less than $1000, possibly some instruments built by amateur builders or under special circumstances.

4. Inexpensive, old, handmade: sometimes less than $1000, usually more.

5. Expensive, new, handmade: sometimes as low as $1000, but average bottom is more like $2500.

6. Expensive, old, handmade: four- or five-digit figures.

7. Very expensive, old, handmade: up to $500,000 (more?); a Stradivarius, for example.

Bow prices break down as follows:

1. New or used factory made: from about $30.

2. New, handmade: $400–2000, sometimes as high as $3000.

3. Old, valuable, handmade: up to $50,000 (more?).

While you may find an instrument or bow for less money than listed here, chances are if the instrument is bought from a second-hand store such as a pawnshop or flea market it will need to be set up, which will add to the price, sometimes considerably. For a first violin, in good condition, expect to pay from $100 to $400 for the violin alone, and an additional $40–150 for the bow, if the bow doesn't come with the instrument.

Here's a sampling of instruments available from four mail-order dealers around the country.

Elderly Instruments (P.O. Box 1795, E. Lansing, MI 48823) (September 28, 1980) lists twenty-seven used violins, all but one under $200.

Fiddlepicker (Box 1033, Mountainside, NJ 07092) (1981) lists thirty-three used violins, from $100 to $2000, most priced for under $500.

Gruhn Guitars (410 Broadway, Nashville, TN 37203) (December 8, 1981) lists five used violins, from $150 to $400.

Metropolitan Music (Mountain Rd., R.D. 1, Stowe, VT 05672) (1981) lists new John Juzek imported commercial violins from about $142 to $750.

Brands and Builders

Because so many violins have been built over the years by so many violin makers and manufacturers, it is impossible, in this space, to list or recommend "brands" or builders. Entire catalogues have been devoted to the purpose of listing instruments and builders, and identifying instruments is a highly developed skill. The following information, however, should simplify the task of choosing an instrument.

NEW VS. OLD

Although the best violins were built many years ago, new and more recent instruments can be excellent.

Often the biggest difference is that the older instrument has been played on a lot and its tone has developed. The situation with bows is similar. According to Joseph Gold, a San Francisco violinist, "some of the finest bow makers in the world are in New York, San Francisco, Los Angeles, and Chicago, and of course in France. Their bows are as good and just as beautiful as the old bows."

COMMERCIAL

Commercial—factory-made—violins range from terrible to very good. Although presently instruments built in the Orient are suitable for schoolchildren and not much else, undoubtedly these violins will improve in the same way that products such as Japanese guitars, cameras, and cars have improved over the years. Really cheap violins can sometimes be improved by replacing the pegs, tailpiece, and strings.

COPIES AND LABELS

Ever since the golden age of the violin, luthiers have copied or emulated the instruments of the masters. Some copies are so good that only an expert can tell they are copies. And some copies are so good they have become quite valuable themselves. Most copies have been built by factories, however, which may produce thousands of imitations of a particular old instrument.

Nothing is wrong with replicating a good instrument, but luthiers and manufacturers have gone a step further, often forging the label of the original maker or in some cases actually stealing an original label and putting it into their own instrument. To this day dealers must contend with people bringing "Strads" in and refusing to believe the deceptions; although authentic old violins do turn up now and then, the occurrence is extremely rare. Many labels on copies are more honest, stating, for example, "Copy of Stradivarius, 1714. Made in Czechoslovakia."

Handmade violins generally bear the luthier's name on the label, along with the year of production and sometimes the city or country of origin, with or without mention of the original inspiration—if there was one. Keep in mind that plenty of handmade instruments do not have the maker's name on the label and that violins with fake labels should be avoided only when they are poor instruments or when it turns out you may be overpaying.

Accessories

Rosin. Rosin is rubbed on the bow to create friction with the strings. A package of rosin costs between $1 and $4.

Shoulder Rest. A shoulder rest is indispensable for comfort. Some rests are extremely hard and painfully uncomfortable. The Wolf Super Flexible ($21.50) is quite good. Some players make their own shoulder rest.

Fine Tuners. A violin set up with gut strings has a fine tuner attached behind the bridge on the (metal) E string to help fine-tune without turning the peg. When the violin is set up with four steel strings for country or bluegrass you may want fine tuners ($1.50–6.00 each) on all four strings.

Mute. A mute softens the sound, cutting volume and also drastically modifying the tone; some mutes make the sound barely audible. A mute is useful if you want to practice quietly. There are three types: a sliding mute (Roth-Sihon, about $2.50) that's permanently attached to the string and may chew up the strings; a standard wood (or plastic) mute ($1.25–2.00) that's clipped on; and a practice mute ($10–15), which allows you to "play" in almost total silence.

Discography

OLD TIME

Ashby, John, & the Free State Ramblers. *Fiddling by the Hearth* (County 773)

Camp Creek Boys. *Camp Creek Boys* (County 709).

Cockeram, Fred, Tommy Jarrell, and Oscar Jenkins. *Down to the Cider Mill* (County 713).

Echoes of the Ozarks, Vols. 1–3 (County 518–520).

Fraley, J. P. *Wild Rose of the Mountain* (Rounder 0037).

Hell Broke Loose in Georgia (County 514). Georgia fiddle bands, 1927–1934.

Jarrell, Tommy. *Sail Away Ladies* (County 756).

Kessinger, Clark. *The Legend of Clark Kessinger* (County 733).

Old-Time Fiddle Classics (County 507).

Old-Time Fiddle Music from Kentucky, Vols. 1–3 (Morning Star 450003–450005).

Round the Heart of Old Galax, Vols. 1–3 (County 533–535).

Schwartz, Tracy. *Look Out, Here It Comes* (Folkways 2419).

Smith, Fiddlin' Arthur. *Fiddlin' Arthur Smith*, Vols. 1 & 2 (County 546 & 547).

Stripling Brothers (County 401).

Texas Farewell (County 517)

Thomas, Buddy. *Kitty Puss* (Rounder 0032).

BLUEGRASS, JAZZ, SWING, TEXAS STYLE

Baker, Kenny. *Portrait of a Bluegrass Fiddler* (County 719). One of the all-time great bluegrass fiddlers.

Berline, Byron. *Dad's Favorites* (Rounder 0100) and *Outrageous* (Flying Fish 227). An excellent contemporary bluegrass/country fiddler, formerly of the Country Gazette.

Clements, Vassar. *Hillbilly Jazz* (2-Flying Fish 101) and *Vassar Clements* (Mercury 1022). Clements has a style that combines diverse influences (bluegrass, country, blues, jazz, swing) and makes him a much-sought-after session man.

Forrester, Howdy. *Stylish Fiddling* (Stoneway 168).

Grappelli, Stephane, with Django Reinhardt. *1935—First Hot Club Recordings* (GNP 9023E). Grappelli, one of jazz's greatest violinists, plays with great feeling, panache, and fine technique.

Kosek, Kenny, with Matt Glaser. *Hasty Lonesome* (Rounder 0215); Kosek with Breakfast Special, *Breakfast Special* (Rounder 3012).

Spicher, Buddy. *American Sampler* (Flying Fish 021).

Texas Fiddle Favorites (County 707).

Texas Hoedown (County 703).

Venuti, Joe, with Eddie Lang. *Stringing the Blues* (CBS 2-CSP JC2L-24). Venuti is a great, thoroughly enjoyable jazz violinist.

See Appendix A for more recordings that include bluegrass and old-time fiddlers.

IRISH

Burke, Kevin. *If the Cap Fits . . .* (Mulligan 021).

Doherty, John. *John Doherty* (Gael-Linn 072 & 073).

Gavin, Frankie. *Frankie Gavin* (Shanachie 29008).

Keane, Sean. *Gusty's Frolicks* (Claddagh 17).

Kelly, John and James. *The Best of Traditional Irish Music* (Tara 1008).

O'Keefe, Padraig, Denis Murphy, and Julia Clifford. *Kerry Fiddles* (Topic 309).

Paddy in the Smoke (Topic 176).

Peoples, Tommy, and Paul Brady. *The High Part of the Road* (Shanachie 29003).

BLUES

Armstrong, Howard, with Martin and Bogan. *Barnyard Dance* (Rounder 2003).

Batts, Will. *Low Down Memphis Barrelhouse Blues* (Mamlish 3803).

Brown, Clarence Gatemouth. *Blackjack* (First American Records), *Anthology of American Folk Music* (Folkways 2952), *He Was Loved by All the People* (Testament 2205), and *I Can See My Baby in My Dream* (Storyville 180).

Cage, Butch. *I Have to Paint My Face: Mississippi Delta Blues* (Arhoolie 1005) and *Blues 'n' Trouble* (Arhoolie 1006).

Chatmon, Lonnie. *Mississippi & Beale Street Sheiks* (Biograph 12041) and *Stop and Listen: The Mississippi Sheiks* (Mamlish 3804).

Chenier, Morris "Big." *Bon Ton Roulet* (Arhoolie 1031).

Clay, Beauford. *Blues 'n' Trouble*, Vol. 2 (Arhoolie 1012) and Blind James Campbell (Arhoolie 1015).

Collins, Chasey. *Jug, Jook, & Washboard Bands* (Blues Classics 2).

Martin, Carl. *The Chicago String Band* (Testament 2220).

Pierce, Charlie. *Jug, Jook, & Washboard Bands* (Blues Classics 2).

Sims, Henry "Son." *Mississippi Blues 1927–1941* (Belzona L1001).

CAJUN

The Balfa Brothers Play More Cajun Music (Swallow 6019).

The Balfa Brothers Play Traditional Cajun Music (Swallow 6011).

Bergeron, Shirley and Alphee, with the Veteran Playboys. *Cajun Style Music* (Lanor 1001).

Cajun Sole by Mamou Cajun Band (Swallow 8001).

The Cajuns. *Songs, Waltzes, Two-Steps* (Folkways RBF 21).

Hackberry Ramblers. *Louisiana Cajun Music* (Arhoolie 5003).

Louisiana Cajun Music, Vols. 1–5 (Old Timey 108–111 & 114).

McGhee, Dennis, and S. D. Courville. *The Traditional Cajun Fiddling of Dennis McGhee and S. D. Courville* (Morning Star 16001).

SWEDISH, CAPE BRETON, FRENCH-CANADIAN, UKRAINIAN, INDIAN

Beaudoin, Louis. *La Famille Beaudoin* (Philo 2022).

Campbell, John. *Cape Breton Violin Music* (Rounder 7003).

Carignan, Jean. *Jean Carignan* (Philo 2001). French-Canadian fiddler.

Folk Fiddling from Sweden (Nonesuch 72062).

Holland, Jerry. *Jerry Holland* (Rounder 7008). Cape Breton fiddler.

Master of the Sarangi (Nonesuch 72062). The *sarangi* is an Indian bowed instrument.

Menuhin, Yehudi, Ravi Shankar, and Alla Rahka. *West Meets East* (Angel 2294). A pioneer recording.

Ukrainian-American Fiddle & Dance Music 1926–1934, Vols. 1 & 2 (Arhoolie 9014 & 9015).

CLASSICAL

Heifetz, Jascha. *Encores* (RCA LSC–3233E). Impeccably performed miniatures.

Milstein, Nathan. *Sonatas and Partitas for Violin Unaccompanied* (Deutsche Gramophone 3-DG 2709047). According to Kenny Kosek, "the greatest fiddle tunes ever." According to most classical music lovers, among the greatest, most inspired and inspiring music ever composed.

Perlman, Itzhak. *Caprices*, by Niccolo Paganini (Angel S-36860). Paganini, who perfected much of modern violin technique, practiced in secret and reputedly was in cahoots with the devil. The twenty-four caprices, which are studies as well as show pieces, still challenge violinists, as undoubtedly they were meant to, and probably were written as virtuoso pieces for the composer himself.

Bibliography: Instruction, Styles, Tunes

With one exception, the books in this section use only standard music notation.

Allen, Ward. *Canadian Fiddle Tunes*, 2 vols. Don Mills, Ont.: BMI Canada, 1956.

Brody, David. *Kenny Baker/Fiddle*. Oak, 1979. The style and repertoire of a bluegrass great.

Christeson, Robert P. *The Old-Time Fiddler's Repertory: 245 Traditional Tunes*. University of Missouri Press, 1973.

Feldman, Allen, and Lamonn O'Doherty. *The Northern Fiddle*. Belfast: Blackstaff Press, 1979. Fiddle tunes, text on Irish music, photographs.

Glaser, Matt, and Stephane Grappelli. *Jazz Violin*. Oak, 1981.

Glaser, Matt. *Teach Yourself Bluegrass Fiddle.* AMSCO, 1978. Good if you already play violin.

Glaser, Matt. *Vassar Clements/Fiddle.* Oak, 1978. Similar to the Brody book, for Clements.

Kaufman, Alan. *Beginning Old-Time Fiddle.* Oak, 1977. Tablature and music. Includes bowings. Excellent book for beginners.

Kosek, Kenny, and Stacy Phillips. *Bluegrass Fiddle Styles.* Oak, 1978. Seventy tunes; styles of twenty-five players.

Krassen, Miles. *Appalachian Fiddle.* Oak, 1973. Good book on old-time fiddling but contains no bowings.

Lieberman, Julie Lyonn. *Blues Fiddle.* Mel Bay, 1981. Beginning to advanced levels. A fine book on blues fiddlers (some of whom are included in the blues fiddle discography) and their music.

Liebermann, Julie Lyonn. *New Age Violin.* Mel Bay, 1982. Beginning to advanced levels. How to improvise in various styles: jazz, blues, swing, rock, Indian, pop.

Lowinger, Gene. *Bluegrass Fiddle.* Oak, 1974. Beginning to intermediate levels. A very popular book by a musician who has played with Bill Monroe and the Bluegrass Boys.

O'Neill, Francis. *O'Neill's Music of Ireland: Eighteen Hundred and Fifty Melodies.* Daniel Michael Collins, 1963. This is the classic collection.

One Thousand Fiddle Tunes. M. M. Cole, 1967. A popular collection.

Reiner, David. *Mel Bay's Deluxe Anthology of Fiddle Styles.* Mel Bay, 1979. A fine collection of tunes in various styles: Texas, cajun, Irish, bluegrass, Swedish. Tape available.

Townsend, Grahm. *Grahm Townsend's Canadian Country Fiddle Tunes,* 2 vols. Scarborough, Ont., Canada: Berendol Music.

Williamson, Rob. *English, Welsh, Scottish, and Irish Fiddle Tunes.* Oak, 1976. Over one hundred tunes. Includes soundsheet.

INSTRUCTION RECORDS AND TAPES

Glaser, Matt. *Texas and Swing Fiddle Styles.* Homespun Tapes, Box 694, Woodstock, NY 12498. Six cassettes for the player "with a basic knowledge of fiddle technique." Includes transcriptions.

Kosek, Ken. *Bluegrass and Country Fiddle.* Homespun Tapes. Six cassettes demonstrating bowing, fingering, tunes, and other matters. Includes transcriptions.

Schwartz, Tracy. *Learn to Fiddle Country Style* (Folkways 8359). Record.

Traditional Cajun Fiddle (Folkways 8361). Record.

Bibliography: History, Construction, Appreciation, Fiddlers, Violinists

Ahrens, Pat. *Union Grove: The First Fifty Years.* Unior Grove Old Time Fiddle Convention, 1975. Photos, history, lists of winners, trivia, interviews—all having to do with the famous fiddlers' gathering.

Bachmann, Alberto. *An Encyclopedia of the Violin.* Da Capo, 1966. History, famous violinmakers, construction, violinists, and violin music. Good, if rather prosaic, sourcebook.

Bachmann, Werner. *The Origins of Bowing and the Development of Bowed Instruments Up to the Thirteenth Century.* Oxford University Press, 1969.

Balfour, Henry. *The Natural History of the Musical Bow.* Longwood Press, 1976. Interesting study of ancient and "primitive" bowed instruments.

Engel, Carl. *Researches into the Early History of the Violin Family.* Amsterdam Antiqua, 1965.

Peterlongo, Paolo. *The Violin: Its Physical and Acoustic Principles.* Crescendo, 1979. Quite good.

Robert, Ronald. *Making a Simple Violin and Viola.* North Charles, Vermont: David and Charles. The instruments described in this book look strange but are easier to build than "real" violins.

Sloane, Irving. *Making Musical Instruments.* Dutton, 1978. This book has a section on building a Norwegian violin—a Hardanger fiddle. Even if you don't want to build one, you'll want to see the photos of these beautiful instruments.

Wechsberg, Joseph. *The Glory of the Violin.* Viking Press, 1973. A highly recommended layperson's guide to construction, music, violinists, violins, and history.

Magazines

The Devil's Box, The Tennessee Valley Old Time Fiddlers Association, Rt. 4, Madison, AL 35758. $6/year (quarterly). An excellent magazine just for fiddlers.

Frets, P.O. Box 28836, San Diego, CA 92128. $18/year (monthly). Columns by Tom Hosmer (instruments) and Byron Berline (music and other matters), as well as interviews with, and articles about, fiddlers and violinists. Good coverage and slanted toward bluegrass, Dawg music, jazz, and country.

Journal of the Violin Society of America, 408 S. Landsdowne Ave., Landsdowne, PA 19050. $25/year for dues (quarterly). Of interest to the serious musician. The VSA also sponsors conventions, exhibitions, and competitions for violin makers.

Sing Out! 505 Eighth Ave., New York, NY 10018. $11/year (bimonthly). Articles of interest to fiddlers appear more than occasionally.

Treoir, c/o John Droney, 70 Westminister Dr., West Hartford, CT 06107. $6/year (bimonthly). Promotes Irish music and culture in the U.S.

Festivals

There are so many conventions you can almost pick a region and find out where the fiddlers' conventions are and just go. And if there are old people whose fiddling you like, go up to them and say, "Gee, I wonder if I could come over and tape some tunes." . . . It's wonderful to hear the contests, because then you hear everyone who's there.

—Liz Slade

Usually the range of talent is so great that no matter how bad you are, there's bound to be somebody who's worse.

—Kenny Kosek

OLD TIME AND BLUEGRASS

Brandywine Mountain Music Convention, Concordville, Pennsylvania. July. Write: Carl Goldstein, Box 3504, Greenville, DE 19807. A favorite of many old-time-music enthusiasts.

Grand Masters Fiddling Championships, Nashville, Tennessee. June. Write: Fan Fair, 2804 Opryland Dr., Nashville, TN 37214.

National Old Time Fiddlers' Contest, Weiser, Idaho. June. Write: Judee Parsons, 8 E. Idaho, Weiser, ID 83672. What Kosek considers a really serious gathering.

Old Fiddlers Convention, Galax, Virginia. August. Write: Oscar Hall, 328-A Kenbrook Dr., Galax, VA 24333. One of the best known conventions.

Old Time Fiddlers Convention, Union Grove, North Carolina. April. Write: J. Pierce VanHoy, P.O. Box 38, Union Grove, NC 28689. The oldest continuously held such convention in the country.

See Appendix E for more festivals and conventions.

BLUES

Blues fiddling is an obscure and fairly defunct artform, but check the blues festivals anyway. They're listed in Chapter 3.

CAJUN

Contraband Days, Lake Charles, Louisiana. April/May. Write: Marilyn Ehmke, Box 679, Lake Charles, LA 70602.

Festival Acadiens, Lafayette, Louisiana. September. Write: P.O. Box 52066, Lafayette, LA 70501.

French Acadian Music Festival, Abbeville, Louisiana. April. Write: Robert Prejean, 209 N. Bailey Ave., Abbeville, LA 70510.

The Gumbo Festival, Bridge City, Louisiana. October. Write: Mrs. Elaine Boatwright, Box 9069, Bridge City, LA 70094.

New Orleans Jazz and Heritage Festival, New Orleans, Louisiana. April. Write: Festival, Box 2530, New Orleans, LA 70176.

Rayne Frog Festival, Rayne, Louisiana. September. Write: Hilda Haure, Box 383, Rayne, LA 70578.

SWEDISH

Duluth Summer Festival of the Arts, Duluth, Minnesota. June/July. Write: Karen Griffith, 301 W. St. Marie St., Duluth, MN 55803.

Scandinavian Mid-Summer Fest, Fergus Falls, Minnesota. June. Write: Fred Sailer, 202 S. Court, Fergus Falls, MN 56537.

Svenskarnas Dag, Minneapolis, Minnesota. June. Write: Iner Johnson, Minneapolis Parks and Recreation Department, 250 S. 4th St., Minneapolis, MN 55401.

Swedish National Federation—Midsummer Festival, Shrewsbury, Massachusetts. June. Write: Elaine Stromberg, 43 Rockdale St., Worcester, MA 01606.

Organizations, Schools

For a free list of organizations, write the Archive of Folk Song, Library of Congress, Washington, DC 20540, and ask for the list of "North American Folklore and Folksong Societies, and Fiddlers' Associations."

Ali Akbar College of Music, 215 West End Ave., San Rafael, CA 94901. Classes in Indian music. Source of information for those interested in learning more about playing Indian music on the violin.

CHAPTER 7

THE MOUNTAIN DULCIMER

The best theory on the origin of the mountain or Appalachian dulcimer is that it has roots in the New World but originated in the New World. Immigrants seem to have built instruments that look and sound different from similar European instruments but follow the same basic principle of stretching strings over a fingerboard mounted on the soundboard. It is almost as if the early builders were building from memory rather than from actual examples.

Because the dulcimer has always been a folk instrument, growing up in rural sections of the southeastern United States, it has never quite assumed a standard shape and size, as have so many other instruments. The dulcimer tradition specifies inspiration and improvisation rather than slavish imitation. And as soon as you say, "Now here is what a dulcimer should sound like," or "Here is the best way to build a dulcimer," you come across an instrument you like better or a builder with a different way of doing things.

Dulcimer players differ from one another in much the same way. Whereas, for example, Earl Scruggs

projected a sound in his early years that is the standard by which all bluegrass banjo players are judged, no dulcimer player has ever achieved or may even try to establish a definitive style.

The dulcimer used to be strummed or played with a noter and quill or pick; now it's also fingerpicked and flatpicked. To meet the demands of players, builders have been changing the instrument. Madeline MacNeil, a performer and the editor of *Dulcimer Players News*, says, "I could put a limit on where the builders might be going and five days from now see someone going beyond that limit." So far the modifications have been relatively straightforward: a larger body for players wanting more volume, bracing for players who like the sound of thinner wood, a longer fingerboard for those desiring a more brilliant sound. You also hear of players' requests for "a dulcimer that sounds like a guitar," a request that some players, though grounded in a tradition rooted in experimentation, view with displeasure. After all, if you want a dulcimer that sounds like a guitar, they say, why not get a guitar? But try telling that to a Californian: they have their own notion of innovation!

INTERVIEW
WITH
JEAN RITCHIE

By her own admission, Jean Ritchie is not a virtuoso on the dulcimer. Technically she has been surpassed by many younger players. But no one has done as much as Jean Ritchie has to spread the gospel of the dulcimer, the people's instrument. Whether or not she is single-handedly responsible for the current dulcimer revival is debatable; however, when people began exploring the roots of American folk music they found Jean Ritchie, who, it turned out, had been there all along.

How do you regard the tremendous up-surge in interest in the dulcimer?

Well, my reaction to it is one of pleasure and happiness. All my life I've been trying to tell people how easy the dulcimer is to play; it's been a crusade with me ever since I started playing on stage for people—playing for people, my father would say, as opposed to playing for yourself. And people always say, "That looks very hard to play." Actually, anyone can play it; anyone who has an ear, who can hear right notes and wrong notes, can play this thing, 'cause it's very, very simple. So the fact that it has caught on around the country makes me feel very good.

Is the appeal of the dulcimer different today from what it was in the past?

Yes, in the sense that it's considered more of an instrument now than it was. I play it very basically, the way an untrained person would play it—untrained musically, that is—because I know nothing about written music. But it appeals to trained musicians now more than it did in the past because they've taken it and pushed it beyond its limitations and made it more flexible.

Doesn't that imply there aren't limitations?

Oh, yes, there were—there are—limitations. The way the dulcimer is played traditionally. It has a diatonic scale, so that in order to change modes you have to retune for each one. But the way people play, using chords and fingerpicking and so on—especially the chording with the left hand—has allowed them to go over the second, third, and fourth strings and get notes that the traditional musician would not get. If the player uses a noter and goes up and down only on the first string, he wouldn't get those notes.

Were there progressive styles among dulcimer players in the past?

No, not really, to my knowledge. People just played the dulcimer in the old way. The way I've

heard people play has just been with the noter and the pick, and they've gone up and down the first string. A person who did play a little bit differently was Jethro Ambergy of Heidman, Kentucky—he's a distant cousin of mine, and the one who inherited Eddie Thomas's dulcimer pattern and sort of took over after Eddie died. Jethro was a banjo player, you know, so he used a little bit of a different fingerpicking kind of style, but the left hand was the same; he didn't go over onto the nonmelodic notes and get different notes.

Why is the dulcimer appealing increasingly to trained musicians?

Well, people are always looking for a unique sound, and I think the dulcimer has a sound that no other instrument has. You couldn't substitute a guitar or a banjo or a fiddle or anything else for the dulcimer. People who want that sound play the dulcimer, at first probably to get the unique sound, and then they realize that it's capable of more than they thought it could do and they go on to develop their style.

A number of dulcimer players, especially on the West Coast, are turning the dulcimer into a sort of guitar, putting on six strings, making the body very large [Jean laughs at this point]. Does that strike you as silly?

"Silly" is maybe not the word I'd pick. I think if you change the dulcimer physically, then it's not a dulcimer any more, but if you use it the way it is, then you can play it any way. Your playing style is your own—there really are no rules or anything. There's an old, untutored way of playing it, which people call the traditional style, and that's that; but no one's going to put you in jail if you go beyond that. But as far as the body of the instrument is concerned, if you make it chromatic, if you put little notes in between . . .

The six and a half fret . . .

Oh, not just the six and a half fret—that was

just an accident that somebody made.... I've seen someone who's done the whole fretboard that way and made it chromatic as a guitar or anything else... but then it's not a dulcimer; it's not the instrument it started out to be; it's more like, well, an example would be the Hungarian zither: that's a dulcimerlike instrument where chromatic notes have been added. That takes it out of the realm of the open-scaled instruments from the Middle Ages, which is what a dulcimer is.

Is part of the definition of dulcimer "a stringed instrument that can be built however you want to, or almost however you want to"?

No, if you change the frets, then you have a different instrument.

Do too many players spend their time on technique and fancy fingerwork and forget the music?

You can't put limitations on players—if they're not good singers and they don't feel like singing, you can't say they should sing too. But my personal feeling is...I love the songs. Anything that I do, in concert or teaching people, is to teach them the songs. The dulcimer to me is another voice that goes along and helps teach the song, helps set forth the song. I never obscure the song with playing. There's a funny story I remember about Doc Watson. He and I were playing at, I guess it was Gerdes Folk City, a long, long time ago—Doc's first gig on his own. I was playing a song on the guitar—"A Pretty Fair Miss 'Aworkin' in the Garden." After about three or four nights, I was a little embarrassed at even pickin' up a guitar with Doc around, so I said, "Why don't you play the guitar for me when I sing this song, instead of my playing it?" And he said okay. It came time for the song, and he picked up the guitar and played the song exactly the way I played it, note for note—he didn't vary it a bit. I think he even put in my mistakes [laughter]. So afterwards I said, "Hey, how come you didn't play something flashy?"

He said, "That's all that song needs." At the same time it was a tribute to his greatness, I guess, and also a compliment to me, that I found the *right* accompaniment for the song, so I appreciate that. I remembered that, later on, when I felt like apologizing for my guitar playing. And I think I would give the same advice to dulcimer players. You can get all kinds of hot licks—I think with any instrument that has to come in the development of playing. The whole guitar era, the dulcimer era, you know, it starts out as a simple little thing, oompah, oompah. I remember when the first guitar came into Kentucky, and everybody around us played oompah, oompah, and accompanied the songs. Well, now if you go into the same place, you'll see people play the guitar like Chet Atkins. It has to come, with any instrument. Musicians will take it and develop and push it and experiment with it—a full cycle. I think that's what's happening now with the dulcimer; among singers at least, you'll have all this flashy playing developed and it gets flashier and flashier and people get in more notes per measure than [laughter]... The Irish dance tunes now are gettin' pushed so fast that dancers could never keep up. Technical excellence just reaches a point after awhile where everybody rebels and says, "Hey, where's the song, what's this all about?" Among singers that's what happens, I think. Some of them get carried away with their accompaniments and with trying to keep up with all the hot licks, but the ones with integrity eventually stop and say, "Well, what is this—is it just to play fast or to play flashily—is that what it's all about?" You have to listen to the words, and you have to listen to what the song's trying to say, and I think that people should use the dulcimer or any instrument that they play to help their songs speak—communicate—not just to say, "Hey, look, I can play better and faster than you do."

What are you doing differently today from the past? I assume you still tour a lot.... Are you saying something different in your music today, is it more refined...?

Let me think about that. I guess the big change

is that I'm writing songs now, about current happenings. Strip-mining, mine safety, abuse of the world. And, well, I'm a lot more *relaxed* than I used to be. I know what I can do and what I can't do. I get on stage now . . . and I pick my stages very carefully. I don't just take any job that comes up. One thing I've learned is which audiences I can reach and which I can't. . . .

Who is your best audience?

I guess a community audience of all ages is good for me. I like college audiences too, but usually they are also thrown open to the community and you have a mixture of kids and grandmothers and college and high school students and it's sort of family oriented. . . . I know what I can do and what I want to say, and I've reached the point where it doesn't bother me an awful lot if people don't like it . . . if they don't like it, that's their problem. So I'm just very relaxed about the whole thing now. I don't like to strive and struggle to put a point across—I don't want to be in a position where I have to sell my product. That's not a cop out, I don't think. It's just a realization of who you are and what you can say and do.

Do people still see the dulcimer as an exotic instrument?

Well, it's a handle to hang it on, I guess—Jean Ritchie, famous dulcimer player. And then that gets all the people to come out who play dulcimer and so on. It's a thing that gets me a lot of work and publicity and notice, but I try to give them more than just a few licks on the dulcimer.

Is the dulcimer symbolic of a simpler way of life?

It is to us simple dulcimer players [laughter]. No, as a matter of fact, when I do workshops, and there are a lot of other dulcimer players in the workshops who play in much more advanced styles—Leo Kretchner, Roger Nicholson, Lorraine Lee—and I'm just sort of the M.C.—the thing I try to tell people—there are always twenty-five or thirty or one hundred people clutching their dulcimers and looking nervous hearing all these people playing in these fancy styles—I'll just try to get the point across

throughout the workshop that anyone can play, and don't *ever* feel that you *can't* play because you heard someone play better than you, because the dulcimer's an instrument that sounds good even when played simply. So then we'll tune up together—all one hundred of us—and just play "Simple Gifts" or something like that. I just tell the people, "Now, play! No matter if you make mistakes. We're all playing together . . . you can't go too wrong on the dulcimer because it sounds pretty good no matter what you do . . . so if you play something that you think's an awful discord, why, no one's going to know you did it." And that business of all playing together always does something for people. If it was recorded, it would sound God—awful. . . . But it seems to fill a need for them: they can say later, "I played my dulcimer with a hundred people", or "I played dulcimer with Jean Ritchie." Then they'll go home encouraged and their playing may get better or maybe it won't, but anyway they'll feel better about it. That's one of the main things I like about the dulcimer.

Do you think as many people are going to keep playing dulcimer now or do you think part of it is slightly faddish—people who are really interested will stick with it and a lot of people will drop out?

I think you said it. I once talked to old Francis McPeake in Belfast when we were over there in '52. We said "Hello, we'd like to hear you play," and he said, "I thought you'd be coming pretty soon, because every twenty years I get out my pipes [laughter]." So I think it goes in waves. Right now the lap dulcimer, as they call the Appalachian dulcimer in Kentucky, has had a great big upsurge and is still coming up around the country. But just take it in one place, say, Louisville, where a lot of my friends live. There are a lot of dulcimers being played . . . but now there's a big hammered dulcimer surge, and last time I was there I heard people asking about Irish harp [laughter]. . . . The Gaelic harp is sort of following the hammered dulcimer, and after that I'm sure it's going to be the harpsichord. Those kinds of people are going to go on to that, and then, *their* children will go back to the dulcimer.

Selecting a Dulcimer

Playability and pleasing tone are the main requirements of the dulcimer hunter. Because the dulcimer "industry" is dominated by individual builders and by a few small shops, considerable variation exists in both instruments and standards. Some builders really try to build a playable instrument, while others build attractive instruments better suited to hanging on the wall. So, although dulcimers are still quite inexpensive for the most part, do a thorough job of checking out the one you plan to buy.

PLAYABILITY

Tuning. To help you evaluate the quality of the pegs and the sound, have someone tune the instrument or do it yourself. Tune the bass strings to a specific pitch—D, for example. Then fret the string at the fourth fret and tune the middle string to that note. Then play the bass string at the seventh fret and tune the top string to that note.

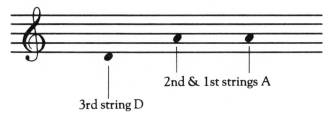

2nd & 1st strings A

3rd string D

Dulcimer tuning.

The pegs should be easy to tune and the strings should stay in tune (although new strings take some breaking-in until they can hold the pitch for any length of time). Because the dulcimer is retuned more frequently than almost any other instrument, not to get it in tune but to change the tuning (the relationships between the pitches of the strings), the tuning apparatus must work smoothly and easily. Wooden and mechanical friction pegs are quite common on dulcimers and acceptable, if they work. However, wooden pegs are definitely harder to use than banjo pegs, and both are harder to use than guitar machines, which a lot of instruments have. If you may be discouraged by friction pegs, buy a dulcimer with guitar machines, or ask the builder to install them. Or install them (from $4.50 per set of six) yourself. Another option is to install better-quality friction pegs (for example, Grover Statite, about $15).

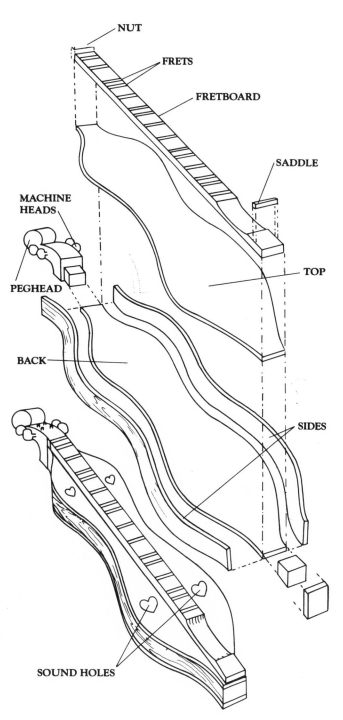

Dulcimer schematic.

Fingerboard. The dulcimer has no neck, only a fingerboard and a head. Sight down the fingerboard from either end to make sure it is straight. The fingerboard itself should either be flat or exhibit a slight dip. To test the condition of the fingerboard, press the bass string simultaneously at the first and last frets; when the fingerboard is correctly curved, the clearance between the string and the top of the seventh fret will be about the thickness of a business card, perhaps a little more. Perform the same test on the fourth string or the third set of strings; the clearance should be the same, maybe a little less. A flat fingerboard has no clearance, but if the fingerboard is warped in either direction, you will see too much clearance or the string will be bowed upward by a hump in the fingerboard.

The fingerboard ought to be smoothly finished and comfortably wide, too, so that your fingers don't run into each other.

Action. Check the action by playing at the bottom and top of the fingerboard and on all the strings, or just press the strings at the top and bottom of the fingerboard. Check the action at the nut by pressing each string between the second and third frets and making sure the clearance over the first fret is about the thickness of a business card. Action at the bridge and nut can be fairly easily adjusted.

Intonation. First, make sure the bridge is positioned. Lightly touch the first string over the twelfth fret with a finger of your left hand and then pluck the string with your right hand until you hear the harmonic; you may have to adjust the position of the finger on the string. Then depress the string all the way to the fret and play that note. The two pitches should be identical. Perform the same test on the string or set of strings nearest you. When the notes are different, the bridge is in the wrong place: too close to the tail when the fretted note is flat, too far from the tail when the fretted note is sharp. Should the bridge seem out of place and moveable, simply adjust it until the two notes are identical. Should the bridge be either glued to the fingerboard or actually wedged into a slot in the fingerboard, it can still be repositioned, but obviously much less easily. In order to check the accuracy of the fret positions the bridge has to be accurately placed, so if for some reason you cannot move the bridge, you

Capritaurus dulcimer.

are taking a chance that the scale may not be accurate. On a dulcimer this is far more likely than on an instrument like a guitar that is usually built in a huge factory.

Once the bridge is in place, work your way up the scale on each string, a note at a time, to make sure the scale is correct. If you have any doubts, either return the instrument or take it to a qualified repair-person or an experienced player for advice.

Frets. Make sure the frets are smooth, rounded, and flush with the sides of the fingerboard; they should also be firmly embedded in their slots and not rattle. Make sure none stick up higher than others, or you may get string buzz. Check for buzzing by playing your way up the fingerboard, a note at a time, the same way you checked the actual fret positions. On some traditional dulcimers the frets may actually be heavy staples that extend only under the string nearest you.

Number of Frets. Dulcimers have different numbers of frets, but some instruments have a traditional scale and others add what are called a 6½ fret and sometimes a 13½ fret, which enable you to switch modes or keys more easily. For a beginner, an instrument without the extra frets is okay. You can always add extra frets later on, or even remove them.

Scale Length. The average scale length is from 26 to 28 inches. Since some of the spaces between frets on the dulcimer are rather large, a scale on the short side lends itself more to people with small hands; a long scale may be difficult to play.

Dulcimer Days festival.

CONDITION AND STRUCTURAL INTEGRITY

Carefully inspect the seams, look for cracks, make sure the instrument is solidly constructed. Make sure the fingerboard is firmly attached to the top.

MATERIALS

Although each wood has a characteristic sound and responsiveness, much depends on the way the wood is worked and on the design of the instrument. The most common woods are native American hardwoods such as walnut, cherry, and maple. Builders also use rosewood, koa, butternut, poplar, redwood—almost any available wood. Many traditional builders will make the entire dulcimer from one type of hardwood, but just as often you find instruments with a softwood top and hardwood back and sides. As a rule of thumb, the harder the wood, the brighter the sound; a softwood top tends to sweeten the sound and somewhat increase the volume and responsiveness.

The nut can be anything hard, such as bone, ivory, plastic, or wood; the fingerboard can be any kind of hard wood. Some builders overlay the fingerboard with rosewood.

Dulcimers are built with both solid and laminated woods, though almost all instruments above a certain quality are built of solid wood. Because the surface area of the dulcimer is so small, and because the soundboard, for example, is bisected by the fingerboard, which essentially cuts down on the vibrating ability of the top, you need not avoid laminated wood.

SHAPE

The hourglass shape is the most common, with the teardrop and elliptical shapes also popular. Other shapes are fiddle, lute, and oblong. Shape affects sound. A dulcimer with a big end and a small front, like the teardrop, ought to have a big bass and a small treble; an hourglass ought to have a more balanced sound throughout its range. Many factors are involved, however, so don't go by size alone when considering tone and volume.

SIZE

Two dulcimers identical in every way but size ought to reflect the difference in their volume: the large instrument will be louder. But a dulcimer that is large and also uses heavy, unresponsive wood will have a soft, muddy sound, whereas a smaller dulcimer built with thin, responsive wood will be loud and penetrating.

Hourglass-shaped dulcimer, by Bonnie Carol. The wood is quilted maple.

NUMBER OF STRINGS

Dulcimers usually have three or four strings, three being the more traditional; some instruments have more, even six. Most dulcimers have a nut with extra notches so that strings can be shifted to different configurations.

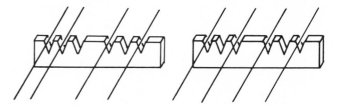

Dulcimer stringing arrangements.

DESIGN FEATURES

Many dulcimers have a hollow fingerboard, which makes an instrument more responsive. Sometimes a scalloped fingerboard is used. Some instruments have fine tuners behind the bridge to facilitate tuning on instruments with friction pegs; the fine tuners are either of the violin type or else they are slide beads.

SOUND

There is no ideal dulcimer sound for everyone; each person has a different idea of what they like, whether it's a small, mellow sound or a large, bassy sound. Two important qualities of sound are responsiveness and balance. A very responsive dulcimer seems to play itself; you touch the string, and the sound develops instantly. An unresponsive instrument fights itself, withholding its sound. A thick, heavy instrument might be unresponsive because the wood is so massive it takes a long time to begin vibrating.

> Madeline MacNeil: "I sing with the instrument and I have a very strong voice, and I also have a tendency to play instruments lightly, so I need an instrument that will do some of the work for me. I recently got a dulcimer, and my criteria for it was that I wanted volume and, of course, response and sweetness. Volume and sweetness are not too easy to get."

Balance, of course, means a good, full sound whether you're in the low or the high registers. You'll just have to try an instrument to see if it's balanced. A balanced sound is highly desirable for a fingerpicker, especially one who plays over the entire fingerboard.

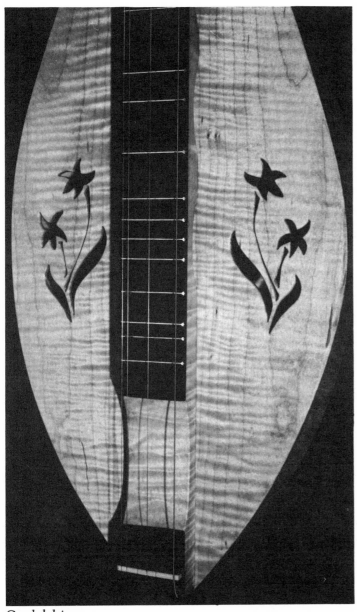

Carol dulcimer.

COSMETICS

Traditionally, the physical appeal of the dulcimer has depended heavily on the grain of the wood, the finish, the shape and general proportions, the pegs, and the design of the peghead rather than on binding or fancy inlays. However, dulcimers are now built with fingerboard inlays, fancy soundholes, abalone purfling, and other touches adopted from other instruments.

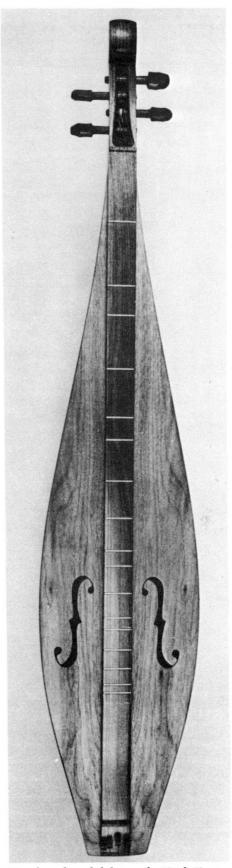

Teardrop-shaped dulcimer, by Keith Young.

COURTING DULCIMER

A courting dulcimer has two fingerboards and an oversized body and is intended to be played by two people at the same time. It is said that parents know their sons and daughters are safe from the temptations of the flesh as long as the music the young 'uns are playing on the dulcimer can be heard.

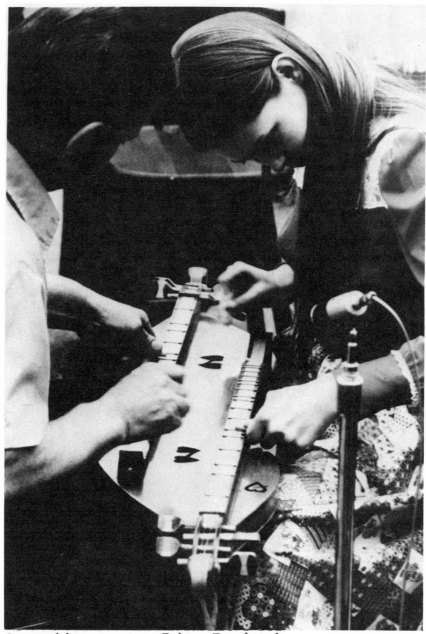

Courting dulcimer in action at Dulcimer Days festival, Coshocton, Ohio.

Money Matters

One great way to get your first dulcimer is to buy a kit. The investment of time and money is small, and regardless of the quality of the instrument, you will find much pleasure in playing something you built with your own hands. In addition, a kit becomes a finished instrument worth about twice its original investment.

Once you become more experienced, the sky is the limit in regard to buying a dulcimer—it really depends on how much money you have and how serious you are. Extremely nice, playable dulcimers are available for under $100 and even for quite a lot less. For someone who plays for fun, which is what most dulcimer players do, an instrument costing under $250 should be more than adequate for quite a while. Like other instruments, dulcimers begin to get fancier and fancier after a point, so a good chunk of the price goes for cosmetics. Bonnie Carol, for example, builds dulcimers which are both beautiful-looking and eminently playable, and charges $500 to inlay an abalone border on one of her instruments—more than the price of the "dulcimer itself." You might want to try decorating a plainer instrument yourself, using materials and designs obtained from the mail-order dealers (see Chapter 1).

Kits, Materials

There are dulcimer kits for every level of woodworking ability. Difficulty is inversely proportional to price; the less work you have to do, the more you pay. On the easiest kits, only assembly and finishing are required: the parts are precut and the fingerboard fretted. On the hardest kits, instructions can be tough to follow and cutting and shaping may be required. Some "white" instruments have also been listed; these are preassembled and just need sanding and finishing. Information on building a dulcimer from plans or from specially available wood is also provided. Plans and kits are listed from easiest to hardest.

Dorogi, Ellicott Rd., Brocton, NY 14716. Instruments available "in the white."

Here, Inc., 29 S.E. Main St., Minneapolis, MN 55414. Instruments available "in the white."

Black Mountain, P.O. Box 779, Lower Lake, CA 95457. Kits. Some household tools (screwdriver, hammer) needed. Prefretted fingerboard. Assembling and finishing required. Extremely clear plans and directions. Recommended for the total novice.

Musical Traditions, 514 Oak St., Sandpoint, ID 83864. Kits. Necessary tools include saw and drill; basically simple tools, but a rather complicated list (a strip of tire, for example, may make a good, cheap clamp, but it may be easier to buy a clamp than hunt around for a tire). Prefretted fingerboard. Assembling and finishing required. Clear, comprehensive plans and instructions. Designed for the beginner.

McSpadden, The Dulcimer Shoppe, Drawer E, Highway 9 North, Mountain View, AR 72560. Kits. Necessary tools include hammer, file, screwdriver, and clamps. Preslotted fingerboard needs fretting. Assembling, trimming edges, fretting, and finishing required. Top and back are preshaped but must be trimmed. Plans and instructions are very clear. Good for a beginner.

Here, Inc. 29 S.E. Main St., Minneapolis, MN 55414. Kits. Tools needed include saw, clamps, drill, file, and plane or Surform. Preslotted fingerboard needs fretting. Top and back are oversized; must be trimmed; sides are prebent; head needs to be shaped or cut, depending on kit model. Although fairly clear, the instructions have too many options, and are confusing and wordy. For the person who has some woodworking experience (and may have built a kit already).

Hughes, 4419-C W. Colfax, Denver, CO 80204. Kits. Necessary tools include file, screwdriver, and plane or Surform. Fingerboard is preslotted but not prefretted. Top and back must be cut to shape; sides must be bent. Clear, simple, concise plans and instructions, ideal for the person who doesn't like to read and doesn't need to be shown every step in excruciating detail.

Bednark, Box 13, Centerville, MA 02632. Kit or plans. Required tools include saw, clamps, and drill. Extremely clear and easy-to-follow plans and instructions. You can buy either the entire kit or just the plans ($10) and then buy the wood yourself. Write for more information.

Folk Roots, Box 153, Felton, CA 95018. Kits. Necessary tools include hammer, coping saw, file, and screwdriver. Fretboard is preslotted but not pre-fretted. Top and back are cut to shape; sides must be bent. You can make a teardrop or hourglass shape with this kit, which is a good option. The plans and instructions are generously illustrated but confusing. The kit is not recommended for a novice woodworker or for anyone not good at reading directions.

Gurian Guitars, Box 595, West Swanzey NH 04369; **Buck Musical Instrument Products,** 40 Sand Rd., New Britain, PA 18901. Materials. Both companies offer all the materials required to build a dulcimer "from scratch": soundboards, sides, fingerboards, hardware. This is the least expensive way to build a dulcimer, short of locating and milling your own wood (which may actually be more expensive).

Dulcimer Brands, Builders, and Manufacturers

Autorino (The Butternut Shoppe, Rt. 9W North, RD1, Box 387C, Kingston, NY 12401). Michael Autorino is a well-known builder who has been in business since the 1960s. Order direct.

Berch (2876 Arthur Kill Rd., Staten Island, NY 10309). Doug Berch, who has built dulcimers since 1978, aims for a good balance of volume and tone and uses voiced (tuned) bracing, graduated tops, and other means to achieve his ends. He also does custom work. Order direct; delivery takes two weeks. Lifetime warranty.

Black Mountain (P.O. Box 779, Lower Lake, CA 95457). Black Mountain, founded in 1971, employs three builders and turns out over one thousand dulcimers per year. Model 56 is "mellow," model 58 "fuller," and model 51 "brighter with more carrying potential," says a spokesperson. These are good instruments for the money. Available through dealers and from Black Mountain; direct delivery takes two weeks. Lifetime warranty on finished dulcimers and on materials for kits.

Blue Lion (Star Route, Box 16-C, Santa Margarita, CA 95453). Begun in 1975, Blue Lion completes one

hundred dulcimers per year. States a spokesperson: the model IIR "is designed for the best players and the most complex music styles, and visually to have the look and feel of custom, one-of-a-kind instruments but with a lower price." *Frets* magazine rated the Blue Lion very high. Available through dealers or from the manufacturer; direct orders take one to two weeks to fill.

Buck (Buck Musical Products, 40 Sand Rd., New Britain, PA 18901).

Capritaurus dulcimers. Note different pegheads.

114

Capritaurus (Box 153, Felton, CA 95018). Four builders work in this shop, which was established in 1969 and now makes 150-300 dulcimers each year—essentially customized Folk Roots dulcimers. Michael Rugg of Capritaurus says these dulcimers "are designed for the contemporary player wanting a warm, strong bass and good overall volume." Available through dealers or directly from the manufacturer.

Peghead, Capritaurus dulcimer.

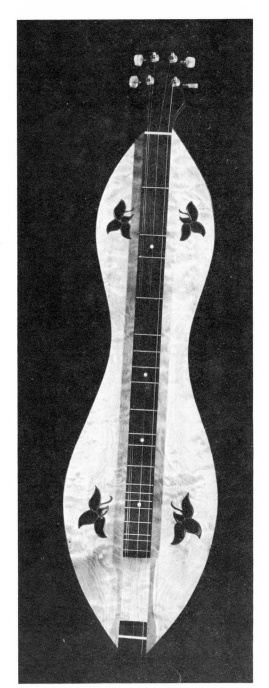

Carol dulcimer.

Fiddle shaped dulcimer (really a modified hourglass), by L. O. Stapleton. The wood is East Indian rosewood.

Carol (Wallstreet, Salina Star Route, Boulder, CO 80302). Bonnie Carol has been building fine dulcimers since 1973 and completes about thirty-five per year. She seeks "resonance, sustain, a balanced bass and treble sound, and enough volume to be heard when played acoustically with other acoustic instruments." She often uses "exotic woods with fancy grains and figures" and builds scalloped fingerboards too. Various options available. Purchase through dealers and from Carol. Lifetime warranty.

Deering dulcimer.

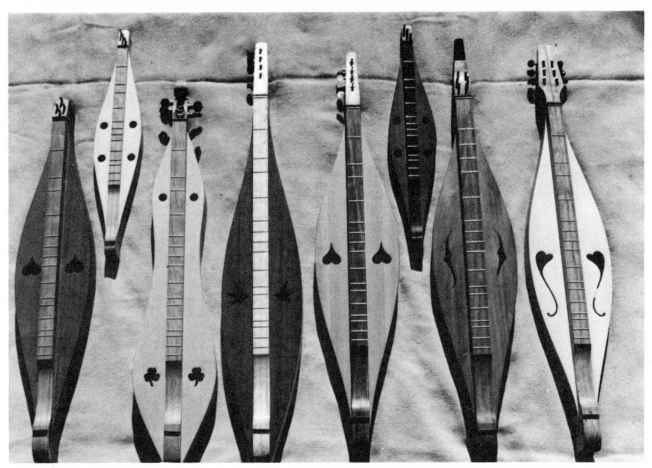

Ewing dulcimers.

Deering (Deering Banjo Company, 3615 Costa Bella St., Lemon Grove, CA 92046). Decent, inexpensive dulcimers. Available through dealers or from Deering; one-month delay on direct orders. One-year warranty.

Dorogi (Ellicott Rd., Brocton, NY 14716). Dennis Dorogi, a respected builder, has been doing business since 1970 and completes three hundred instruments each year. Order through dealers or directly from the builder.

Ewing (2318 E. Rahn Rd., Kettering, OH 45440). Ron Ewing has been building dulcimers since 1973 and completes twenty-four to thirty-six per year. He says he is a "semicustom builder" who aims for a sound that is "typically bright, with modest to good volume. I build the instrument to suit the person, if I can. My aim is to build attractive, quality instruments that are affordable for most people." Available through dealers or from Ewing; allow two weeks for delivery on direct orders.

Farkleberry Farm (Rt. 1, Swans Rd., Newark, OH 43055).

Folk Roots. See Capritaurus for address. Vital statistics of the business differ somewhat from those of Capritaurus.

Glenn (Rt. 1, Sugar Grove, NC 28679). Leonard and Clifford Glenn are longtime builders of more-traditional dulcimers than most. Order direct.

Green Mountain (33 Buell St., Burlington, VT 05401). Jerry Rockwell has been building dulcimers since 1971 and established Green Mountain in 1979. He completes sixty instruments per year. His dulcimers have a rather contemporary look and are nicely finished. Rockwell says his "larger instrument has a very rich bass but it doesn't boom or detract exceedingly from the high-end response. The smaller, reverse-curve hourglass has less bass, more high end. The sustain on both instruments is better than

Green Mountain dulcimer.

average." Available through some Vermont dealers and from Green Mountain; direct orders take one to two weeks to fill.

Harmon (10370 Hosberry Lane, Pensacola, FL 35204). Loran Harmon has been building instruments since 1966 and completes 250 per year. He aims for a sharp, crisp, clear, uncluttered sound. The Hourglass model is semicustom. Order direct; delivery takes one to two weeks. Lifetime warranty.

L. Harmon and dulcimers.

Here, Inc. (29 S.E. Main St., Minneapolis, MN 55414). The philosophy of this well-known company, which was started in 1968 and builds two hundred instruments a year, "is to get people playing music for themselves. As long as we can make it, we'll continue to be about fifty percent educational institution and fifty percent business. We sell mainly folk instruments to folk." Available through dealers or from Hughes; direct orders filled in one week.

Hughes (4419-C W. Colfax, Denver, CO 80204). Hughes Dulcimer Company was established in 1965

and has six employees. It's a well-known company with a diverse line of dulcimers. Order through dealers or from Hughes.

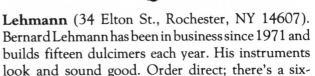

Jeffreys (232 W. Frederick St., Staunton, VA 24401). A. W. Jeffreys Jr. has been building dulcimers since 1956; his family have been assisting him since 1962. One hundred fifty instruments are made each year. Jeffreys aims for a traditional sound and look. Order direct; delivery takes less than two weeks.

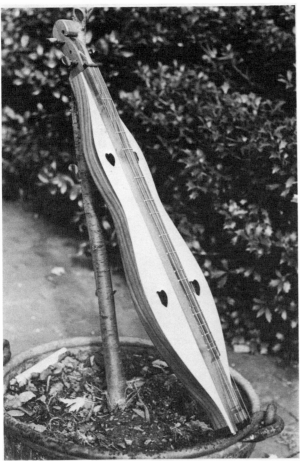

Jeffreys dulcimer.

Kelischek (Workshop for Historical Instruments, Brasstown, NC 28902). Many builders have "trained" with George Kelischek, who founded his workshop in 1955 and builds, besides dulcimers, lutes, viols, psalteries, hurdy-gurdies, and many other instruments. Order direct. Catalogue: $2.

Ledford (125 Sunset Heights, Winchester, KY 40391). Homer Ledford has been building dulcimers since 1946 and finishes 150-200 per year. He's a traditional builder. Available from some Kentucky dealers and from Ledford; direct orders are filled in one month.

Lehmann (34 Elton St., Rochester, NY 14607). Bernard Lehmann has been in business since 1971 and builds fifteen dulcimers each year. His instruments look and sound good. Order direct; there's a six-month wait. Lifetime warranty.

McSpadden (The Dulcimer Shoppe, Drawer E, Highway 9 North, Mountain View, AR 72560). Lynn McSpadden & Co., founded in 1962, has six to seven employees; McSpadden has been called the Henry Ford of the dulcimer. His dulcimers have a good reputation and are reasonably priced. Available from dealers or from McSpadden.

Mize (Rt. 2, Box 288, Blountville, TN 37617). Robert Mize, who has been making dulcimers since 1969 and completes 130 per year, says he "strives for the traditional old mountain dulcimer sound." Order direct; delivery takes two to four weeks. Two-year warranty.

Montague (16 Patriot Rd., Tewksbury, MA 08176). Write Fred Montague for information.

Musical Traditions (514 Oak St., Sandpoint, ID 83864). Musical Traditions was founded in 1970 and changed hands in 1978. There are five employees, producing six hundred kits and six hundred finished instruments per year. John Rourke of MT says "we are after a loud, clear, well-balanced sound. We especially want the instuments to compete with other folk instruments. Our dulcimers are geared to the beginner who wants a quality instrument that retains its value." Available from dealers and MT; delivery on direct orders takes two to three weeks for all models except the Jean Ritchie, which takes one to two months.

North Country (709 Spice St., Pittsburgh, PA 15214). NCD, established in 1975, produces one hundred dulcimers per year. Robert Hutchinson of NCD states: "We are primarily interested in an instrument that can blend well with a band; therefore our dulcimers tend to sound a bit 'trebly.' They come

Mize dulcimers.

across exceptionally well through amplified systems. Our dulcimers are designed by a professional dulcimer player and are overbuilt to put up with 'road abuse' without sacrificing any liveliness of tone.... Most people who purchase our dulcimers are buying a second or third instrument. We make a svelte, flashy, highly untraditional dulcimer." Add $70 for an electrified dulcimer. Order direct.

Stapleton (Hillbilly Dulcimer & Craft Shop, 201 Midland Ave., Springdale, AR 72764). L. O. Stapleton, who has been building dulcimers since 1977, says, "I am always looking for something unusual in the wood, such as high figuring, crotches, flaming, mottling....I'm not bashful about decorating my instruments....I can't see why an instrument can't be pretty as well as good....I never make any two alike, so I guess each could be called original....I use five basic shapes....hourglass, boat, teardrop, elliptical, and fiddle." Write for information.

Southern Highlands (1010 S. 14 St., Slaton, TX 79364). Stinson Behlen has been making instruments since 1951. On his acoustic model he says he aims for a "powerful, brilliant" sound. Add $40 for an electronic pickup. Order direct.

Wurtz (2503 Medcliff Rd., Santa Barbara, CA 93105). Write Howard Wurtz for information on his instruments.

Young (3815 Kendale Rd., Anandale, VA 22003). Keith Young, who has been building instruments since 1964, describes his typical customer as a "professional or beginner who wants a perfectly adjusted, easy-to-play dulcimer with a full, round sound." Various options are available. Young offers a free lesson with each dulcimer. Order from the builder.

Stapleton dulcimer.

To locate other dulcimer builders, some of whom may live in your area, check crafts fairs and shops as well as music stores. Also check the ads in *Dulcimer Players News*. Some of the dulcimer instruction books list builders, but many of the entries are dated: the builders have moved or are no longer in business.

Discography

Clayton, Paul. *Dulcimer Songs and Solos* (Folkways 3571).

Freeman, Alan, and Frank Beal. *Black Mountain Dulcimer* (write: Sidetrack, P.O. Box 273, Grantsville, WV 26147).

Hellman, Neal, Michael Rugg, Robert Force, Albert d'Ossche, Bonnie Carol, and Michael Hubbert. *Pacific Rim Dulcimer Project* (Biscuit City 1314).

Lee, Rick and Lorraine. *Contrasts* (Front Hall 014).

Leibovitz, Jay, and Leo Kretzner. *Pigtown Fling* (Green Linnet 1019).

MacNeil, Madeline. *Strawberry Fair* (Troubadour 7) and *Many Butterflies* (Roots and Branches 001).

Meyer, Fred, with Doug Berch and others. *Gnawbone* (Midwest Coast 101).

Pribojszky, Matayas. *Citeraszo: The Sound of the Zither* (Qualiton SLPX 16602).

Niles, John Jacob. *The Ballads of John Jacob Niles* (Tradition 1046). Niles, a singer and collector, plays a giant dulcimer that's not especially prominent in his music.

Ritchie, Jean. *High Hills and Mountains* (Greenhays 701) and *Clear Waters Remembered* (Geordie SES97014).

Rockwell, Jerry, and Mary Ann Samuels. *Mountain Dulcimer and Psaltery Instrumentals* (Traditional).

Roth, Kevin. *The Mountain Dulcimer Instrumental Album* (Folkways 3570).

The Simmons Family. *Stone County Dulcimer* (Simmons 112).

Stamper, I. D. *Red Wing* (June Appal 010).

Bibliography: Instruction, Songs, Tunes

Hellman, Neal. *Life Is Like a Mountain Dulcimer*. The Richmond Organization. A good book for beginners that is somewhat more ambitious than the Murphy or Ritchie offerings.

Hornbostel, Lois. *The Irish Dulcimer*. Mel Bay. 1979. Tablature and music. Intermediate level. Quite good. Aside from the introduction, entirely a collection of tunes.

Lapidus, Joellen. *Lapidus on Dulcimers*. ALMO, 1980. Tablature. Basic information; interesting tunings; section on jazz; photos of the author's instruments. Soundsheets included.

Lee, Lorraine. *An Elizabethan Songbook*. Communications Press, 1977.

Murphy, Michael. *The Appalachian Dulcimer Book*. Folksay Press, 1976. Tablature and music. Beginning level. Very good.

O'Neill, Francis. *O'Neill's Music of Ireland: Eighteen Hundred and Fifty Melodies*. Daniel Michael Collins, 1963. The classic collection of tunes is an excellent source for experienced players.

One Thousand Fiddle Tunes. M. M. Cole, 1967.

Pacific Rim Dulcimer Songbook. Dusty Moose Publishers, 1977. Goes with record of same name.

Ritchie, Jean. *The Dulcimer Book*. Oak, 1974. Tablature and music. Interesting historical information, photos, personal notes, tunes, basic instruction. Recording available. Recommended.

Richie, Jean. *Jean Ritchie's Dulcimer People*. Oak, 1975. Tablature and music. Intermediate level. Sketches on builders and players, some instruction, music, section on building a dulcimer. A wonderful compilation of dulcimer lore.

Rockwell, Jerry. *Chordal Explorations for the 3-String Dulcimer: Ionian Tuning GCG*. Crying Creek Publishers 1978 (write: P.O. Box 8, Highway 32, Cosby, TN 37722). Beginning or intermediate levels. Good for the ambitious beginner or the person who has mastered the basics.

Bibliography: Construction

Kimball, Dean. *Constructing the Mountain Dulcimer*. David McKay, 1974. This is the best, most comprehensive book on how to build a dulcimer.

Magazines

Dulcimer Players News, P.O. Box 2164, Winchester, VA 22601. $6/year (quarterly). A beautifully done little magazine that lists festivals, new books and records; publishes songs and tips; gives you the lowdown on instruments and repairs, and much, much more. Lots of ads for builders. *DPN* is *the* resource center for current news on the dulcimer.

Frets, P.O. Box 28836, San Diego, CA 92128. $18/year (monthly). Two colums of interest to dulcimer players. One, by Michael Rugg, is usually technically or historically inclined; the other, by Mary Faith Rhoads, is more musically inclined.

Sing Out! 505 8th Ave., New York, NY 10018. $11/year (bimonthly). Of particular interest to dulcimer players because of the focus on traditional music and because of the amount of music published.

Festivals: Mountain Dulcimer and Hammered Dulcimer*

Most of these festivals include activities for both kinds of dulcimers. Write for details.

Annual August Festival, Elkins, West Virginia. August. Write: August Heritage Arts Workshop, Davis and Elkins College, Elkins, WV 26241.

Annual Cosby Dulcimer Convention, Cosby, Tennessee. June. Write: Folk Life Center of the Smokies, P.O. Box 8, Cosby, TN 37722.

Annual Cranberry Hammered Dulcimer Gathering, Binghampton, New York. July. Write: Bob Wey, 21 Redcoat Lane, RFD 3, Plainville, MN 02762.

Annual Downeast Dulcimer Festival, Bar Harbor, Maine. July. Write: Eddie and Anne Damm, 118 Ledgelawn, Bar Harbor, MN 04609.

Annual Kentucky Music Weekend, Louisville, Kentucky. August. Write: Metro Parks, attn. Nancy Barker, P.O. Box 13334, Louisville, KY 40213.

Annual Walnut Valley Festival, National Mountain and Hammer Dulcimer Championships, Winfield, Kansas. September. Write: Bob Redford, Box 245, Winfield, KS 67156.

Dulcimer Days, Coshocton, Ohio. May. Write: Roscoe Village Foundation, 381 Hill St., Coshocton, OH 43812.

Dulcimer Days Festival, Overland Park, Kansas.

*Reprinted by the kind permission of *Dulcimer Players News* (Spring 1981); originally compiled by Jane Jones.

June. Write: Harvey Prinz, 9540 Walmer, Overland Park, KS 66212.

The Dulcimer Fair, Burlington, Vermont. September. Write: Jerry Rockwell/Mary Ann Samuels, 33 Buell St., Burlington, VT 05401.

Bob Evans Farm Dulcimer Festival, Rio Grande, Ohio. July. Write: Bob Evans Farm Dulcimer Festival, Bob Evans Farm, Box 33D, Rio Grande, OH 45674.

Great Black Swamp Dulcimer Festival, Lima, Ohio. May. Write: Michael Wildermuth, 3160 Zurmehly Rd., Lima, OH 45806.

Kindred Gathering, Talent, Oregon. July/August. Write: Willy Sears, 10798 Yank Gulch Rd., Talent, OR 97540.

Nonelectrified Musical Fun Fest, Evart, Michigan. July. Write: E. A. Cox, Box 136, Byron Center, MI 49315.

Old-Time Music Festival, Waynesville, Ohio. June. Write: Ed Simpkins, P.O. Box 591, Middletown, OH 45042.

The Original Dulcimer Players Club May Meeting. May. Write: Paul Gifford, 1046 Withington, Ferndale, MI 48820.

Pine Mountain Festival, Pine Mountain State Park, Kentucky. September. Write: Dick Albin, Box 271, Stanton, KY 40380.

The Southeastern Dulcimer Festival, Helena, Alabama. May. Write: Charles Ellis, Rt. 1, Box 473, Helena, AL 35080.

Southern Regional Mountain and Hammer Dulcimer Convention and Contests, Mountain View, Arkansas. Write: The Dulcimer Shoppe, Drawer E, Highway 9 North, Mountain View, AR 72560.

CHAPTER 8

THE HAMMERED DULCIMER

Every time I play for people who've never heard one before, they're enchanted, they want to know, What is that, Why have I never heard one before? And that's just the way I felt when I first heard a hammered dulcimer. As more people are exposed to it, that sort of reaction is going to get bigger and bigger.

—Sam Rizzetta

Despite their sharing of the word *dulcimer*, hammered and mountain dulcimers are two entirely different instruments. The hammered dulcimer is played with hammers instead of being plucked, it is constructed very differently, and its ancestors—at least over the past thousand or so years—are different. Dulcimer authority Sam Rizzetta has pointed out that the hammered dulcimer, being the older instrument, ought to be called simply "dulcimer," while the other instrument ought to be prefaced by the adjective "plucked" or "mountain" or "Appalachian" (or "fretted" or a lot of other names). We'll follow that from here.

The roots of the dulcimer go back at least to eleventh-century Persia. During the Moslem occupation of Spain and then during the Crusades, instruments of all kinds began filtering into Western Europe, among them the ancestor of both the Persian dulcimer, the *santur*, and the psaltery and dulcimer—the *qanun*. Around the fifteenth century, the psaltery began to fade in popularity in Europe and the dulcimer, which sometimes seems like little more than a hammered psaltery, became popular.

Also around this time it appears that builders were experimenting with keyboard versions of two popular stringed instruments, namely, the dulcimer and the psaltery. Although calling the piano a mechanized dulcimer (both use hammers) and the harpsichord a mechanized psaltery (both use plectra) is not totally accurate, a superficial examination of the instruments will show the similarities. Soon the superior flexibility, volume, and doubtless charm and novelty of the keyboard instruments pushed their brethren out of the picture. The earlier instruments continued to live on, but were no longer as important as they once were.

Eventually the dulcimer found its way to the New World, and being portable eventually found its way out West on wagon trains (can you imagine a grand piano in a covered wagon!), where it was sometimes called a lumberjack's piano. Around the turn of the nineteenth century, dulcimers were popular enough to appear in the Sears catalogue, selling for about $10. Even Henry Ford was a dulcimer fan, and he played one in a square-dance orchestra. However, once again the dulcimer began falling into obscurity, and only in the past ten years has it again been making a comeback. Says Rizzetta:

Some of the hotbeds of current popular interest in the hammered dulcimer have grown out of areas where there were Irish and English players. Michigan is probably the largest hotbed of that sort. I lived in Michigan in the middle sixties and that is where I got going with the dulcimer. There were clubs of old-time players. People would come to the club meetings and hear the music, and eventually these meetings grew into festivals, which now draw ten thousand people during the summer-

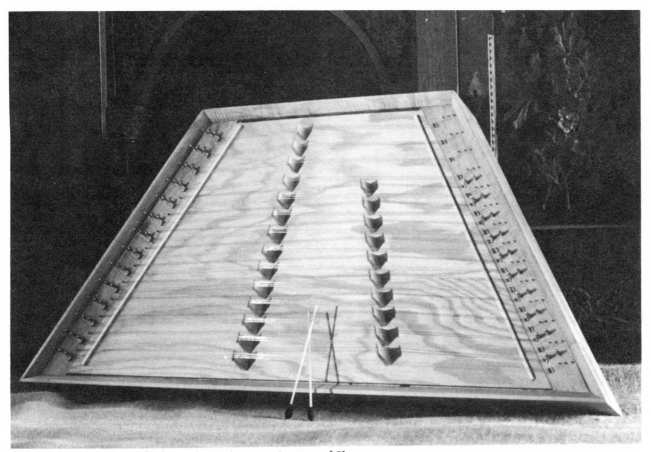

Dulcimer with a separate bridge under each course, by Rose of Sharon.

time. And it means more and more people who play music get smitten with the idea of taking up the dulcimer themselves. When I was in Michigan, it was pretty unusual to get more than a dozen players at that sort of meeting, and now there are clubs that have hundreds of members. So I think it was almost the creating of a social occasion for dulcimer music that has led to Michigan being maybe the foremost hotbed.

Sam Rizzetta.

All kinds of people are playing the dulcimer. Says Rizzetta:

> The hammered dulcimer's popularity in the sixties partly grew out of the interest in string-band music, fiddle tunes, banjo tunes. That kind of music—very fast, melodic—fits the dulcimer well and sounds great. The dulcimer was used for a much wider variety of things in the past, but this seems to be what got it off the ground in this current revival. Now, what's happening is that people are seeing that the dulcimer can be a more versatile . . . instrument, so they're trying it in the kinds of music they like. We're seeing experimentation with the dulcimer. It's been used for recordings in rock 'n' roll, bluegrass, country and western, western swing, jazz, ragtime. I think we're going to see an extension of that—people just trying more things with the dulcimer. What I hope to see is that it will just be accepted as another musical instrument. You won't think of the dulcimer as something you just play fiddle tunes or dance music on, but when you want the dulcimer sound you can put it into any kind of music. I think that in the next five years or so we're going to see a breakout of dulcimer within one particular idiom as far as national music and popular music. I wouldn't be surprised if that turned out to be country and western.
>
> The dulcimer is going to become more of a musical presence and less of a fad. It's going to grow to the point where fewer people are building them as a hobby and buying one and not playing it much. The people who *do* buy them will be doing more and more wonderful things with them.

Various other kinds of hammered dulcimers are still played in other parts of the world and also in this country. There's the Greek *santouri* and the Persian *santur,* and the Hungarian *cimbalom.* Sometimes you can hear the Greek dulcimer in Greek restaurants or Greek festivals. The *santur* is primarily a classical instrument and is harder to hear live, but some universities have classes in Persian music or even, as does U.C.L.A., some fine Persian musicians on staff and concerts of various kinds of ethnic music. The cimbalom might be found in gypsy orchestras entertaining in restaurants and nightclubs and can occasionally be heard in a piece of classical music.

Selecting a Dulcimer

More than anything, a dulcimer should be structurally sound and easy to tune.

STRUCTURAL INTEGRITY

Dulcimers average fifty to one hundred strings, which means great stress on the instrument. Sight down the bridges; do they sag? Do the parallel sides of the frame sag? Are the pin blocks warped or the joints opening up? Does the instrument feel solid and sturdy? On good instruments the frame will probably be braced. Since more strings means more stress, the more strings an instrument has, the stronger it should be. Used instruments may have a sagging soundboard; often, however, the instrument settles and some warpage occurs, but then goes no further.

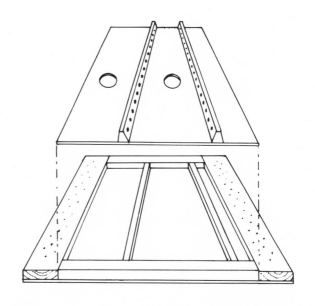

Dulcimer schematic.

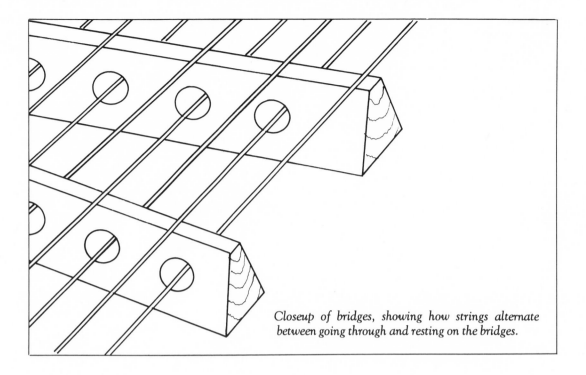

Closeup of bridges, showing how strings alternate between going through and resting on the bridges.

TUNING UP

Dulcimers come with one, two, or more bridges. Two—a bass bridge and a treble bridge—is the most common. Some instruments have additional, small bridges that give chromatic notes and extend the range. Check the bridge positions. The interval between the two sides of the treble bridge is usually a fifth. Even if you do not go through the laborious procedure of tuning each string, check the position of the bridges by tuning the strings to some pitch and making sure the interval at each set of strings is correct. (If you do plan to tune all the strings, find out from the builder what range to tune in.) Adjusting the bridge position, should the interval be off, is easy—just loosen the strings and move the bridge. Some instruments have individual bridges for each set of strings, so that it may only be a matter of loosening a few sets of strings. At any rate, before you can actually tune up, the bridges must be in the right place. Make sure the tuning pins do their job, since tuning one hundred strings—or just fifty—is not easy. Once the dulcimer is in tune, and barring a lot of traveling or rough handling or climatic extremes, a dulcimer should stay in fairly good tune for a month or two, requiring only minor adjustments. New dulcimers go out of tune until they settle, however.

SOUND

The sound was unlike anything I'd ever heard. It's a combination of a very string sort of sound—bell-like or harplike—and a very percussive sound. . . . that's what captivated me. That's the real reason for the dulcimer's revival. When people hear it, it's not hard to be captivated.

—Sam Rizzetta

Instant, amorphous harmonies tend to exude from it; it just sits there and sings. If you don't know what I'm talking about, seek out a bunch of people playing music and place your hammered dulcimer in a room with them. Now, don't play a note on the dulcimer, just put your ear up close to it. You can hear it humming along. Maybe it doesn't know the words, but that's not the point. The point is the amazing resonance derived from the sheer number of strings.[1]

—Peter Pickow

The dulcimer ought to sound bright and have just enough sustain to give the sound that "amazing resonance" but not enough to smear the sound and turn the instrument into an echo chamber; the sound ought to have a moderately quick decay. Some instruments, however, have a harsh, hard, brittle sound. Compare instruments to see what all this means.

STRINGS

Dulcimers are built with different numbers of strings and courses. Instruments with twelve treble courses and eleven bass courses are becoming a kind of norm, but some instruments have no bass courses, which is perfectly acceptable. Don't get fewer than twelve treble courses or the range will be limited. More courses extends the range, but so can different tunings and special bridges.

Bass and treble courses usually have two to four strings each, but the bass courses often have more than the treble. Two is minimum, or else you won't get much of that "amazing resonance." Because the higher-pitched strings have less sustain than the lower strings, three or four strings per treble course may help balance the overall sound, making the volume and tone fairly consistent from the lowest note to the highest. The greater the number of strings, too, the heavier the instrument (it has to be stronger and larger).

SHAPE AND SIZE

Most modern dulcimers are trapezoidal, but the actual shape of a trapezoid is unimportant. Volume is roughly proportional to size, but convenience is inversely proportional. Most dulcimers are of the table-top variety, convenient for traveling. Large dulcimers at one time were common parlor instruments, in much the same way the piano is a common "parlor" instrument today.

MATERIALS

Due to the strength of plywood, the dulcimer is one stringed instrument where laminated wood is as desirable or good as solid wood for certain parts. The top can be softwood or hardwood, solid or laminated. The back is often solid or laminated cherry, walnut, birch, or maple. And the pin blocks can be either solid or laminated; hard maple is excellent, and

Hammered dulcimer, by Capritaurus.

laminated hard-maple blocks, similar to those used in pianos, may be used.

The bridge or bridges should be a hardwood such as maple or rosewood and capped with an even harder material, anything from wood to steel (welding rod is frequently used). Rizzetta uses different materials to cap the individual bridges on his instruments to try to balance the overall sound— a hard material on the high strings brightens the sound and a softer material on the low strings reduces the tendency to oversustain. Caps also prevent the strings from biting into the bridge.

HAMMERS

There are basically three kinds. A flexible hammer has a nice, vibrant sound, the "prettiest sound possible" (Rizzetta). A stuff hammer has a hard, woody sound but is versatile since you can easily control its bounce; a stiff hammer facilitates fast playing. A hammer somewhere in between is hard to control and makes an "in between" sound.

The ends of the hammers control the tonal nuances. Hard wood gives a hard, bright, tinkly sound; felt gives a soft, piano- or harplike sound and also more sustain. Felt tips are good for soft, slow pieces and for vocal accompaniment. Leather comes in different hardnesses and is about halfway between felt and bare wood.

Instruments are usually supplied with hammers. Try them for a while and then experiment with others; try as many as possible. In selecting an instrument, try to play with the hammers you probably will use for a while. Making your own hammers is quite common.

Money Matters

The cheapest way to obtain a dulcimer is to build one from scratch, using, for example, the plans drawn up by Sam Rizzetta. The biggest problem is making the instrument structurally sound (as you can see by reading the Howie Mitchell booklet listed in the bibliography); otherwise, the task is fairly simple compared with that of building a violin or guitar. The second cheapest way—and the best for most people—is building from a kit, which doubles in value when completed. Several dulcimer kits are partially preassembled.

Compared with mountain dulcimers, hammered dulcimers are somewhat more expensive on the average, but the prices are comparable to those of inexpensive to moderately expensive guitars or mandolins. It's important to buy an instrument with a warranty of at least six months, and preferably a year; if the instrument hasn't collapsed by then, it probably won't.

Kits

All of the following kits can be built by someone with only basic woodworking skills. Perhaps the most work involves shaping, sanding, and finishing. Kits are ranked from easy to hard in terms of the amount of work required and also in terms of the clarity of the instructions; the more work the manufacturer does for you, the more the kit costs. Two "non-kit" kits are also included—the Here, Inc. assembled instrument that only needs sanding and finishing, and the do-it-yourself Gurian. Gurian Guitars will supply you with the wood and hardware you need to build a hammered dulcimer.

Capritaurus, P.O. Box 153, Felton, CA 95018. Save $60 over the price of a finished instrument.

Here, Inc., 29 S.E. Main St., Minneapolis, MN 55414. "In the white." Save money by doing the sanding and finishing yourself.

The following two kits are similar in difficulty, though I have not seen the Bednark instructions.

Bednark, Box 13, Centerville, MA 02632. Semi-Kit (SK-1). Required tools include hammer, screwdriver, and wire cutters. Frame is preassembled; holes are drilled. Work: mount top and bridges; hammer in pins; attach strings; sand and finish.

Dusty Strings, 1848 N.E. Ravenna Blvd., Seattle, WA 98105. Tools include hammer, wire cutters, saw. Back, rails, and pin blocks are joined. Holes are predrilled. Work is similar to Bednark SK-1; some trimming required. Instructions/plans are extremely lucid, ideal for someone with minimal woodworking experience. The owner's manual, though well intentioned, could be more complete and easier to read.

The following kits are similar in difficulty. I have not seen the Hughes or Bednark instructions. Aside from sanding and finishing, all require some final trim work, as the wood is often rough cut.

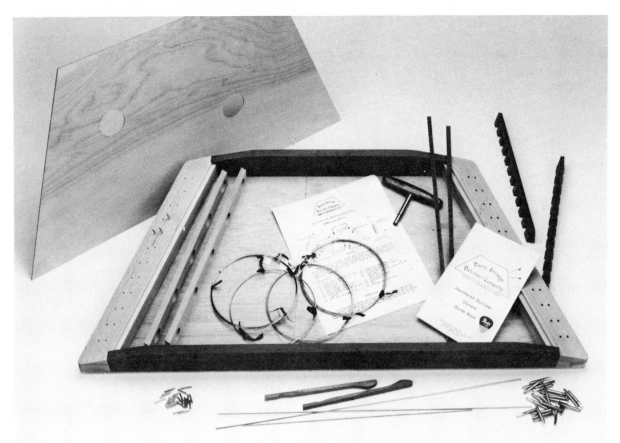

Dusty Strings dulcimer kit.

Fogel, Box 174-D, Deale, MD 20751. Required tools include rasp, knife, plane, wood wedge, hammer, clamps, wire cutters. Holes are predrilled. Instructions are excellent. This is a model instruction guide; each step is generously illustrated as well as timed, so that you know exactly how long each operation takes; basic and tuning information provided. According to Fogel, "even people with no woodworking experience can be playing their own hand-built dulcimer after about twenty hours of construction." A good kit for someone who likes guidance but wants to do some woodworking too.

Hughes, 4419-C W. Colfax, Denver, CO 80204. Required tools include a knife, plane, file, and coping saw. Minimal woodworking required; time: fifteen to twenty-five hours. If the instructions are anything like those for the Hughes mountain dulcimers they are probably clear, short, and simple, good for the person who doesn't need excessive guidance.

Bednark. K1. Required tools include clamps, plane, chisel, hammer, wire cutters, screwdriver. Holes are predrilled.

Here, Inc. For an additional $60, the Here, Inc. kits described below are available with the holes drilled for the pins, all the parts precut, and the pin blocks mounted.

Here, Inc. 95HK requires more work than 100HK because it is constructed differently. Required tools include drill or saw, hammer, pliers, wire cutters, clamps, crosscut saw. Holes not predrilled. Very detailed instructions; hard to read because the type is single spaced and in italics; illustrations could be more clear. Extensive instructions on tuning included. A good kit for someone who wants to do most of the work herself or himself.

Gurian Guitars, Box 595, West Swanzey, NH 03469. For about $60 you can purchase all the materials needed to build a hammered dulcimer. The wood is cut so that you can build an instrument that follows Gurian's specifications. Order the Rizzetta leaflet or use the Fogel book for plans.

Dulcimer Brands, Builders, and Manufacturers

Note: Warranties may only cover assembled and finished instruments.

Autorino (The Butternut Shoppe, Rt. 9W North, Rt. 1, Box 387D, Kingston, NY 12401). Michael Autorino is a well-known builder. Order direct.

Bednark (Box 13, Centerville, MA 02632). Thomas A. Bednark, formerly a partner in Cuttyhunk Instrument Kits, has been building dulcimers since 1977 and works alone, turning out fifty instruments each year. Available through dealers or from Bednark himself; when ordering from the builder, allow two weeks for delivery. The SK-1 is guaranteed one year.

Beriyth (JeananLee Dulcimer Shop, P.O. Box 8, Highway 32, Cosby, TN 37722). Available only through JeananLee's. Three-year warranty.

Capritaurus (P.O. Box 153, Felton, CA 95018). A highly regarded outfit. Order direct.

Clayton and Wizmer (5280 S. 7 Rd., #8, Arlington, VA 22204). Bob Clayton and Ralph Wizmer produce about fifteen instruments each year. Extras—stands, fancy hammers and veneers—are available. Available through some Washington, DC stores or direct from the manufacturer; direct delivery takes ten to ninety days. Fiver-year warranty.

Dorogi (Ellicott Rd., Brocton, NY 14716). Dennis Dorogi, a highly respected luthier, has been building dulcimers since 1970 and works alone. Available from dealers or from Dorogi.

Dulcimerseed (5520 Soquel Dr., Soquel, CA

95073). Denis Murphy has been building instruments since 1971 and completes fifty per year. He states: "I have chosen to produce (in a one-at-a-time manner) an instrument that is free of gimmicks and follows a traditional line." Special effort goes into constructing a truly portable instrument: "The volume of our instruments competes with that of instruments twice the size and weight." Murphy also builds *santurs*. Available through dealers and from Dulcimerseed; direct delivery takes one to eight weeks, depending on the model.

Dusty Strings (1848 N.E. Ravenna Blvd., Seattle, WA 98105). Dusty Strings Dulcimer Company has been in business since 1977, employs six builders, and produces 275 instruments a year, of which 50 to 60 are kits. Custom work is available. Dusty Strings aims for a "well-balanced, rich, full-bodied sound," and its instruments "are being played by rank beginners with no prior musical background as well as by multitalented musicians. Available through dealers in California, Washington, and Oregon, and directly from the manufacturer; direct orders take two to three weeks to fill. Two-year warranty.

Fogel (Box 174-D, Deale, MD 20751). Rick Fogel has been building dulcimers since 1975 and completes about forty per year. Available through some mail-order dealers and direct from Fogel; delivery from Fogel takes two months for a finished instrument. Lifetime warranty.

Hale (The Well-Traveled Clavier, P.O. Box 516, Patagonia, AZ 85624). R. P. Hale has been building keyboard instruments since 1975, dulcimers since 1980. He works alone and builds fifteen dulcimers per year, by commission only. Hale has been experimenting with various designs, including a tapered soundboard. He aims for a balanced, penetrating, resonant sound. His instruments are for the "serious beginner, professional, or traditional player," and he does "not sell furniture or wall-hanging instruments." Available only from the builder.

Here, Inc. (29 S.E. Main St., Minneapolis, MN

55414). A well-known company, Here, Inc. has been manufacturing dulcimers since 1975. The instruments are on the light side, and the 300HD can be built as a suitcase-type dulcimer with the cover part of the frame. Available through dealers and Here, Inc; direct orders take two to four weeks to fill.

Hughes (4419-C W. Colfax, Denver, CO 80204). Hughes Dulcimer Company, another well-known manufacturer, has been building dulcimers since 1965. Available from dealers and Hughes.

Kelischek (Rt. 1, Brasstown, NC 28902). Founded in 1955, the Kelischek Workshop has specialized in unusual instruments and historical reproductions and has trained luthiers. Order direct. Catalogue: $2.

Magic Mountain (Saga Musical Instruments, P.O. Box 2841, South San Francisco, CA 94080). Available from Saga and dealers.

Montague (16 Patriot Rd., Tewksbury, MA 01876). Custom instruments. Write Fred Montague for information.

Neptune Rising (P.O. Box 834, New Glarus, WI 52574). Custom instruments. Write Dennis O'Brien for information.

Rizzetta (P.O. Box 87, Valley Head, WV 26294). Sam Rizzetta, who has been building dulcimers and other instruments since 1959, is perhaps the most respected authority on dulcimers in the country. His instruments, of which he builds thirty to fifty each year, are in great demand. He also builds a Hungarian cimbalom. Order direct; delivery time is two years. Lifetime warranty.

Rose of Sharon Instruments (The Road to the Oblong Valley, Sharon, CT 06069). Roger Williams has been making dulcimers since 1980 and works alone. Options include a painted soundboard (with motifs), a spruce or cedar soundboard, and solid-color sides. Available direct from Rose of Sharon.

Round (6470 8th Ave., Grandville, MI 49418). Donald Round of the Round Family Dulcimer Company has been building dulcimers since 1971 and completes seventy-five to one hundred per year. Round, who has a fine reputation, aims for a "crisp, clear sound." Replacement strings are free to customers. Available direct from Round; immediate delivery.

Stapleton (201 Midland Ave., Springdale, AR 72764). Says L. O. Stapleton, who has been building dulcimers since 1978, "these are one of a kind. Most have marquetry or mother-of-pearl inlaid on the front rail." Available direct from Stapleton. Lifetime warranty.

Bibliography: Instruction

Hughes, Norman. *The Hammered Dulcimer*. Mel Bay. 1979. A very basic book.

Mason, Phillip. *The Hammered Dulcimer Instruction Book*. Communications Press, 1977. Tablature and music. A good book.

Pickow, Peter. *Hammered Dulcimer*. Oak, 1979. Tablature and music. Beginning level. Instruction and tunes. A very good book, but a total novice may need a few more pointers to get started.

INSTRUCTION TAPES

Dusty Strings Dulcimer Co. Cassette. (See p. 000 for address.)

Fogel, Rick. *Traditional Music*. Cassette. Four of the tunes included are notated in tablature in Fogel's dulcimer kit instructions.

Round, Donald. Cassette.

Bibliography: Construction, Theory, History

Fogel, Rick. *Physics, Music Theory and the Hammered Dulcimer*. Rick Fogel Printing Service, 1979.

For the person who wants "to concisely connect physics, music theory and the hammered dulcimer," says the author. This is a bit formally written but worthwhile.

Fogel, Rick, and N. A. Martin. *Building a Hammered Dulcimer: Do-Kit-Yourself.* R. F. Printing Service, 1980. The instruction manual accompanying the Fogel kit also contains some information on tuning and tunings as well as the tablature and music for the four tunes on his cassette *Traditional Music.* Fogel also has plans for building a dulcimer from scratch; write for information.

Holmes, Michael (ed.). *The Hammer Dulcimer Compendium. Mugwumps* Magazine, MIH Publications, 1977. A collection of articles on history, playing, and other matters. Recommended.

Mason, Phillip. *How to Build a Hammered Dulcimer.* Blue Ridge Dulcimer Shop, 1977.

Mitchell, Howard W. *The Hammered Dulcimer: How to Make It and Play It.* Folk-Legacy Records FSI 43, 1972. A classic collection of Mitchell's early experiments building dulcimers that is useful for the would-be dulcimer builder but not really a how-to book.

Rizzetta, Sam. *Hammer Dulcimer: History and Playing.* Smithsonian Institution Leaflet 72-4, 1972. Free, and good.

Rizzetta, Sam. *Making a Hammer Dulcimer.* Smithsonian Institution Leaflet 72-5, 1972. A free pamphlet of use to the would-be builder.

Stein, Eva. *The Hammered Dulcimer and Related Instruments: A Bibliography.* Archive of Folk Song, Library of Congress, 1979. Very good, and free.

Magazines

Dulcimer Players News, P.O. Box 2164, Winchester, VA 22601. $6/year (quarterly). The premier source of information on dulcimers: recordings, classifieds, festivals, news, tunes, and instruction. Recommended.

Frets, P.O. Box 28836, San Diego, CA 92128. $18/year (monthly). Two columns of interest: by Michael Rugg (speculative, musicological) and Mary Faith Rhoads (practical); sometimes the roles reverse.

Sing Out! 505 8th Ave., New York, NY 10018. $11/year (bimonthly). Occasional articles of interest. Worthwhile.

Discography

AMERICAN DULCIMER

American Hammered Dulcimer (Troubadour 6). A good sampler, with a jam-session quality.

Carter, Dorothy. *Troubadour* (Celeste 1003) and *Wailee Wailee* (Celeste 1004).

Daglish, Malcolm, and Grey Larsen. *Banish Misfortune* (June Appal 016). Lots of Irish tunes.

Looman, Patty, and Russell Fluharty. *Dulcimore* (Page Publishing SLP 602).

McCutcheon, John. *The Wind That Shakes the Barley* (June Appal 014) and *Wrystraw: From Earth to Heaven* (June Appal 028).

Mitchell, Howard W. *The Hammered Dulcimer: How to Make It and Play It* (Folk Legacy FSI 43). Mitchell has been a key figure in the dulcimer revival.

Parker, Chet. *The Hammered Dulcimer* (Folkways 2381).

Rizzetta, Sam, with Trapezoid. *Three Forks of Cheat* (Troubadour 1). Dulcimer ensemble.

Round, Jay. *One Time Friend* (Turnaround 5003).

OTHER DULCIMERS

Feldman, Zev, with Andy Statman. *Jewish Klezmer Music* (Shanachie 21002). Klezmer, the music of the Eastern European Jews, reflects various musical influences, including gypsy, Hungarian, Romanian, and Middle Eastern. Feldman plays *santouri*, a Middle Eastern hammered dulcimer.

Moschos, Aristidis. *Solo Santouri* (EMI Col 2J054-70264). Greek dulcimer.

Racz, Aladar. *Cimbalom* (Hungaroton LPX 11981). One side is classical music (for example, Scarlatti); the other, folk. The folk side contains a series of improvisations on Romanian folk melodies that is extraordinary. The cimbalom has a more muted, less resonant sound than the American dulcimer and sounds a little like an early piano.

Rastegar, Nasser. *Music of Iran: Santur Recital*, Vols. 1-3 (Lyrichord 7135, 7165-7166), and *The Persian Santur* (Nonesuch H-72039). Excellent performances.

Festivals

See Chapter 7 for dulcimer festivals.

*Wes Linenkugel at Dulcimer Days, Coshocton, Ohio. Note
tuning wrench in upper left-hand corner of dulcimer, ready
for action.*

CHAPTER 9

THE AUTOHARP*

Like most musical instruments, the Autoharp has had its share of fame and failure. Ever since its invention in 1881, the Autoharp has gone through periods when the manufacturer couldn't build. But one time, just twelve years after the first production model was completed, the manufacturer actually closed down![1] Autoharps have been used by polite society, in the classroom, and in rural areas of the South; sometimes the Autoharp is called an Appalachian harp, even though its inventor, Charles Zimmerman, lived in Philadelphia. Although there have always been respected players—Sarah and Maybelle Carter, Kilby Snow, and Pop Stoneman among others—finding them has often been a problem, as Mike Seeger, of the now-defunct New Lost City Ramblers, relates:

I had asked Pop Stoneman if there were other Autoharp players, and he said, "Yeah, the best one is Kilby Snow." Kilby was then living near Fries, pronounced "freeze" (or "fries" depending on the time of year!). [Pop Stoneman] thought it was a big joke that Kilby *Snow* lived in "freeze". Anyway, within a very short while, a few months, I was down there visiting with Wade Ward and went to see Kilby. It was a real chase to find him. He was a very elusive person. He wasn't one of those people who leave tracks in the places that you usually find tracks. So I eventually found him a couple of miles from Wade Ward's house near Independence, Virginia, after following him from Fries to Galax and back to Independence. He was working there putting up a concrete block building and he had his harp with him in a

*Autoharp is a registered trademark of Oscar Schmidt International.

Henry J (that's a car from the early 50's). He had his work clothes on and his hands in the concrete, and we just had a little talk, and then he just kind of cleaned off his hands a little bit and pulled out his harp and played me tunes right there![2]

One reason the Autoharp languished in obscurity may be that seious musicians did not take it seriously and were put off by presumably built-in limitations. After all, the Autoharp was invented for easy playing; unfortunately, some thought the instrument so easy to play they called it names: "idiot zither" is especially poignant. Recently, however, the Autoharp has been taken up by ambitious, adventuresome musicians who have been developing its potential by inventing new techniques, playing more challenging music, and modifying the instrument to alter the sound and facilitate new techniques. Bryan Bowers, the most prominent of the new generation of Autoharp players, says, "I played a regular harp for about three or four years. Then I started realizing that there were a lot of things that I perceived as shortcomings and I started changing them. It's not a process that started and stopped. It's still changing."[3]

In the strictest sense, the word *Autoharp* should be used only when speaking about the instrument manufactured by Oscar Schmidt, since Autoharp is a trade name and has been since its invention one hundred years ago. However, Autoharp is commonly used to refer to any brand of *chorded zither* in much the same way resophonic guitars are called Dobros regardless of who makes them. To avoid the confusion that would arise when other brands are discussed—for example, a Chromaharp (brand) Autoharp—*harp* or *chorded zither* will be used except when the Autoharp Autoharp is meant.

The principle of the harp is simple. Thirty-six (sometimes thirty-seven) strings are usually tuned chromatically over a range of approximately three octaves. Chords are played by depressing bars that damp some strings and allow other strings to vibrate when the harp is strummed or picked. When the C major bar is pressed, for example, only the notes in a C major chord will sound.

Although the harp has traditionally been used to play chordal accompaniment to popular and folk songs, it can be used to play any kind of music, depending on the interests of the player and his or her ability to adapt the instrument. Some musicians are playing fiddle tunes, for example, others, jazz.

Selecting a Harp

CHORDS

Harps come with different numbers of chords. Autoharps, for example, have twelve, fifteen, or twenty-one chords; Chromaharps, five, twelve, fifteen, and twenty-seven; Autorino Harps, fifteen. The more the chord bars, the more keys you can play, the greater the harmonic flexibility, and the more chord combinations possible. A twenty-one-chord harp lends itself well to melodic playing (such as fiddle tunes), though most melody players prefer fewer chord bars because there is more room to move the fingers. A harp with fewer chord bars has other advantages. The unused strings can be tuned in unison with their neighbors, to give a fuller, special sound; playing in special tunings is easier; and a musician planning for any reason to remove chord bars will save money by initially buying a harp with fewer bars.

Instruments with only a few chord bars—like the six some players use—also have their disadvantages. You can play in only one key, and the variety of chords is limited. You may have to purchase several instruments to keep from boring yourself, your audience, and your musical companions. As soon as the guitarist or banjo player you're with shifts into any key but the one you have chords for, you're out of luck. Bryan Bowers:

> I bought twenty-four [instruments] at a clock from the factory and I have ones people have given to me. I carry about six on stage nowadays. I have a bunch at home that I string up and set up different ways...thirty.[4]

Modifying the harp is nothing new, as Bowers learned by watching old-time musician Kilby Snow:

> I'd been listening to his music because Mike Seeger had turned me on to it. Mike Seeger had worked with Kilby and had produced at least one, and I believe two of his albums on Folkways. Of course I had heard Kilby on record, but I was up in New York visiting some people, and I heard he was in town at the Navy Pier in a folklore society sponsored situation. So I went down there.
>
> Well, Kilby Snow was playing, and he was just wonderful! I thoroughly enjoyed it, so after his set I went up and was talking to him a little

Bryan Bowers, at the Walnut Valley Festival, Winfield, Kansas.

bit. I didn't tell him I played the harp or anything else. I was just talking to him, and I asked him if I could look at his harp, and he said, "Sure." So I picked up the harp and started looking at it. Of course, he had the chord bars moved upwards so he could play down below them. I'd been moving my chord bars down so I'd have room to play up top! Well, I looked at it and everything and by and by said to him, "Mr. Snow, how come you moved your chord bars up?" figuring he would say, "Well, that's cuz I like to play down at the bottom." Instead, he turned to me and said, "Well, I moved them up because you can't get any music up there at the top!" It was great! So I didn't even tell him. I

didn't tell him where I'd been playing the Autoharp. What was I gonna say? So I just said, "Yes, sir, okay, Mr. Snow!" I sure wasn't about to argue with him![5]

For a beginner, a twenty-one-chord harp is probably the best investment. The difference in price between such an instrument and one with fewer chord bars is insignificant, and the advantages are significant. According to Becky Blackley, editor of *The Autoharpoholic*, a magazine devoted exclusively to harps: "Because the twenty-one-chord harp is far more versatile than the other models, no matter what direction the player takes, this harp can 'travel' with him. The chords are easily rearranged, interchanged, or modified as the player begins to discover his or her individual needs. To convert to fewer bars is fairly easy (and fairly inexpensive), but to convert from a twelve- or fifteen-chord model to the twenty-one is tricky and expensive. In the long run it is a better investment."

A further consideration is the chords themselves. Production instruments like the Autoharp and Chromaharp offer little choice unless you want to buy extra chord bars and construct your own chord configuration. Instruments built by individuals or small shops often come with a choice of chords.

NUMBER OF STRINGS

The standard number is thirty-six, but some non-commercial harps have thirty-seven or whatever number you want.

MATERIALS

Most production models are built of laminated wood, some have a solid wood top, and one—the Autoharp Centurion—uses all solid wood except the pin blocks, which are laminated. Nonproduction instruments usually are constructed entirely of solid woods, except for the pin blocks, which are laminated. The best pin blocks are maple, the best tops spruce. According to Blackley, "laminated pin blocks are very important in keeping the instrument in tune."

STRUCTURAL INTEGRITY AND CONDITION

The harp should be sturdy. Production models and instruments constructed by reliable, well-known builders are all reliable. A good warranty is especially

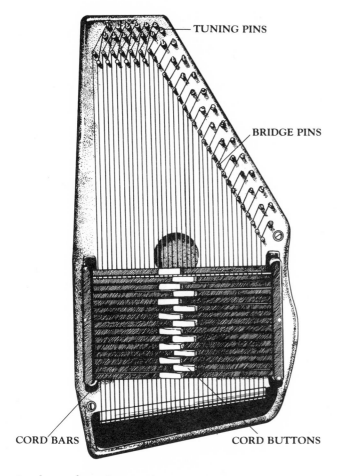

- TUNING PINS
- BRIDGE PINS
- CORD BARS
- CORD BUTTONS

Autoharp schematic.

desirable from an individual builder. Make sure the moving parts work smoothly. On a used instrument check the joints, especially at the hitch pin block to make sure they are sound; also check the felts to make sure they aren't worn (but new felts are easy to obtain and install).

TUNING

Bryan Bowers: "I tune to the last minute. I tune each harp three times before I walk on the stage. I usually start about an hour before the show. I tune the whole batch of harps, take a break, go through them again, take a break and then tune them *again* just before going on. I tune them to themselves. When I first put on a new harp I'll tune it to the pitchpipe, but after awhile when it gets settled in I just leave it."[6]

Although tuning a harp is time-consuming, it's a good way to find out how well the instrument holds up under normal string tension, to evaluate the tone, and to make sure the tuning pins turn easily and don't slip.

There are different tuning systems. Most common is standard equal temperament, the system of the guitar, piano, and most other instruments and the one explained in the Michael King article below. Another system is diatonic equal temperament; the result here is a scale similar to that of the mountain dulcimer. And still another is diatonic just intonation; here the pitches are more exactly ("justly") related to one another and the sound is more harmonious. In order to tune this special way, the instrument must be physically modified. "Just intonation also has a serious disadvantage," says harpmaker and player Keith Young. "It is fine if you are playing solo, but sounds out of tune when you play with other instruments that are equal tempered (which includes all fretted instruments)."

On Tuning* by Michael King

Place the Autoharp flat on a table-top or desk with the strings vertical: bass strings left, treble strings right. The only equipment required is the tuning hammer provided by the manufacturer and a tuning/pitch aid. Although there are many types of tuners available, I have found that the round chromatic pitchpipes (sold at any music store) are more than adequate. By holding the pitchpipe in your mouth, you can sound the pitch continuously while having both hands free: left hand for plucking the string and right hand on the tuning hammer.

Start with the highest octave "C" and carefully fit the tuning hammer on the tuning pin. Be absolutely sure the hammer is "seated" on the pin before turning. Otherwise, the squared area on the pin can strip away. Sound the pitchpipe and then pluck the string and *listen*. If the string is flat (too low), *gently* turn the hammer clockwise until you reach the pitch. If the string is sharp (too high), turn the hammer counter-clockwise until the string is flat, *then* bring it up to pitch. Somehow it seems easier for many people to tune *up* to pitch, rather than down.

With the pitchpipe still sounding "C", follow the same procedure and tune the next lower "C" string, and the next lower, until all the "C" notes are tuned. This method will evenly and gradually distribute the string ten-

*Reprinted from *The Autoharpoholic*, Vol. 1, No. 2 (Summer 1980). © 1980 by i.a.d. Used by permission. All rights reserved.

sion on the harp and make the instrument less likely to shift out-of-tune. Simply work down by octaves until all the strings have been tuned, going next to "B", "A#", etc. The interval of one octave is usually fairly easy to hear when tuning.

New Autoharps often come with some of the lower plain strings tuned quite sharp, so special attention is required with them. The strings have a "memory" and, if tuned sharp for very long will tend to go sharp again even after repeated tunings. I find that by gently stretching the string by placing two fingers under and tugging when the string is below pitch and tuning it up and repeating the process several times will "settle" the offending string.

When the octave tuning process is completed, you may have to "temper" and fine-tune by ear. Make several chords and strum all the strings, and you may have to slightly retune certain notes to blend with the chords.

You can spot-check certain key notes by pressing two chord bars together. For example, press "C# maj" and "F maj" and you will hear only "C" notes, common to both chords; "F maj" and "Bb maj" give you only "F" notes; "Bb maj" and "Eb maj" give "Bb", and so forth. Depending on the chord layout of your Autoharp, any tonic (I maj) chord and subdominant (IV maj) played together will block all notes but the scale tone of the tonic chord.

Above all, do not rush the tuning process and be patient. If you have a problem with relative pitch, remember: A sense of pitch can be learned and developed. . . .

Money Matters

The price range of harps is small compared with that of other musical instruments, running from about $150 for a factory-built imported instrument to about $1000 for a custom-made American instrument; the selection of brands and models is also limited. However, the most expensive production model, the Autoharp Centurion, lists for only $270; anything more expensive is built by an individual luthier. By contrast, $270 will buy an inexpensive beginners' guitar, $1033 the least expensive Martin guitar. Custom-made guitars can cost $3500 or more.

Custom Harps

Who buys handmade and custom harps? Autorino Harps, which are handmade but built on a standard model, "are bought mainly by people who are performing," says Michael Autorino. Tom Morgan, another harp builder, says he builds for "the discriminating player." And Dennis O'Brien, a custom builder, believes beginners should consider custom instruments: "These [cheap] instruments are difficult to play, difficult to tune, don't stay in tune, and sound terrible—just what the beginner needs, right? . . . a person learns an instrument to make music, which will, hopefully, awaken the soul, loosen us up, and let us merge a bit. . . . But the music reaches the soul through the ear, so the instrument should sound not okay but good."

Harp Builders, Brands, and Manufacturers

Autoharp (Oscar Schmidt International, 1415 Waukegan Rd., Northbrook, IL 60062). Oscar Schmidt has produced Autoharps for over fifty years, and more Autoharps are sold than all the other brands combined. The newest model is the Centurion. Becky Blackley says, "I prefer the standard models for melody playing because of the brighter sound, and the Centurions for vocal accompaniment because of the rich, mellow sound." Sold through dealers. Six-month warranty.

Autorino Harp (The Butternut Shoppe, Route 9W North, RD#1, Box 387C, Kingston, NY 12401). Michael Autorino, who has been building instruments since 1965, is a respected craftsman. Order direct.

Chromaharp (Various distributors, including C. Bruno & Son, 20 Old Windsor Rd., Bloomfield, CT 06002; and Peripole, Browns Mills, NJ 08015). Chromaharps are imported from the Orient. Prices vary greatly between distributors. Sold through dealers, including Peripole. Three-year warranty from C. Bruno.

Mary Morgan with Morgan harp.

Morgan (Rt. 3, Box 147-1, Dayton, TN 37321). Tom Morgan is a long-time builder of harps.

Neptune Rising (P.O. Box 834, New Glarus, WI 52574). Dennis O'Brien has been building his harp about three years and completes twenty instruments a year, all strictly custom instruments: the harp "assumes the shape and size desired by the musician. He or she determines the number of strings and how they are tuned as well as the number of chords and how they are arranged...." Ordering "through personal contact is best," O'Brien says, but a few stores carry his instruments. Delivery on direct orders takes six to eight weeks. Lifetime warranty.

Young (3815 Kendale Rd., Annandale, VA 22003). Keith Young has been building his "Appalachian folkharp" for eight years and produces seventy instruments each year. Available from Young; delivery takes six months. One-year warranty.

Accessories

Tuning Wrench. Harps usually come with a standard tuning wrench, but some players use a star wrench.

Chord Conversion

You can change the total number of chords on most harps, or you can just change the chords. Oscar Schmidt offers kits for converting a twelve-chord instrument into a fifteen-chord one and vice versa, or for converting an instrument into a twenty-one-chord model. Prices range from $34 to $45. Single chord bars are $3 apiece, and custom chord bars (you tell them the chord you want) are $5. Individual builders also sell chord bars.

Discography

Bluestein, Gene. *Sowin' on the Mountain* (Fretless 141).

Bowers, Brian. *The View from Home* (Flying Fish 037) and *Home, Home on the Road* (Flying Fish 091).

Carter, Maybelle. *Mother Maybelle Carter* (2-Columbia CG-32436) and *Mother Maybelle Carter and Her Autoharp* (Smash MGS-27025; out of print). Records by the Carter Family and by its individual members change labels and go in and out of print too often for comfort. You're bound to hear at least a little Autoharp on any record you find.

Couton, Patrick, and Georges Fisher. *Autoharp ce Soir* (Iris TR 1012).

Fingers Akimbo. *Cowtowns and Other Planets* (Biscuit City 1319).

Jones, Clayton. *Traditional Autoharp* (Sunny Mountain EB 1006).

Hammered Dulcimer Reunion (Take II Productions 001).

Music of the Ozarks (National Geographic Society 703).

Snow, Kilby. *America: Country Songs and Tunes with Autoharp* (Folkways 3902).

Snow, Kilby, Ernest Stoneman, and Neriah and Kenneth Benfield. *Mountain Music Play on the Autoharp* (Folkways 2365). Recommended as a first record.

Waldron, Betty and Mark. *Parlor Picking* (Outlet STLP 1028).

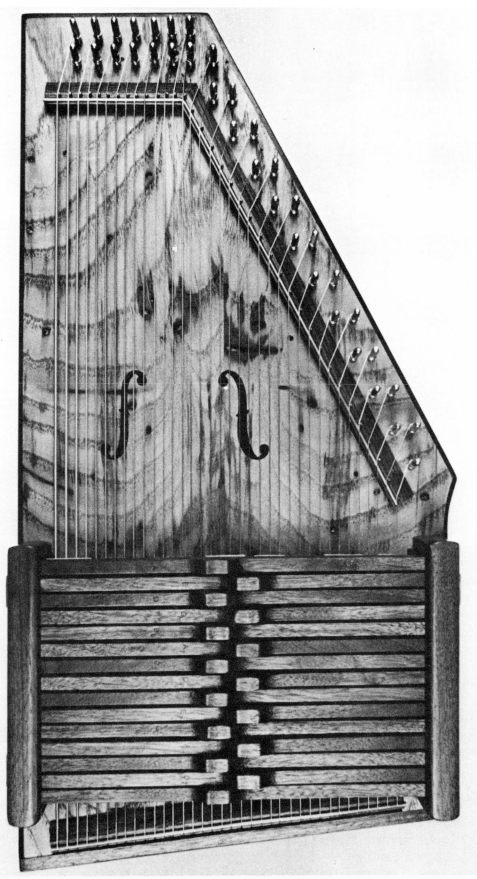

Harp, by Keith Young.

Bibliography: Instruction

All of these books are recommended.

Jones, Clayton, and Barbara McClintock Koehler. *Traditional Autoharp.* Mel Bay, 1978. Tablature and music. Beginning level. Accompanying record available from Sunny Mountain Records, P.O. Box 14592, Gainesville, FL 32604.

Peterson, Meg. *The Complete Method for Autoharp.* Mel Bay, 1980. Music. Beginning to intermediate levels. Thorough treatment of the instrument; applications to blues and reggae; melodic playing.

Peterson, Meg. *The Many Ways to Play the Autoharp.* Vols. 1 & 2. Oscar Schmidt, 1966. Beginning through intermediate levels.

Taussig, Harry. *Folk Style Autoharp.* Oak, 1967. Tablature and music. Also contains a history of the instrument.

Bibliography: History, Players, Repairs, Modifications, Tunings

Benson, Peter. "No More Grooves." *The Autoharpoholic,* Vol. 1, No. 3 (Fall 1980), p. 11. How to eliminate grooves in the chord bar felt.

Blackley, Becky. "Custom Chording Your Autoharp." *Frets,* November 1980, pp. 36–37.

Blackley, Becky. "How to Convert Your Harp to the Diatonic Scale." *The Autoharpoholic,* Vol. 2, No. 1 (Winter 1981), pp. 21–22.

Blackley, Becky. "How to Tighten Up the Playing Action." *The Autoharpoholic,* Vol. 1, No. 3 (Fall 1980), p. 21.

Blackley, Becky. "View from the Top: Interview with Bryan Bowers." *The Autoharpoholic,* Vol. 2, No. 1 (Winter 1981), pp. 8–11.

Bowers, Bryan. "Teach-In: Tuning the Autoharp." *Sing Out!* Vol. 24, No. 1 (March-April 1975), pp. 13–14.

Coats, Art and Leota. "Bryan Bowers." *Frets,* May 1979, pp. 13–14.

Moore, A. Doyle. "The Autoharp: Its Origin and Development from a Popular to a Folk Instrument." *New York Folklore Quarterly,* Vol. 19, No. 4 (December 1963), pp. 261–274. This excellent article is reprinted in the Taussig book.

Padgett, Woody. "Diatonic Just Tuning." *The Autoharpoholic,* Vol. 2, No. 1 (Winter 1981), pp. 18–19.

Magazines

The Autoharpoholic, 190 Santa Clara St., Brisbane, CA 94005. $10/year (quarterly). Interviews, how-to, reviews, etc. Infused with great energy and enthusiasm and highly recommended.

Frets, P.O. Box 28836, San Diego, CA 92128. $18/year (monthly). Occasional articles of interest.

Festivals

International Autoharp Championship, Winfield, Kansas. September. Write: Walnut Valley Association, Box 245, Winfield, KS 67156. Coincides with the National Guitar Flat-Picking Championship (and other events).

See Chapter 6 and Appendix E for other festivals; some of these have special activities for harp players.

CHAPTER 10

THE
HARMONICA

We tend to think of the harmonica as a Western instrument, even an American invention, associating it with the cowboy, with the open road, with various symbols of our country. But the harmonica as we know it originated in Europe early in the nineteenth century and is based on an instrument very likely of Chinese origin that first appeared about two thousand years ago In spite of this long, exotic history, the harmonica has established itself as a most modern fixture in the musical life of our country. Over a million harmonicas were sold in 1980, probably more than the combined sales of all the other instruments discussed in this book except the violin!

Harmonica virtuosos, while they do not exactly abound, do exist, playing old-time music, blues, jazz, country, and classical music. Yet the harmonica is really more of a people's instrument than anything, an inexpensive passport to simple (and sometimes complex) and thoroughly enjoyable musical pleasures. The harmonica is ideal for the person who likes to figure out his or her favorite tunes in a casual sort of way, and is especially handy while traveling. What better way to enjoy a little music at the beach or in the woods or in some hotel room in a foreign country than to take along a harmonica!

Inside each harmonica is a series of reeds, thin metal strips that vibrate when air strikes them. The principle is similar to that governing single-reed instruments such as the clarinet and saxophone.

M. Hohner, the principal purveyor of harmonicas, lists over fifty different models in its catalogue, but there are two basic types: diatonic and chromatic. Diatonic harmonicas—most of them—will play a diatonic (major) scale in the middle of the instrument and only some notes of the scale on either side. Chromatic harmonicas play a complete chromatic scale and have a sliding mechanism that helps get the additional notes.

Two types of diatonic harmonicas are used for blues and old-time music: the Marine Band and the Blues Harp (the harmonica is often called a harp or mouth organ). Both have ten holes, and Hohner sells them in all twelve keys. The Blues Harp is specially built to facilitate the note-bending used by blues players but is otherwise the same. Since each harmonica plays fully in only one key, you will need several if you plan to play with other musicians, use songbooks, or play along with records. For old-time music, important keys are C, D, G, and A; for blues, various keys are used, but E and A are good to begin with.

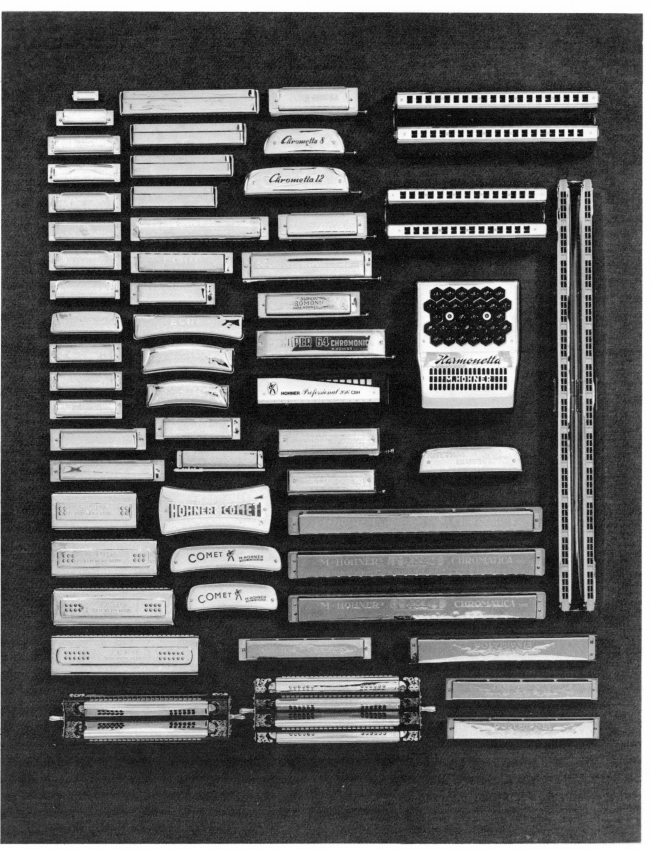

Hohner harmonicas.

Hohner Marine Band harmonica.

Brands and Prices

Hohner (Andrews Rd., Hicksville, NY 11802). Hohner harmonicas are imported from Germany and have been manufactured since 1857.

HH-1896 Marine Band—$9.75
HH-532 Blues Harp—$10.25

Should you wish to experiment with other harmonicas, see your local music store or write Hohner for its catalog.

Accessories

Hohner Harmonica Holder—$7.50. This apparatus is a collar with a holder for the instrument; by freeing your hands it enables you to play harmonica while playing another instrument, for example, guitar.

Harmonica Belt—$8.50. A belt to hold all your harmonicas (Bob Dylan used to have one). If you have lots of harps, this can be handy, but for just a few, pockets are as convenient.

Bibliography: Instruction, Tunes

Glover, Tony. *Blues Harp.* Oak, 1975. Tablature.
Glover, Tony. *Blues Harp Song Book.* Oak, 1975. Tablature.
Morgan, Tommy. *Blues Harmonica.* Gwyn, 1971.
Terry, Sonny, Kent Cooper, and Fred Palmer. *The Harp Styles of Sonny Terry.* Oak, 1975. Music and a long interview with Terry, who is one of the greats. Tablature. Have fun with the tablature.
Heaps-Nelson, George, and Barbara McKlintock Koehler. *Mel Bay's Folk and Blues Harmonica.* Mel Bay, 1976. Tablature and music. Although this book is fairly good, the "blues" part of the title is misleading: the book contains little on blues playing. Good discography.

Discography

BLUES

Butterfield, Paul. *The Paul Butterfield Band*

(Elektra 7294) and *East-West* (Elektra 7315). Butterfield and his band are excellent. The first album is Chicago blues; the second, a combination of Chicago blues with the more experimental title cut.

Harmonica Blues Great (Yazoo 1053). A good anthology of prewar blues players.

Horton, Big Walter, and Carey Bell. *Big Walter Horton with Carey Bell* (Alligator 4702).

Little Walter. *Boss Blues Harmonica* (Chess 2CH60014), *Best of Little Walter* (Chess LP1428), *Quarter to Twelve* (Red Lightnin' 002), *Little Walter* (Chess 2ACMB 202*), *Blues and Lonesome* (Roi du Blues 33.2007), and on *Chicago Blues* (Blues Classics 8). One of the greatest Chicago bluesmen. The Chess albums (some others may be available) are the best, but may be hard to find.

Lowdown Memphis Harmonica Jam 1950-55. (Nighthawk 103).

Miller, Rice (Sonny Boy Williamson). *This Is My Story* (Chess 2CH50027), *King Biscuit Time* (Arhoolie 2020), *Sonny Boy Williamson and the Yardbirds* (Mercury 61071), and *Portraits in Blues*, Vol. 4 (Storyville 158). Sonny Boy 2, as he is called, was a first-rate player. Other recordings are also available.

Reed, Jimmy. *The Best of Jimmy Reed* (2-GNP 10006).

Sam, Peg Leg (Jackson). *Medicine Show Man* (Trix 3302).

Terry, Sonny, and Brownie McGhee. *Midnight* (2-Fantasy 24721) and *Back to New Orleans* (2-Fantasy 24708). Sonny Terry plays a countrified blues as opposed to the urban blues of the Chicago musicians. He and Brownie McGhee, an excellent guitarist, make an enjoyable team and do a lot of performing.

Wells, Junior. *Blues Hit Big Town* (Delmark 640)

and *Hoodoo Blues* (Delmark 612). Another well-known Chicago musician.

Williamson, John Lee ("Sonny Boy"). *Sonny Boy Williamson*, Vols. 1-3 (Blues Classics 3, 20, & 24). Known as Sonny Boy 1, although he was born after, and died before (1948), the other Sonny Boy (who died in 1965), John Lee Williamson was one of the most important blues harpists. He was instrumental in establishing the Chicago blues sound.

OLD TIME MUSIC

The Crook Brothers and the McGhee Brothers. *Opry Old Timers* (Starday/King 182).

The Five Harmaniacs (1926-1927) (Puritan 3004). Country-oriented vaudeville.

Foster, Garley. *The Carolina Tar Heels* (Folk-Legacy 124).

Foster, Garley and Gwen. *The Carolina Tar Heels* (Old Homestead 113).

Pioneer Grand Ole Opry Performers 1925-34 (Nashville: The Early String Bands, Vols. 1 & 2) (County 541 & 542). Many cuts feature harmonica (The Crook Brothers; Dr. Humphrey Bates; and DeFord Bailey, who's actually a blues player).

The Red Fox Chasers (County 510).

Ernest V. Stoneman and the Blue Ridge Corn Shuckers (Rounder 1008).

Festivals

Some of the festivals listed elsewhere in this book feature events of interest to the harmonica player. Check Chapters 3 (section on blues festivals), 6, and 7 and Appendix E.

CHAPTER 11
⤥ THE BASS ⤦

By definition, the bass is somewhat subservient; after all, the bass line in a piece of music does provide a foundation. Yet without the bass, many a tune or symphony would crumble. So though supportive, bass players are by no means subservient. According to Molly Mason, a bassist who plays bluegrass, country, swing, and old-time music, "bass playing is more of a function—it's *what* you play more than the instrument you're playing." But since low pitches are harder to hear than high ones, the bass is hard to hear and is thus less well suited to frontstage playing in the kinds of music, like bluegrass, that involve what is almost nonstop playing. Says Mason, "there isn't room for the band to stop in bluegrass and old-time music for the bass to take a break"; she does take small lead breaks occasionally, however. Possibly for this reason bluegrass and old-time bassists have been content lurking in the shadows, providing the kind of rhythmic support that allows the guitarist to play lead lines and not just rhythm. "I'd say the function is pretty limited," says Mason. "Most people use the old 'clamp your finger on the A note and just hold it there through the whole song.'" Of course, we're speaking only of a certain kind of music. Jazz bassists

do a lot more; some are as famous in their own right as soloists or rhythm players as any saxophonists or trumpeters; and a few are leaders of groups.

The current niche for the bass in old-time music and bluegrass is admittedly small, but a few enterprising jazz players have shown that there is always room for a good musician. In addition, there is a lot of territory to explore. One area is progressive bluegrass; another, Dawg music, which displays its bluegrass influences even though it's strayed in jazz domains.

The bass (also called double bass, contrabass, or string bass), is a member of the violin family—the largest and "lowest member," in fact. It can be plucked or bowed, but in old-time music and bluegrass it is plucked (sometimes slapped); jazz players usually pluck the instrument, but many also use a bow in special circumstances. Classical bassists use the bow more often than not. Because some of the best jazz bassists have classical training, and others have simply wanted to explore the use of the bow, bowed jazz bass has become a lot more common in recent years.

Guild makes an acoustic bass guitar for those who don't want to bother with a regular string bass.

148

INTERVIEW WITH MOLLY MASON

Despite the rather small role of the bass in bluegrass and old-time music, do you like what you do?

I played guitar for about eight years before I ever tried playing bass, and my interest always kind of ran to the bass line of chord progressions. I would pay a lot of attention to the bass line to get my own bass lines just right and my bass notes just right. So I had the function of a bass player way before I even picked up the bass. It came very naturally to switch over, because I was doing the same thing I was doing playing rhythm guitar.

Is switching to bass easy?

It takes a lot of the same concentration. You have to concentrate on the downbeats, because that's generally what you're playing. On rhythm guitar, and for some kinds of music, the back beats are more important, like in swing and Texas-style guitar backup; in some old time and some bluegrass the strum is at least equally important to the bass notes.

Do you ever feel ignored?

No, I guess I feel in the background, but I don't feel left out or ignored, because that's where I'm supposed to be. And if I didn't want to be there, I'd better get a mandolin or a fiddle. It doesn't bother me, because over the years that seems to be my function—to play the background for whatever else is going on. I just don't have that desire to play lead. It's fun, I play a tiny bit, but I get much more satisfaction out of being the other half. That's just my personality. It's just as vital, and it takes just as much effort to be really good at it, yet it takes a different sort of talent to be able to hear somebody who's playing lead to figure out what they need and fit yourself around what they do to make them sound the best. You have to be flexible. And some people's personalities are geared to that and some to being the other, the one who's playing the lead. I'm the other way; I'm real comfortable with what I'm doing.

What's the hardest thing about playing bass?

For me, providing a really good, steady rhythm. Playing bass seems to take enormous energy. Is that true? I used to play along with records when I was learning. It took months for my right hand to be able to play a steady rhythm for more than a minute or two at a time—my hand would cramp up.

Selecting a Bass

Keep several things in mind when looking for a bass to use in playing bluegrass, old-time, or acoustic country music. First, you probably will not need a full-size instrument. A three-quarter-size bass, possibly even a half-size bass, will do just fine. Second, a bass made of plywood is more than adequate. A carved, solid-wood bass is expensive, and using one to play, say, bluegrass, is something like buying a tuxedo in order to ride a bull at a rodeo. Third, the bass is so large that you can overlook scars and problems that you couldn't overlook when buying a violin. Small defects make less difference on a bass because they get swallowed up by the immensity of the instrument.

Read the violin chapter, but take the information with a grain of salt.

Brands and Money Matters

Be on the lookout for old Kay basses, and also for basses made by King and American Standard—all plywood instruments. Kay has been taken over by Englehart. Also look for German plywood basses. Expert to pay an average of $500 for a used bass in good condition, but you may wind up paying as much as $800 if the bass needs extensive work, which is a lot of money to spend for an instrument unless you're really serious. A real bargain would be something costing $250–300. By comparison, however, a carved-top bass will cost at least $2000.

Accessories

Mute. A mute cuts the volume of the instrument. Prices range from $5 (Tourte), to $11.85 (Roth-Sihon), to $17.50 (three-pronged ebony mute).

End Pin. The end pin keeps the bass off the ground or floor and elevates it to the right height. You can get one for about $12.50.

Discography

This list contains many jazz albums. For bluegrass albums, most of which include a bass in the lineup, see the discographies in Chapters 4, 5, and 6 and Appendix A.

Brown, Ray, with the Oscar Peterson Trio. *Action* (Pausa PR 7059). Brown is a fine jazz bassist.

Carter, Ron. *Spanish Blue* (CTI 6051). Carter, one of today's premier bassists, has been making forays into bluegrass. This album is jazz.

Confurius, Marty, with Andy Statman. *Flatbush Waltz* (Rounder 0116). Jazz bassist Confurius teams up with mandolinist Statman on this interesting album to explore a variety of styles.

Hayden, Charlie. *Closeness: Duets* (Horizon SP 710). Hayden, another top-notch jazz musician, has played with Ornette Coleman.

Holland, Dave. *Conference of the Birds* (ECM/Warner Brothers 1-1027), *Norman Blake/Tut Taylor/Sam Bush/Butch Robbins/Vassar Clements/David Holland/Jethro Burns* (Flying Fish 701), and with Miles Davis, *Bitches Brew* (2-Columbia PG-26).

Holland, a jazzman with impeccable credentials (e.g., backing Miles Davis), has been making excursions into what can only be loosely called bluegrass/swing-inspired music.

Leopold, Jaime, with Dan Hicks and His Hot Licks. *Striking It Rich* (Blue Thumb 36). Nurtured on classical music, self-taught on jazz bass, Leopold joined up with this eclectic group in the 1960s after a stint with the now defunct Orkustra. Hicks & Co. play a strange blend of Andrews Sisters and western swing.

Mason, Molly, with the Fiction Brothers. *River of Swing* (Flying Fish; to be released), and with Fiddle Fever, *Fiddle Fever* (Flying Fish; to be released).

Mingus, Charles. *Passions of a Man* (3-Atlantic 3–600) and *Better Git It in Your Soul* (2-Columbia CG-30628). Mingus was not only a great jazz bassist and composer but a seminal figure in post-World War II jazz. He epitomized the bassman who wasn't content to stay in the shadows.

Neidlinger, Buell, with Richard Greene. *Ramblin'* (Rounder 0110). Neidlinger specialized in avant-garde music of the "classical" variety when I first heard him over ten years ago. Now he's playing Greene's Dawg-inspired music.

Bibliography: Instruction

Alterman, Ned, and Richie Mintz. *Bluegrass Bass.* Oak, 1977. Tablature and music. Okay book. Out of print but probably available from dealers. Includes soundsheet.

Mason, Roger. *Teach Yourself Bluegrass Bass.* AMSCO, 1978. Music.

Magazines

Downbeat, 222 W. Adams, Chicago, IL 60606. $13.50/year (monthly). Fine jazz magazine.

Frets, P.O. Box 28836, San Diego, CA 92128. $18/year (monthly). There's a column by Ron Carter, but all in all, the bass receives minimal coverage.

Festivals

You'll probably be welcome at most any festival. See Chapters 3, 4, 5, and 6 as well as Appendix E.

CHAPTER 12

THE UKULELE

The ukulele is a guitarlike instrument of Portuguese origin that showed up in the Hawaiian Islands about 1879. It later became popular in the continental United States after the 1915 San Francisco Columbian Exposition. The word *ukulele* means, literally, "jumping flea." After a brief moment in the limelight, the uke slipped out of favor and, despite subsequent changes in the tide, has remained an instrument of limited appeal. Yet because the ukulele is one of the few instruments that wasn't brought out

of retirement during the 1960s and 1970s, sooner or later the jumping flea may be jumping again.

There are several kinds of ukeleles. Tunings are not exactly standardized. The various ukeleles generally maintain the same pitch relationships, but the actual key they're tuned to is fairly changeable. You will notice from many of the following tunings that all bear a relationship to the standard guitar tuning EADGBE, usually a fifth higher. Most unusual about uke tunings is the *reentrant* tuning of the fourth string—it is often higher in pitch than the third and second strings.

The soprano uke has four nylon strings often tuned ADF#B or GCEA:

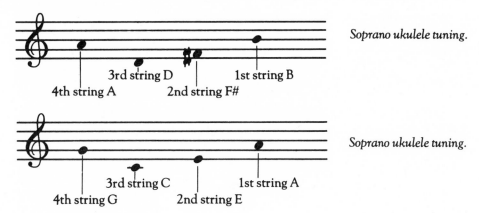

Soprano ukulele tuning.

3rd string D
4th string A   2nd string F#   1st string B

Soprano ukulele tuning.

3rd string C
4th string G   2nd string E   1st string A

The larger, baritone uke is tuned like the top four strings of a guitar:

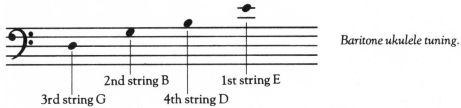

Baritone ukulele tuning.

2nd string B   1st string E
3rd string G   4th string D

The tenor uke can be tuned like the soprano or lower:

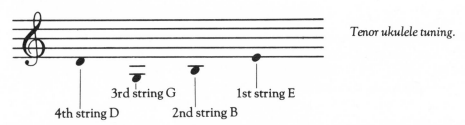

Tenor ukulele tuning.

3rd string G   1st string E
4th string D   2nd string B

There are also three double-string members of the uke family: the liliu, the taropatch, and the tiple. The liliu has six strings, with the top two doubled, and is tuned like a soprano uke. The taropatch, essentially a slightly enlarged soprano uke, has eight strings in four pairs and is also tuned like the soprano. And finally, the tiple has ten metal strings, tuned like a soprano uke and often arranged as follows:

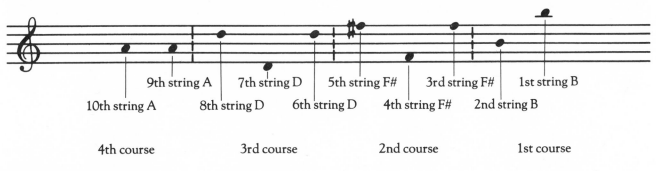

9th string A   7th string D   5th string F#   3rd string F#   1st string B
10th string A   8th string D   6th string D   4th string F#   2nd string B

4th course   3rd course   2nd course   1st course

Tiple tuning.

Selecting a Ukulele

Check the uke or tiple the same way you would a guitar or mandolin, looking for a straight neck and good action. Make sure the bridge is positioned correctly (check the harmonic) and securely attached to the top. Check for loose braces (if there are braces) and listen for buzzing when you strum. Some older instruments use wooden pegs; change them to mechanical friction pegs. Inspect older instruments carefully for hairline cracks, since some tops are extremely thin. Old Martin ukes often have cracked tops, but they can usually be repaired.

MATERIALS

New Martin ukuleles have a mahogany top, sides, back, and neck, and are equipped with friction pegs. Kamakas are made almost entirely of koa. The Martin tiple has a spruce top, mahogany or rosewood back and sides, mahogany neck, rosewood or ebony fingerboard, and geared tuners. Custom, old, and cheap ukuleles may incorporate different materials and hardware.

Brands and Prices

Extremely cheap ukuleles can be found in music stores, pawnshops, and department stores for $15-30, but many are essentially toys. Avoid instruments with a plastic fingerboard or made entirely of plastic. Used Martins are recommended as a good buy; ukes start at about $100, but you may find one for considerably less. Other brands to look for in the way of used ukes are Gibson, Favilla, and Harmony. The only good instrument manufactured in the lower 48 is made by Martin. A lot of ukes imported from the Orient are floating around; some may be worth buying.

Ukulele Manufacturers

Aria (Music Distributors, Inc., 3400 Darby Ave., Charlotte, NC 28216). Aria catalogues list several inexpensive ukes. Since Aria is a reputable company, you might look for these instruments. Write the distributor (Aria is an import) for names of local dealers.

Kamaka Hawaii (550 South St., Honolulu, HI 96813). Kamaka is a well-known firm. Since their instruments are not sold through dealers in the Continental U.S., you'll have to write for information and order directly from the manufacturer.

Martin (CF Martin Organisation, Nazareth, PA 18064). New Martins must be special-ordered through a dealer.

Discography

Early Country Music 1928–31 (Historical 8002). Tiple. Ohta, Herb. A popular Hawaiian musician with many albums on the Surfside label.

Smeck, Roy. *Roy Smeck Plays Hawaiian Guitar, Banjo, Ukulele, and Guitar 1926–1949* (Yazoo 1052) and *The Wizard of the Strings* (Blue Goose 2027). Smeck is around eighty years old and has played vaudeville, the Grand Ol' Opry, and other famous music/entertainment centers. He lives in New York City and gives lessons.

Ukulele Ike. *I'm a Bear in a Lady's Boudoir* (Yazoo 1047), *Shakin' the Blues Away* (Totem 1005), and *I Want a Girl* (Totem 1014).

Bibliography: Instruction

Bay, Bill. *Fun with the Baritone Uke.* Mel Bay, 1961. All of the Mel Bay ukulele books are extremely basic and easy to use.

Bay, Bill. *Fun with Strums—Baritone Uke.* Mel Bay, 1975.

Bay, Bill. *Fun with Strums—Ukulele.* Mel Bay, 1975.

Bay, Mel. *Fun with the Ukelele.* Mel Bay, 1961.

Bay, Mel. *Ukulele Chords.* Mel Bay, 1961.

Reser, Harry. *Broadway Classics for Ukelele.* Warner Brothers Publications.

Reser, Harry. *Broadway Showcase for Ukelele.* Warner Brothers Publications.

Reser, Harry. *Harry Reser's Let's Play the Baritone Ukulele.* Warner Brothers Publications.

Reser, Harry. *6 Magic Chords for Ukulele.* Warner Brothers Publications. Tunes such as "I'm Looking over a Four Leaf Clover" and "Put on Your Old Gray Bonnet."

12 Bob Dylan Hits Playable with Three Magic Chords. Warner Brothers Publications.

Warner Brothers Publications (75 Rockefeller Plaza, New York, NY 10019) has quite a few more instruction books and song collections for the uke.

Bibliography: History

Kanahele, George S. *Hawaiian Music and Musicians: An Illustrated History.* The University of Hawaii Press, 1979. Interesting but will leave the ukulele fanatic or would-be fanatic hungry.

Martin tiple.

CHAPTER 13

THE PSALTERY

The heyday of the psaltery fell approximately between the eleventh and fifteenth centuries. So many representations of the psaltery exist in the art of the period, and in so many different shapes and sizes, that one assumes the instrument was exceedingly popular. Although eventually the psaltery died out in most of Western Europe, two descendants have survived to the present day: the Finnish *kantele* and the Russian *gusli*. In other parts of the world, in countries like Turkey, the *qanun*, the ancestor of the psaltery, continues to be played.

Structurally, the psaltery closely resembles the hammered dulcimer. In fact, the psaltery is undoubtedly the dulcimer's immediate ancestor. Sometimes the instruments look so similar that probably what you call them depends on how you play them; the psaltery is plucked, with the bare fingers or fingerpicks, while the dulcimer, of course, is played with hammers. A good example of this occurs with

the so-called Bob Beers psaltery, a nineteenth-century hammered dulcimer that musician Beers plucked and apparently decided to call a psaltery. Usually, however, modern American hammered dulcimers tend to be larger and heavier, and have more strings, than modern psalteries, all of which are fashioned not after actual surviving medieval or Renaissance instruments (none survive) but after pictorial representations.

Since little is written about how to play the psaltery, you have the field to yourself. Invent your own style, adapt playing techniques of other instruments, listen to medieval music and try to imagine how the psaltery was played, and listen to recordings of the other kinds of psalteries mentioned.

Another instrument played today is the bowed psaltery. This is not a true holdover from the past but actually was invented in the twentieth century, presumably in Germany. And finally, there's the bowharp, a diatonic variant of the bowed psaltery.

Selecting a Psaltery

Look for pretty much the same things you would when buying a hammered dulcimer; sturdiness, then, is very important. The top may sag on some instruments, but this doesn't mean the end of the instrument as long as it is well built.

Most instruments are trapezoidal, but others have one or two curved sides (forming a modified trapezoid).

You should tune the instrument to see how the pins or pegs work and also to evaluate the tone and volume. The psaltery is tuned diatonically. Ask the builder what note to start on at the bottom.

Psaltery Builders

Autorino (The Butternut Shoppe, Route 9W North, RD1, Box 387C, Kingston NY 12401). Michael Autorino is the only person building the Beers psaltery. Order direct.

Bechtel (4224 Red Bud Place, Cincinnati, OH 45229). Ben Bechtel has been building instruments since 1966 and fashions his psalteries after pictorial representations. The wire-string instrument has a full sound and lots of volume. Order direct; allow three to six weeks for delivery.

Capritaurus (Box 153, Felton, CA 95018). Capritaurus has been in business since 1978 and has a good reputation. Order direct; delivery time under thirty days. One-year warranty.

Dorogi (Ellicott Rd., Brocton, NY 14716). Dennis Dorogi has been building instruments (mostly dulcimers) since 1959. Order direct and through some dealers; direct orders filled in under thirty days.

Kelischek (Brasstown NC 28902). George Kelischek has been building a variety of historical instruments since 1956. Catalogue: $2. Order direct.

Larsen (1293 Forgewood Ave., Sunnydale, CA 94086). Gail Ann Larsen has built her psaltery since 1979. Order direct; delivery in less than six weeks. One-year warranty.

Lewandowski (67 Main St., Brattleboro, VT

Psaltery, by Kelischek Workshop.

05401). Lynne Lewandowski has been building psalteries since 1975. Write for information.

Montague (16 Patriot Rd., Tewksbury, MA 08176). Write Fred Montague for information on his plucked psalteries. Order direct.

Samuels (33 Buell St., Burlington, VT 05401). Mary Ann Samuels has been making her psaltery since 1980. Order direct; delivery in less than thirty days.

Stapleton (201 Midland Ave., Springdale, AR 72764). L. O. Stapleton has been making his psaltery since 1978. See p. 000 for a statement of his philosophy and an example of his craftsmanship. Order direct.

Wagner (1717 Ella St., Cincinnati, OH 45223). Russell Wagner has been making medieval and Renaissance stringed instruments since 1973. He is now assisted by his wife, P. J. Order direct; delivery can take up to four weeks.

Discography

Beers, Bob. *The Art of the Psaltery* (Prestige). Unfortunately this album, which features the psaltery as a solo instrument, is out of print; copies can sometimes be found, however.

Beers, Bob and Evelyne. *Evelyne and Bob Beers* (Biograph 12045) and *Walkie in the Parlor* (Folkways 2376). On these recordings the psaltery is primarily used for backup.

The Early Music Consort. The Age of Chivalry (write: Ben Bechtel, 4224 Red Bud Place, Cincinnati, OH 45229). There is one cut of psaltery on this album.

Samuels, Mary Ann, with Jerry Rockwell. *Mountain Dulcimer and Psaltery Instrumentals* (Traditional 610). This record is perhaps the most valuable for those interested in applications of the hand-held psaltery to traditional music.

Smith, Betty. *For My Friends of Song* (June Appal 018). This recording features the Bob Beers psaltery.

A Very Special Night at the Seraglio (Musical Heritage Society 3290). One cut on this recording of classical Turkish music features the *qanun* (psaltery). Recommended.

Bibliography: History

Andersson, Otto. *The Bowed-Harp: A Study in the History of Early Musical Instruments.* (William Reeves, 1930.)

Panum, Hortense. *Stringed Instruments of the Middle Ages.* (Greenwood Press, 1970.) This is one of the best sources on the psaltery; numerous pictorial representations are included.

Marcuse, Sybil. *A Survey of Musical Instruments.* (Harper & Row, 1975.) Contains an excellent section on the psaltery.

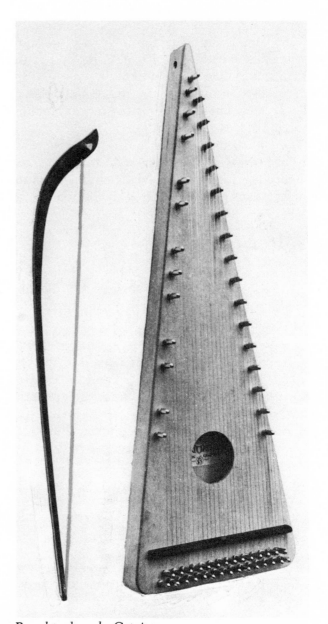

Bowed psaltery, by Capritaurus.

Magazines

From time to time articles or information on the psaltery appears in such magazines as *Frets, Sing Out!*, and the *Folk Harp Journal* [P.O. Box 161, Mt. Laguna, CA 92048. $8/year (quarterly); this is an excellent magazine, by the way].

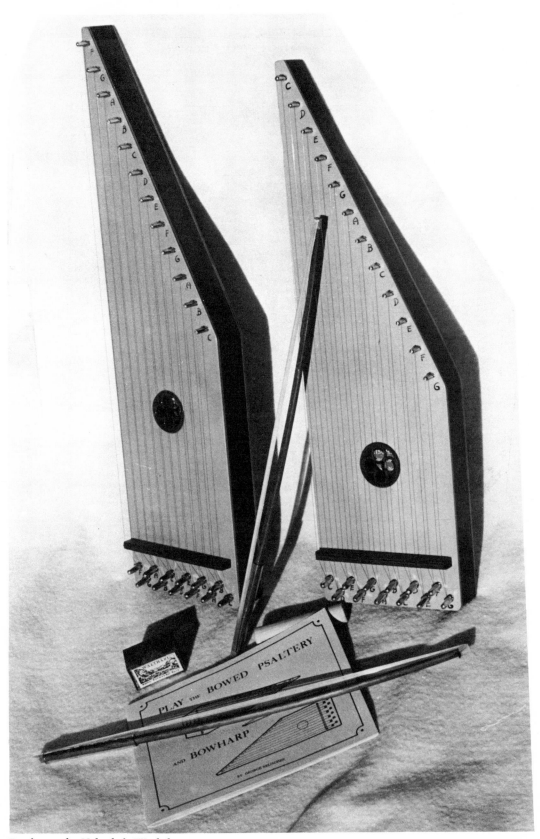

Bowharps, by Kelischek Workshop.

CHAPTER 14

THE BALALAIKA

The balalaika, of course, is the Soviet Union's best known native instrument. Unfortunately, it is often associated with the kind of superficial music you'd imagine hearing in some Moscow restaurant where everything is bad except the vodka. But when you start listening to really good balalaika orchestras and soloists, you will discover that this little instrument has astonishing possibilities.

Although the balalaika, which resembles a mandolin in sound and size but not in shape, has been around for quite a while, the golden age of the instrument was from about 1895 to 1920, during

which time Andreyeev, an aristocrat who loved Russian folk music, transformed the balalaika into its present form. He wanted to leave some features but change enough others so that the instrument would be able to hold its own on the concert stage. He refined the instrument, enlarged the body to give it more volume, lengthened the fingerboard to extend the range, and fixed the tuning. Andreyeev also developed a whole range of balalaikas, patterned after the instruments in a mandolin orchestra, going from piccolo (smallest) to contrabass—in all, six sizes.

The balalaika has a "dual nature" and is equally at

Alexander Eppler, a Seattle musician and instrument builder, with balalaika.

home with both classical and folk music, much like the violin. The balalaika is also deceptively simple looking, having only three strings, two tuned to the same note. But to Peter Rothe, a balalaika player and builder who lives in San Pedro, California, the balalaika has "lots of challenges." Mastering the basic skills isn't difficult, but going beyond *is*, because the instrument is so "primitive."

Although the balalaika is built in various sizes, most common is the prima balalaika, the solo instrument. The bottom two strings are usually nylon and the top plain steel; the bottom two strings are usually tuned to the E below middle C, the top string to the A a fourth above. The total range is three octaves. Sometimes the strings are tuned in a triad, and folk tunings also exist. The combination of metal and nylon strings allows for unique effects such as the appearance of two voices of entirely different coloration. All in all the balalaika's sound and technique are not too exotic, but exotic enough to be of interest to traditional American musicians.

Selecting a Balalaika

The biggest problem in selecting a balalaika is to find one to select. Although some of the instruments found in stores or mail-order catalogs are functional, most would probably be more useful hanging on the wall. Many are built in one or two Soviet factories by the hundreds of thousands and sell for under $50. Other instruments, made in Italy, have six steel strings; this is obviously an imposter. The cheap Russian instruments, really meant to be souvenirs, can be distinguished by orange stain on the marquetry, back, and neck; by their cheap look and poor finish; and by their price: good balalaikas cost more. Nevertheless, in the beginning you may have to settle for second-best.

Once you lay your hands on a balalaika, inspect it in much the same way you would a guitar or mandolin.

Tuning Machines. Older instruments were made with wooden pegs similar to those on a violin; newer instruments have geared machines.

Neck. The neck should be straight and the fingerboard flat. Because a balalaika player does a lot of sliding with the left hand and uses the left thumb constantly (Rothe has a huge callus on the first joint of the thumb), the neck should be thin (⅝ of an inch including the fingerboard) and preferably *unfinished.*

Frets. Again, because of the left-hand technique, the fret ends should be extremely round and polished. They may have to be reworked by a repairperson.

Action. The balalaika is often played quite forcefully; therefore, to prevent string buzz, the action must be high. Because Rothe likes a loud, brilliant sound, he likes a high bridge. "For me," he says, "the quality of the sound has become the ultimate esthetic." The freestanding bridge that should come with the balalaika is relatively easy to work with.

Construction. The top is raised, as on a Martin mandolin. The back is vaulted like the back of a bowlback mandolin or bouzouki but in a less exaggerated manner; the back and sides are thus one and the same. The overall shape of the body is triangular.

STRINGS

The most important strings, says Rothe, are the nylon ones, since obtaining brilliance with these is harder than with the metal string. He uses nylon guitar G (third) strings. For the metal string he recommends an unwound, .012″ banjo string or, what amounts to the same thing, a .012″ (light-gauge) steel-string, guitar high E (first) string. Once the E strings are accounted for, everything else takes care of itself.

MATERIALS

On the finest instruments, the top is solid spruce, the fingerboard is ebony, the neck is ebony or rosewood, and the back is hard maple. On instruments that are good but not as good, the neck may be maple. The string can be maple, rosewood, or ebony; ebony has the most brilliant tone. Harder woods are preferred for the neck of the balalaika than for the neck of other fretted instruments so that the neck can be very thin while still being strong.

Brands and Prices

The Stradivari of the balalaika was Nalimov, and one of his instruments is worth the equivalent of a good vintage Martin guitar. In the 1920s a German named Zimmerman made fairly good copies of Nalimovs. Today, a Soviet-built "Artist" model, which is a decent factory instrument, costs between $125 and $300, if you can get one—in this country you might find a used one. A premium handmade Soviet or American instrument costs $600–700. Look for a used Hoffner, a respectable, less expensive German instrument that is no longer made.

Discography

Feoktistov, B. *Folk Balalaika* (Westminister Gold 8263).

Moscow Radio Folk Instrument Orchestra. *Airwaves Concert* (Westminister Gold 8258).

Necheporenko, P. *Music of Sergei Vasilenko: Concerto for Balalaika and Orchestra* (Westminister Gold 8222).

Rozhkov, M. *Mikhail Rozhkov.* (Melodyia C 20-7861-62(a)). Folk and light-classical music.

Tikhonov, A. *Russian Balalaika* (Melodyia CM 02167-68(a)). Tikhonov is first chair of the Osipov Russian Folk Orchestra, one of the two leading orchestras of its kind in the Soviet Union (the other is the Andreyeev). Recordings of both groups are available on the Melodyia label as well as on Monitor.

Virtuosi of the Accordion, Balalaika, and Domra (Monitor 515E). The domra is another Russian folk instrument; it is similar to, but older than, the balalaika. This is a good record to get a taste of Russian music.

Melodyia records can be ordered through Four Continent Book Corporation, 149 Fifth Avenue, New York, NY 10010, if you cannot find them at your local music store.

Bibliography: Instruction

Dorozhkin, Alexander. *Elementary Method for the Balalaika*. Henry Adler, 1964 (dist. Belwyn-Mills).

Organizations

The Balalaika and Domra Association of Americas, 3319 W. 3 St., Chester, PA 19103, publishes a newsletter, which costs $7.50/year (bimonthly).

CHAPTER 15

❦ STRINGS ❦

Picked, Plucked, Strummed, and Hammered Instruments

Strings. Some musicians violently assert there are no good strings, others swear by a particular brand or type of string, and still others use whatever is handy. What are the differences in strings?

GAUGE

Gauge is the thickness of a string, and strings come in four standard gauges for six-string flattop guitars and fewer gauges for other instruments. Tension corresponds to gauge with nylon strings—high tension is the equivalent of heavy gauge, medium tension of medium gauge, and so on. Richard Johnston, of Gryphon Stringed Instruments in Palo Alto, California, points out that "it is extremely important to find out what sizes the strings actually are, because manufacturers do not agree as to what constitutes a light set of strings or extra-light or medium." String gauge is important for several reasons. First, strings exert tension on the top and neck of an instrument. Second, gauge affects sound and volume. Third, gauge correlates with string buzz. And fourth, string gauge affects playability.

When selecting a gauge for a fretted instrument, especially a steel-string guitar, try to find the gauge best suited to the particular instrument. Sometimes the manufacturer suggests a gauge, sometimes not. Compromises in gauge must sometimes be made. Says Johnston, "If you have a large, relatively stiff-topped guitar, you may want to use medium-gauge strings even though you would prefer to use lights, because the medium gauge strings will make your guitar sound much more efficiently in terms of what you are playing. If you're playing a really light, old guitar, you might want to use silk and steel or extra-light strings, even though you would prefer the stiffness of a light or medium set—for two reasons. One is that the extreme tension of the heavier strings might pull your guitar apart, might damage it permanently. And second, extreme tension often makes the guitar sound really crashy, as if it's on the verge of blowing up."

WINDINGS AND MATERIALS

Strings are either plain steel or nylon (unwound) or steel or nylon wrapped with another material(s) (wound); most instruments use both: usually unwound for the treble strings, wound for the bass strings. Steel strings can be wound with silk or a synthetic and with metal (compound, or silk and steel, strings) or with various alloys, including brass, bronze, and Monel (an alloy formed primarily of nickel and copper). Nylon strings are usually wound with metal (copper, silver, bronze, etc.), but sometimes the treble strings are wound with plastic or nylon.

One major problem in choosing strings is knowing what you are buying. Manufacturers and packagers seem to use terms like *brass* and *bronze* interchangeably. GHS, for example, which is a reputable company, markets a Bright Bronze™ string that is actually, according to a company spokesman, brass. Other companies don't even know what it is they are selling. Be wary of terms like 90/10 brass, 90/10 bronze, 80/20 brass, 80/20 bronze, and so forth, because for all we know the brass may be bronze or the bronze, brass!

Materials have different characteristics. With wound strings, generally the harder the alloy, the longer-lasting the string; but durability and performance are not always compatible. For wound metal strings, Monel is the hardest winding and has the most consistent tone over time; but its sound is not especially popular. Phosphor bronze strings have a consistent tone over time and are extremely popular. Bronze is similar to phosphor bronze but not quite as durable. Brass is very bright at first but may deaden quickly. Silk and steel strings are light and bright, may deaden quickly, and are easy to play and thus good for beginners. Unwound strings sound virtually the same in the same gauge regardless of brand. For wound nylon strings, the differences in alloy may be less significant than the design of the string.

BRANDS

According to Johnston, "A lot of people come up with a catchy idea for packaging or for describing their strings, or have a couple of famous people they know quite well, so they come up with a string brand. They have one of the major manufacturers make a lot of strings with this packaging, and if they do a lot of advertising in the trade journals, suddenly guitarists are walking into stores asking, 'Do you have these new Zippo guitar strings?' Despite the hundreds of brands of strings on the market, there are no more than ten manufacturers in this country producing strings, and of those, two or three have very low production and don't count for a very significant percentage of the sets of strings sold. The core material—in other words, the material for the unwound strings and the core of the wound strings—all comes from two or three sources, and manufacturers who produce strings usually use more than one of these sources. There are many manufacturers of the material for the wrapping, and so there's going to be tremendous variation there in terms of where the material comes from, the alloy, etc.... Usually the differences in strings are in the gauging. A lot of string packagers order the strings with a slightly different gauging than the old standards. They may adjust the alloy in the bronze."

One thing to guard against is buying what your hero buys, or what the hero in the ad endorses. Johnston says, that "for all the sets of strings we've had around here that for one reason or another were unpopular, there's always someone—and usually more than one person—that feels that [one] particular string is the best. It's also true that what works well for a hero may or may not work well for you. For instance, he may be wealthy enough to have his strings changed every one or two days by a roadie, whereas for you it's important that a string last for a long time. Maybe for the hero a set of strings that sounds really bright and brilliant but doesn't last a long time is just what he needs. But for you, whose guitar may sound bright and brassy even with dead strings, a set that sounds even brighter and brassier is exactly what you don't need. Furthermore, you probably can't afford to change strings every few days." Johnston also adds that "many guitarists who have played the same guitar for a long time have a favorite brand of strings. But they often feel that another brand sounds best to them when they change guitars. After selling guitar strings for over ten years I can only conclude that which string sounds best is purely personal preference. Choosing strings is more a matter of finding a set of strings that you like that consistently sounds good on your guitar and not a situation where it can be narrowed down to saying that one set of strings is definitely better than another."

LONGEVITY

According to Johnston:

"The most important thing to remember when thinking about what set of guitar strings you should buy is that the individual guitarist, and the conditions under which he plays, are the primary factors in determining how long the strings will last. That means that comparisons between different brands are difficult because the conditions are rarely the same. For example, some guitarists who play every day can leave a set of strings on their guitar for several months; the strings, although they won't sound new, will still sound relatively live. Other guitarists reduce a set of strings to something sounding like old rubber bands in a matter of days or even of hours. It's as much body chemistry as playing style, and guitarists who are what we call string killers don't necessarily have sweaty hands that are always dirty. However, in general, a person whose hands perspire a lot will kill strings much faster than the guitarist who has relatively dry hands, and that's especially true of high-stress situations, such as playing on stage. This means that if you put a new set of strings on your guitar in wintertime, keep your guitar in a room with dry heat, and don't let others play your guitar, the strings may last for months and months and still sound great. However, if you put on a new set of strings at ten o'clock in the morning—even the same brand—go off to the beach, play guitar off and on all day, loan your guitar to other people to play, your new set of strings may be totally dead by four o'clock in the afternoon. Radically different conditions such as these account for most of the very strong opinions among guitarists that we hear as to which strings last longest.''

WHEN AND HOW OFTEN TO CHANGE STRINGS

When and how often you change strings depends on whether you like the sound of new or played-in strings, how fast you wear out strings, how much money you have to spend on strings. Knowing *when* to change strings is a matter of looking and listening for signs—the guitar won't play in tune, the sound is dead, the strings are frayed.

Some owners of very inexpensive guitars change strings frequently (to get the sound of new strings) and buy the most expensive strings. Says Johnston: "If you like a new set of strings, then you'll probably want a set of strings that is relatively inexpensive and change them more often. You need to remember that the money you spend on strings in two years could go toward buying a new guitar. You've got to decide if you want to spend a lot of money to have your inexpensive guitar sound like it does with new strings, or if you want to change strings as seldom as possible and buy a guitar that's going to sound better even if the strings are dead.''

> Never use nylon strings on a flattop guitar or steel strings on a classic guitar. Steel-string guitars are built to take some tension from the strings; insufficient tension may backwarp the neck. Nylon strings will not be loud enough on a flattop guitar. Steel strings may literally pull a classic guitar apart, since classic guitars are designed for much lower-tension strings.

STRING GUIDE

Strings for all instruments can be bought singly or in sets.

Banjo: Five-String (Bluegrass and Open-Back). Since only one banjo string is wound, the main differences between brands are the gauging and materials. Well-known brands include D'Addario, D'Angelico, Dean Markley, Earthwood, Ernie Ball, GHS, Gibson, La Bella, Liberty, Stewart-MacDonald, and Vega. Prices range from about $3.50 to $4.80 for the typical set of strings, with La Bella's special nylon-silver-plated strings running $8.31 a set and the gut-silver-plated strings running $10.70 a set; these expensive sets are especially made for open-back banjos. D'Addario and GHS have the largest selection of strings.

Banjo: Four String (Tenor). Brands include D'Addario, Ernie Ball, Stewart-MacDonald, and Vega; prices go from $3.50 to $4.25 per set.

Chorded Zither. Both La Bella and Oscar Schmidt strings sell for about $25 per set.

Dulcimer: Hammered. Unwound strings can be bought as musical-instrument wire. The manufacturer may provide extra strings, may provide free strings when you need them, and should suggest the gauges to use. WARNING: If the manufacturer does not provide you with information on the different gauges, ask, or measure the gauge (string diameter) yourself. Even a small difference in string diameter, when multiplied by the forty to one hundred strings on the dulcimer, can result in significant, possibly damaging, additional stress.

Dulcimer: Mountain. Dulcimer sets are packaged by D'Addario ($3.20), Darco ($2.95), and Martin ($2.50) (and by some dulcimer manufacturers), but many players use banjo strings.

Guitar: Classic. Brands include Arabesque, Augustine, Aranjuez, D'Addario, La Bella, and Savarez. Prices range from $7 for a set of Aranjuez strings to $30 for a set of the highest-priced D'Addarios. The average price for inexpensive strings is $7–10; for more expensive ones, $10–15.

Guitar: Six-String Flattop. Silk and Steel: Brands include Martin, Martin Marquis, D'Addario, Earthwood, D'Angelico, and Guild. Prices range from $6.25 for a set of Earthwoods (which are made in regular, soft, and extra soft) to $9 for a set of D'Addarios; the average price is about $8 per set. *Metal Wound:* Brands include the above brands plus Darco, Ernie Ball, Fender, Gibson, and La Bella. Prices range from $6 for a set of Earthwoods to $8.25 for a set of bronze D'Addarios, with the average price about $7.25 per set. Especially good selections are offered by D'Addario, Guild, and Martin, which package brass as well as bronze strings.

Guitar: Twelve-String Flattop. Silk and Steel: Brands include D'Addario, D'Angelico, Darco, Guild, and

Martin, and prices range from $9 for Earthwood soft strings to $14 for Darcos. Average price is $12.30 per set, but Earthwoods seem priced a bit lower than the average price of the other brands. *Metal Wound:* Brands include all of the above except Earthwood, in addition to contributions from Ernie Ball, GHS, Dean Markley, and Martin Marquis (Martin's premium label). Prices go from $9.50 for a set of Ernie Ball bronze lights to $13 for a set of Martin Marquis bronze lights or D'Addario phosphor bronze lights or extra lights. Average price: about $14.40. With the exception of D'Addario and Martin, which package brass and bronze strings, all of the companies package only bronze or phosphor bronze.

Mandolin. Brands include D'Addario, D'Angelico, Darco, Ernie Ball, Dobro, Earthwood, Gibson, Guild, La Bella, Dean Markley, Martin, and Stewart-MacDonald. There's a decent selection of windings—steel, nickel, brass, bronze, and phosphor bronze, but only GHS packages a heavy-guage string. Prices of sets range from $5.10 for Dobro strings to $7 for Ernie Ball and Earthwood strings. Average price: about $6.25.

Psaltery. See *Dulcimer: Hammered.* The only difference is that some instruments are strung with nylon strings. Wire strings are considerably louder.

Ukulele and Tiple. Brands include Martin, D'Adarrio, and La Bella. Martin uke strings cost $2.75 per set, while D'Addarios run $3.20 and La Bellas $2.22. La Bella tenor uke strings are $3.50, baritones $3.75. Martin tiple strings (bronze) are $7.50, while La Bella's "golden alloy" are $6.29.

Bowed Instruments

VIOLIN STRINGS

Most of the guidelines for strings for nonbowed instruments also apply to violin strings. The two main differences are the higher prices and greater diversity of violin strings.

Except for the E string, which is almost always plain steel, violin strings are wound. Windings include gold, silver, and aluminium, and cores are gut, Perlon (a nylon), steel, rope (steel wound on silk or other material), or spiral (steel wound with steel). Gut-core strings are used by most classical violinists and have a warm tone. They also act up under the

effects of varying temperature and humidity. Steel-core strings are used by many fiddlers and have a brighter, larger tone than gut strings, are more immune to the elements, and also can damage an instrument because of the increased tension. According to Tom Hosmer, a repairman in Syracuse, New York, "A properly cut bridge will last no more than one year under this kind of pressure." Perlon-core strings are used and can be used by violinists and fiddlers alike, sound brighter than gut, wear well, and again resist the elements better than gut. Rope-core and spiral-core strings, being primarily steel, have the advantages and disadvantages of steel but are a little closer to gut or Perlon in tone.

Hosmer suggests "that country fiddlers who wish to get away from steel strings try Perlon strings." His "favorite string set for country fiddlers is: a Pirastro Wondertone steel E string, a Jargar A string, a Prim D string, and a Prim G string." Since steel strings come in three gauges, he also advises that "if you must use steel strings, do your instrument a favor—use light-gauge."

STRING GUIDE*

Steel Core. Brands include Supertone ($5.50/set), Supersensitive ($12.05), Pyramid Ultraflex Rope-core ($13.50), Thomastik Precision ($15.00), Pirastro Ultra Sensitive ($16.10), Thomastik Super Flexible ($18.50), Pyramid Soloflex ($20.60), and Thomastik Spirocore ($24.30). Average price: $13.80.

Synthetic Core. Brands include Sensicore ($17.60), Pirastro Aircore ($22.50), and Thomastik Dominant (Perlon) ($24.30).

Gut Core. Brands include Black Label ($18.30), Tricolor ($18.80), Gold Label ($20), Kaplan ($16.30–20.60), and Eudoxa ($16.30). Average price: $18.40.

BASS STRINGS

Read the previous sections for general information on strings. Bluegrass and old-timey bass players generally use steel strings. Brands include Supersensitive ($56.50/set) and Thomastik Precision ($71.20/set); both have a steel core. Bass strings are expensive (these are two of the *least* expensive sets!), so shop around for a good discount. Metropolitan Music Co. (Mountain Road, RD1, Stowe, VT 05672), for example, sells strings at a 40% discount.

*Quotations in this section are from "On Violin Strings," Tom Hosmer's column in *Frets* (February 1981), p. 41.

*Prices are approximate and depend on the makeup of the set, since some strings are only sold singly.

CHAPTER 16

ACCESSORIES

Picks

Picks are either held between thumb and finger or attached to the thumb and fingers. *Flatpicks* come in various sizes, degrees of stiffness, and materials. The standard plastic (often celluloid, a type of plastic) flatpick is made in three standard thicknesses—thin, medium, and heavy—but some manufacturers offer a wider assortment of gauges. Real tortoise shell picks produce a clean tone, last a long time, are large and thick and quite expensive, and are made from an endangered species. Nylon picks are virtually indestructible, produce a smoother sound than plastic picks, and also are produced in various gauges and sizes; some have grips on them. Except for the tortoise shell, the picks are cheap enough so that you can experiment a lot. *Fingerpicks* usually consist of a plastic or metal thumbpick and two metal or sometimes plastic fingerpicks, worn on the index and middle fingers. Fingerpicks come either in one size and thickness or in different gauges and sizes; Dunlop sells "mini-picks" for people with small fingers.

Balalaika. A pick is not used.

Banjo. Use a plastic (or, if you prefer, metal) thumbpick and two metal fingerpicks for bluegrass banjo; Dunlop and National fingerpicks are the most popular. For Irish tenor banjo, use a soft flatpick.

Chorded Zither. Use metal or plastic picks on the first two fingers and a plastic thumbpick; a metal thumbpick, sometimes used, is somewhat harsher sounding. Dunlop brass fingerpicks are more mellow than steel and also more flexible, and they are gauged. The picks should extend past the ends of your fingertips 1/8 to 1/4 of an inch. The more pointed Ernie Ball picks can be good for picking individual strings. You can also use the felt pick that comes with many instruments.

Guitar. Use bare fingers for a classical guitar. Use bare fingers or, more often, picks for a steel-string guitar: a flatpick for single-note playing and strumming, a plastic (or metal) thumbpick and two metal (sometimes plastic) fingerpicks for fingerpicking.

Mandolin. Use a small, stiff pick for bluegrass or old-timey. Beginners may find a more flexible pick easier to use. Also use a flexible pick for Irish music.

Mountain Dulcimer. Traditional players may use a quill. Use any size or gauge of flatpick; medium is good all-around, a long pick good for strumming. Fingerpicks can also be used. Players also make their own picks from milk jugs, coffee can lids, and other objects.

Psaltery. Try bare fingers and various kinds of picks to see what works for you.

Ukulele. Use bare fingers or a special felt pick.

PICKS

Flatpicks

Fender (plastic)—three sizes, two or three thicknesses
Herco (nylon)—light and heavy   } 10–50¢
Dunlop (nylon)—gauged
Real tortoise shell   } $2.00–2.50
Felt

Thumbpicks

Ernie Ball—thin plastic—two sizes
Dobro—plastic—three sizes
Dunlop—metal—one size (right- or left-handed)
Gibson—plastic—three sizes   } 10–75¢
Herco—plastic—two sizes
National—metal
National—plastic—three sizes

Fingerpicks

Ernie Ball—metal—pointed tip
Dunlop—metal—gauged
Dunlop—metal—gauged—minipick   } 25–50¢
Gibson—plastic—three sizes
Herco—plastic
National—metal

Capos

A capo is a device that holds down all the strings at one fret, enabling you to use the same chord patterns in different keys. There are three kinds: simple elastic, Dunlop, and screw or clamp type. Elastic capos are cheap, eventually stretch, and may alter the pitch or distort the sound; the Dunlop is a spinoff of the elastic capo; the screw or clamp capos are good, though some may scratch the instrument.

Balalaika. Capo not used.

Banjo. A regular capo works only on the four main strings of a five-string banjo. The fifth string needs a special capo, either commercial, which requires holes in the side of the neck, or homemade, using H.O. spikes in the fretboard. Ask your dealer or the manufacturer to install spikes or, if you prefer, a commercial capo. Some manufacturers install a capo on their banjos.

Guitar. Any type of capo can be used for a steel-string guitar. Classical musicians normally do not use a capo, but a capo can be used on a classic guitar.

Mandolin. Capo rarely used; most banjo capos will work.

Mountain Dulcimer. An ordinary elastic guitar or banjo capo cannot be used unless the fingerboard is scalloped. Try the Ewing capo, specially designed for the dulcimer.

Ukulele. Capo rarely used.

CAPOS

• *Recommended.*

Elastic
Bill Russell Single Strap Classic Guitar—$1
• Bill Russell Double Strap Six- or Twelve-String Flattop Guitar-$2
Bill Russell Banjo—$1
Bill Russell Single Strap Flattop Guitar—about $1.50

Jim Dunlop
Glassic Guitar (with or without buckle tightener)—about $3
Flattop Guitar (with or without buckle tightener)—about $3

Screw Type
Hamilton KB 19—$3.15
Sabine Banjo or Guitar—$7.95
Saga Banjo—$3.50
Saga Guitar—$3.95
• Shubb Banjo, Classic Guitar, Flattop Guitar—
    $12.95

Clamp Type
Hamilton KB 19A—$3.15

Banjo Fifth-String Capo
Shubb (nickel plated)—$29.50

Dulcimer Capo
• Ron Ewing (2318 E. Rahn Rd., Kettering, OH 45440)—$5

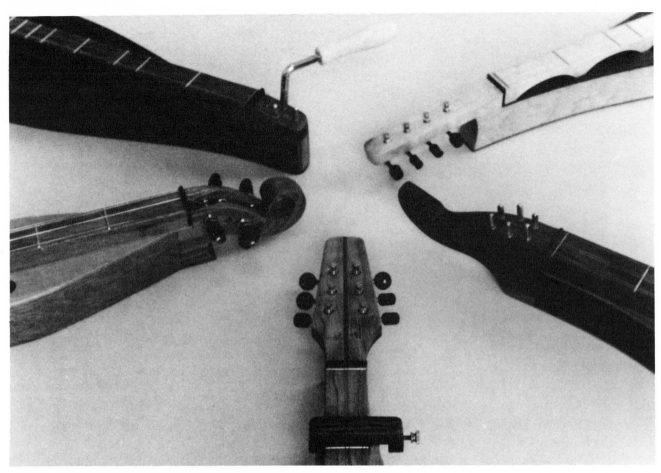

Middle dulcimer shows Ron Ewing's special dulcimer capo.

Tuning Aids

Owning a device that gives you a reference pitch to tune your instrument is essential. There are several choices: a pitchpipe giving just the notes of the instrument; a chromatic pitchpipe, which has a one-octave range and can be used for any instrument; a tuning fork, which gives just one pitch; an electronic device, which gives either a few pitches (as few as one) or any pitch; and any fixed-pitch instrument, for example, a piano. The most accurate and versatile device is electronic; it is also quite expensive. A tuning fork is the next most accurate; pitchpipes, though the least accurate of the devices (next to an out-of-tune piano), are inexpensive and easy to use . . . and entirely satisfactory. A piano is fine (as long as it's in tune).

To use a tuning fork, strike the forked end on a hard but nonabrasive object (the kneecap is perfect). Then stand the end on the bridge of your instrument or on a hard object (or put it against the bone in front of your ear). Tuning forks are made in various pitches, but easiest to obtain are those in A (440 hertz) and E. Since these are not especially helpful for an instrument like the banjo unless you play in special tunings, using a tuning fork means you will have to tune to a fretted note; for example, tune the first E on the fourth string (play the note at the second fret) to get the string in tune.

Although any device will work, here are some recommendations.

Balalaika. Tuning fork at A440.

Banjo. Tuning fork at A440; four-note pipe GDGBD or GCGBD; or still better, so you can easily retune in different tunings, a chromatic pipe.

Chorded Zither. Electronic device; chromatic pitchpipe.

Guitar. Tuning fork at A440 or E; pitchpipe EADGBE.

Hammered Dulcimer. Electronic device; piano; tuning fork or chromatic pitchpipe.

Mandolin. Tuning fork at A440; pitchpipe EADG.

Mountain Dulcimer. Tuning fork at C or other pitch; chromatic pitchpipe.

Psaltery. Any device.

String Bass. Tuning fork at A440; pitchpipe EADG.

Ukulele. Tuning fork at A440 or G; chromatic pitchpipe.

Violin. Tuning fork at A440; pitchpipe GDAE.

Tuning Fork—about $5

Kratt Master Key Chromatic Pitch Instrument (F to F, C to C, or E flat to E flat; C to C is a good choice)—$7

Kratt Pitchpipe (for individual instruments)—about $4.50

Korg Electronic Tuning Device (has a range of seven octaves) WT-12—$230

Straps

You'll want a strap if you plan to play most fretted instruments—especially a banjo—standing up. Avoid straps made of synthetics, which can interact with and ruin the finish of your instrument. Metal buckles can scratch the finish. Following are just a few of the many straps available:

Guild Denim Guitar Strap (2 inches wide)—$5.95

Oscar Schmidt Autoharp Straps—$5 & $15

Silver-Eagle Designs Denim and Leather "Pick-Pocket" Guitar Strap—$17.95

Stewart-MacDonald Leather Banjo Strap—$9.50

Metronomes

A metronome is an electrical or mechanical device that produces a steady, adjustable beat. Rob Sax, a banjo player, recommends a metronome for banjo players because "the most important thing in bluegrass banjo playing is the rhythm." Here are three of the many metronomes available:

Seth Thomas Wind-Up—$30

Taktell Super-Mini Wind-Up—$39

Franz Electric (beats and/or flashes)—$39.

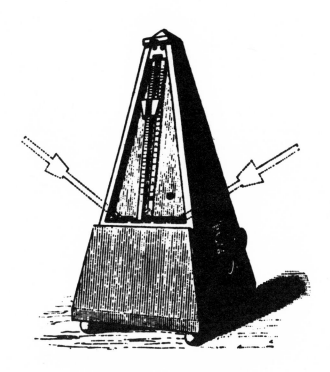

CHAPTER 17

USED AND
❧ VINTAGE INSTRUMENTS ❧

Vintage refers to older American-made fretted instruments, particularly those built before World War II. Although the word *vintage* usually refers to used instruments, it is almost always used to connote value. Valuable old violins may be called "old" or "rare."

According to Hap Kueffner of Mandolin Brothers in Staten Island, New York, "one of the reasons the vintage market ever happened is the big folk boom of the early sixties," and in the past fifteen years prices of vintage instruments have increased up to 1000% —about 250% more than the price of gasoline has increased. Says Pat Conte, a New York musician: "If you were to outfit a bluegrass band now, in 1981, with period instruments, it would cost you twenty thousand dollars."

What makes an instrument valuable? Michael Holmes, editor of *Mugwumps*, a magazine devoted in part to vintage instruments, says "three things . . . make an instrument valuable. Playability, ornamentation . . . and rarity. The most valuable instruments are those which are useable playing instruments."[1] Yet two dealers state emphatically that price may have little to do with what makes an instrument valuable to a musician:

Hap Kueffner: "Playability and sound have nothing to do with it. We sell Lloyd Loar mandolins at anywhere from $5000 to $10,000, depending on their condition, history, price, and ownership."

Matt Umanov (of Matt Umanov Guitars, New York, New York): "Usually instruments are priced according to supply and demand."

According to Stan Werbin of Elderly Instruments in East Lansing, Michigan, "Demand *is* higher with better playability and sound (all else being equal)."

Although Kueffner is correct on one level, as are Holmes and Werbin, the law of the marketplace is still the ultimate determinant. Loar mandolins, for example, are valuable for the reasons Holmes stated, priced, perhaps, according to Kueffner's criteria, and extremely expensive because of low supply and high demand.

Why is there a demand for old instruments?

Matt Umanov: "Some of the demand—a great deal of it—is produced by certain models or makes being used by certain well-known musicians."

Kueffner: "People want to use what their idols use. If your idol is Earl Scruggs and he uses a Gibson Granada, you're going to get a Granada or a copy of a Granada."

Umanov: "Other instruments are known to be intrinsically good, for instance, Martin guitars."

Pat Conte: "There's a certain joy about finding an old instrument in an attic or pawnshop; it possesses some kind of spirit that's truly a link to the music you're after. There's always the joy of finding an old instrument you wouldn't have with a new instrument."

Buying Used Instruments

Condition. Make sure the instrument is in good condition or is worth fixing, and that the price reflects the condition. Keep in mind that most companies' warranties are in effect only through the original ownership of an instrument.

Authenticity. Make sure the instrument is what the seller says it is. Violin dealers usually write a certificate for the valuable instruments they sell, but dealers of fretted instruments do not do this as a rule. Nevertheless, try to obtain something in writing about the instrument; this may help if you want to resell it.

Although there are crooked dealers, according to violinist Joseph Gold "even expert [violin] dealers can make mistakes" in authentication, but "if you buy from somebody who's really reputable, they're right most of the time. The ones who are bad don't know."

Price. Matt Umanov says that "most dealers, being reputable, will have their instruments priced according to what they feel the instrument is worth on the open market. If it's priced way above the market, the only way the customer will know this is by comparison shopping." Since supply and demand vary somewhat from dealer to dealer and from city to city, comparison shopping may involve checking outside your city. Scalpers exist, but they seem to be ignorant rather than greedy.

Sources. "I've scoured a few states down South looking for instruments and never come up with much," says Pat Conte. "People are a lot more antique conscious now and assume that anything old is valuable, which is wrong." Referring to a particular flea-market dealer, George Gruhn of Gruhn Guitars in Nashville, Tennessee, says:

> a lot of the flea market dealers like that do sell such that almost everything they have is overpriced almost ridiculously. The banjos he had for $100.00 were worth $35.00 to $50.00 if you're generous.... and yet there are some bargains.[2]

Pat Conte is similarly generous with pawnshop dealers; he says they are "usually maniacs." Although the best buys probably come from ignorant sellers, the instruments a dealer has are usually going to be playable and set up; that's part of the music dealer's high (or "market") price, in fact. Try every source, but be especially wary of spending too much money at a flea market or second-hand store.

When you do buy from a dealer, you can buy off the wall, of course, but the best way to get what you want is to be very specific. Explains Matt Umanov, "If you want me to locate something for you and keep your name on file you're going to have to be specific."

Gibson A-1 mandolin.

Selmer archtop guitar with cutaway body, slotted head, and oval soundhole.

Selling Your Used Instrument

Before you sell or trade in an instrument, determine its market value and then set your price accordingly. Naturally, this isn't always possible. Says Michael Holmes:

> I've got several items I'd like to get $2000 or $3000 for; unfortunately they're only worth a couple of hundred. There is a very confusing ground here. There is asking price. There is what somebody is willing to pay; and what somebody is willing to pay for it, is what the thing is worth. And that is not what just one person is willing to pay. There's got to be a couple of people willing to pay it.[3]

You will receive more money from a private party than from a dealer because, as Umanov points out, "a dealer is buying for the purpose of resale." For a dealer to be able to resell an instrument at market value, he or she has to buy at considerably less than market value. Peter Tatar, a violin dealer in New York City, says dealers "try to get an instrument for half or less," while George Gruhn says "on most of the things I sell, the average profit margin is something like, pay $350 and sell for $500.00.... Most stores buy at half of what they sell for.[4] Some instruments are very hard to sell because there is a large supply and no demand. Take a $200 guitar, for example. Even if you are asking only $150, I can do better elsewhere. For one thing, the warranty is not valid after resale. And for another, I can buy a brand-new $250 guitar for $150. Tatar, who routinely turns down offers of inexpensive instruments, says "it's a question of supply and demand."

Vega Artist tenor banjo.

Trading-in one instrument for another is another way to part with an instrument. Many dealers make it a policy to take trade-ins on instruments they have sold. For example, Fiddlepicker, a mail-order violin dealer, says in its price list: "Any instrument or bow bought from the Fiddlepicker will be accepted at purchase price against an instrument or bow of greater value." Mandolin Brothers will try to sell on consignment any instrument they sold you, providing it is in good condition. But Paul Braden, of Woodsy's Music in Kent, Ohio, still believes selling for cash is more lucrative for the consumer. Braden's policy on trade-ins depends on his relationship with you, the instrument you are trading in and its condition, and the instrument you are buying. He gives a better trade on an instrument selling close to list price, for example, than on a heavily discounted instrument like a Martin guitar.

RARITY

Pat Conte: "How many prize American instruments are in the class of something like an Italian old master violin? Nowadays when you see 'rare' that might mean there are one hundred fifty original five-string banjos from such and such a year. But when a violin dealer says rare, he *means* rare—like thirteen known. Rarity is a word that's thrown around. As far as I'm concerned, there aren't any really rare American instuments, with few exceptions."

Matt Umanov: "Martin guitars from the 1930s vs. Gibson guitars from the 1930s—there were probably more Gibsons produced; however, there are probably more Martins around, partly because they were more solidly built, partly because since they cost more new they were better cared for. Martin guitars of that period can by and large be sold for more money, more quickly, than Gibson guitars from that period."

Used Instruments

Among used instruments, some good buys are still to be had among old Gibson mandolins that are not F-5s, and also off-name open-back banjos. The demand for the latter is not especially high. More recent Martin guitars—1950s and 1960s—are reasonably priced, but new Martins may be a better buy at the huge discounts often available. And some instruments built by individual luthiers can be a good buy; although they are good, demand is not as high in most cases as for, say, a Martin, since they are less well known.

Sources of Used Instruments and of Information on Used Instruments

Banjo Newsletter, Box 1830, Annapolis, MD 21404. Good classified section (banjos).

Bluegrass Unlimited, Box 111, Broad Run, VA 22014. Good classified section (banjos, guitars, mandolins, Dobros).

Dulcimer Player News, P.O. Box 2164, Winchester, VA 22601. Some classifieds (mountain and hammered dulcimers).

Elderly Instruments, P.O. Box 1795, 541 E. Grand River, East Lansing, MI 48823. Buys and sells fretted instruments and violins. Periodic listings.

Frets, P.O. Box 28836, San Diego, CA 92128. Articles on vintage (fretted) instruments; regular column by George Gruhn.

Gruhn Guitars, 410 Broadway, Nashville, TN 37203. Buys and sells fretted instruments. Certificates. Periodic listings.

Guitar Trader, 12 Broad St., Red Bank, NJ 07701. Buys and sells fretted instruments. Periodic listings.

Mandolin Brothers, 629 Forest Ave., Staten Island, NY 10310. Buys, sells, and appraises fretted instruments. Quarterly listings.

Mugwumps, 1600 Billman Lane, Silver Spring, MD 20902. Almost exclusively devoted to disseminating information on fretted instruments. Classifieds. Back issues available; current issues irregular.

Matt Umanov Guitars, 276 Bleecker St., New York, NY 10014. Buys, sells, and appraises fretted instruments.

Westwood Music, 1100 Westwood Blvd., Los Angeles, CA 90024. Buys and sells fretted and bowed instruments.

CHAPTER 18

CARING FOR YOUR INSTRUMENT

Aside from accidents, theft, and acts of nature, the greatest threat to any musical instrument is climate, and the most vulnerable parts of your instrument are those made of wood. Cold weather makes an instrument contract, hot weather makes it expand, dry weather makes it shrink and crack, humid weather makes it swell and come apart. But by far the greatest threat is not so much weather as weather changes, especially drastic ones. For example, your guitar is cool and dry. You leave it in the sun on a humid day and it swells; then you put it back in a cool place and it contracts. When this cycle happens too often and too fast (or even just once), damage occurs.

Try to store your instrument in a stable environment and at a constant temperature. Keep the instrument away for direct sunlight as much as possible, from radiators, and especially from the inside of a sealed car or the trunk on a hot day, which is by far the worst place to keep an instrument. Use a humidifier in the instrument case or in the instrument itself when the air is dry. Here are some commercial humidifiers:

Dampit—device containing sponge (goes inside instrument), which you moisten: for bass (about $7.50), violin (about $5.50), or guitar (about $6)

Herco Guardfather—moisture-containing substance (goes inside case)—$2.25

Temperature changes can make instruments like chorded zithers, hammered dulcimers, and psalteries go out of tune very easily.

Cases. Instruments need cases to protect them from the elements and from physical damage. A bag is convenient and lightweight but inadequate, especially for serious traveling with a good instrument. A chipboard case, which looks hard from a distance but is actually rather flimsy, is adequate for inexpensive instruments and totally insufficient for hard-traveling; never check your chipboard-cased guitar at the airport, for example. Hardshell cases provide the best protection, and many good instruments come with them. Special flight cases (Anvil: $150–300) are also available for extra protection. Nearly all companies will sell you cases to go with their instruments.

Daily and Periodic Maintenance

Stringed instruments need to be maintained on a daily basis as well as on a periodic basis several times a year. Sweat, friction, moisture, and dust eat away at and dull the finish. Although everyone's body chemistry is different, it is a good idea to wipe off all the wood and metal parts, including the strings and fingerboard, with a soft, slightly damp cloth *each time* you finish playing, before you pack the instrument into its case. Always use soft, natural, unabrasive cloth, such as baby diapers or special instrument-polishing cloths; flannel is good too. Remove the capo from a fretted instrument. Banjo players usually do not clean the head, even when it's dark with dirt; some players actually dirty the head to make it look old.

Chorded Zither. Mike King, a harp player in California, suggests using a metal flute cleaning rod to work on hard-to-reach parts: "Thread a soft cloth through the slot in the end of the rod and slip it under the strings above the chord bars. Use the rod to push the cloth around, but be careful not to scratch the instrument." He also recommends a trumpet or brass mouthpiece brush "to get around and under the strings between the bridge pins and tuning pegs...." King's last suggestion is using a tenor recorder swab: "When you just want to dust under the strings, not polish, this is a great little gadget. It has long, soft threads wrapped around a wire coil that extends past the brush area and becomes a handle. Be sure to get one with a handle long enough so it will go under all the strings from one direction (small recorder swabs are too short)."[1] Becky Blackley, *Autoharpoholic* editor, recommends a complexion brush "because it has soft sable hairs that are long enough to reach through the soundboard from *above* the strings, making dusting the harp a snap! Mine is an old Revlon brush...."[2]

Fretted Instruments. Several times each year, depending on how frequently you play, polish the wood parts of your instrument with special instrument polish. The most important thing about polish is that it contain no silicone; anything too abrasive will damage the finish. Guitar cleaner, if used, should be used with caution because it contains a mild abrasive and will remove the finish if used too often.

Once or twice a year you may want to clean the fingerboard. Use very fine steel wool (0000 grade) and then oil lightly with a little lemon oil, linseed oil, or Gurian fingerboard oil (experts disagree on whether to clean the fingerboard and, if it is cleaned, the type of oil to use—if any). Clean the metal parts of a banjo with a good automotive polish no more than twice a year (if even that much). For banjos with gold-plated hardware, never use polish: wipe with a soft cloth. Avoid getting polish or cleaner on an instrument's strings.

Gurian Guitar Cleaner (2 oz.)—$2.25
Guild Guitar Cleaner/Polish (2 oz.)—$1.50
Gurian Guitar Polish (4 oz.)—$2.25
Martin Guitar Polish (6 oz.)—$2.95
Gurian Fingerboard Oil (2.5 oz.)—$2.10

Herco Acoustic Guitar Maintenance Kit contains polish cloth, humidifier, pegwinder (for changing strings), capo, and pitchpipe in A—$10

Violin. If you take good daily care of your violin, special violin polish is necessary very infrequently; use perhaps once a year. Applying polish with a silk cloth works best. There are many brands on the market; Sacconi Cleaner and Polish ($2.50) is one of the best.

String Bass. See section above on violin.

Harmonica. The M. Hohner company advises harmonica owners to keep their instruments clean: "After playing, tap the harmonica (holes inverted) several times against the palm of your hand. This will eject excess saliva and foreign substance.... Clean playing surface with dry, lint-free cloth and place harmonica back in its case."

Storage

When you aren't using your instrument, put it into its case and leave it in a safe place, away from temperature extremes. When storing an instrument for a long time, loosen the strings but leave them on. Periodically look in on the instrument; temperature and humidity may cause unglued seams and other problems.

Insurance

There are three kinds of policies. The best policy is a special one covering just your musical instrument(s) for the *replacement* value. If, for example, your 1978 Martin D-28 guitar is stolen in 1982, the insurance company will give you the money either to replace it with another 1978 Martin D-28 in similar condition and value or else to replace it with an instrument of comparable value. The precise definition of "replacement value" has to be explored with the agent writing the policy, since it is a nebulous and often misunderstood term. Make sure the agent understands that eventually many instruments begin to increase rather than decrease in value.

The second best policy is a similar one covering your instrument for the current appraised value. The Martin D-28 for which you paid $1200 is now worth $900. If that instrument is stolen, you get $900. The drawback with this policy is that when you look for another guitar, there may be no 1978 D-28s for that or any price, and the cost of a new D-28 is significantly higher. Nevertheless, this is sometimes the only policy available. The third best policy is not declaring the guitar separately but simply including it among your household goods. If your house is broken into and the guitar stolen, your general theft coverage takes care of the instrument. Exactly how much you will receive on your claim depends on limitations in the policy and the value at which you declare the guitar. This sort of policy is okay if you never take the guitar anywhere, but once the guitar leaves the house the policy is probably not in effect. Again, check this out with your insurance agent.

The first and second policies are floaters, that is, they're special policies covering your instrument. Some regular insurance companies write floaters only if you have a standard policy. For example, you could have fire and theft coverage on your apartment and a special floater for your musical instrument.

Once you have found the kind of insurance you want, you'll have to have your instrument(s) appraised in order to determine the premium. Some dealers do appraisals for free, others charge either a flat fee or a percentage of the value of the instrument. An appraisal—written, of course—ought to cost at the very most $50 for an *extremely* expensive instrument.

Shipping and Traveling

When shipping an instrument, loosen the strings, remove the endpin, and pack the instrument, case and all, carefully (make sure the instrument doesn't rattle) into a sturdy box or crate. Always insure the instrument. United Parcel Service is the choice of many, many manufacturers; they're fast, reliable, are quite inexpensive, and take good care of what they transport. For a small additional fee, UPS will pick up in many areas.

Taking an instrument on any kind of public or commercial transportation can be hazardous. Always use a hardshell case unless you know for sure the instrument is going with you and not into a special baggage compartment. On a bus or train you can often take an instrument (except for a string bass) into the passenger compartment and put it between your legs, in the overhead rack, or into an empty seat.

Flying is trickier. When you are going by plane, ask the airline's policy on musical instruments *before* you even make your reservation, or while you are making it. Although the airlines' policies are similar, there are also small variations. American Airlines, for instance, has a special service that allows you to actually accompany the instrument to the baggage compartment. Ask for "escort" at the check-in gate. TWA, on the other hand, has a special place to check valuable baggage, and supposedly the instrument is carried by hand to the plane instead of being loaded onto one of those overloaded baggage wagons. A spokesperson at TWA said they "plaster" the instrument with handle-with-care tags.

Liability seems to vary, but at least TWA and American have good policies. If your instrument is valuable, you can fill out special forms to this effect at the ticket counter. The TWA representative said that if an instrument is damaged beyond repair, they will replace it; otherwise, repairs will be covered. An old, fragile instrument may give you some problems, however, and the airline may be more reluctant to assume total liability. Additional insurance can often be bought at the airport or from your insurance agent.

❦ APPENDIX A ❦

Discography

MOSTLY OLDIES

Many of the following recordings are of music that makes the transition from string-band music to bluegrass. Included also are recordings featuring brother duets.

Acuff, Roy. *Best of Roy Acuff* (Capitol SM-1870).

Armstrong Twins. *Hillbilly Mandolin* (Old Timey 118).

The Bailes Brothers. (Old Homestead 103).

Carlisle, Cliff. *Cliff Carlisle*, Vols. 1 & 2 (Old Timey 103/104).

Delmore Brothers. *Brown's Ferry Blues* (County 402).

Dixon Brothers. *Beyond Black Smoke* (Country Turtle 6000).

Lee, Wilma, and Stoney Cooper. *Early Recordings* (County 103).

Lowe, Bill. *Kentucky Farewell* (Rambling 001).

Maddox Brothers & Rose (1946–51) (2-Arhoolie 5016/7).

Murphy, Jimmy. *Electricity* (Sugar Hill 3702).

Patterson, Ray and Ina. *Songs of Home and Child* (County 737).

Skaggs, Ricky. *Sweet Temptation* (Sugar Hill 3706).

BLUEGRASS: MORE OLD THAN NEW

Allen, Red, and the Kentuckians. *Bluegrass Country* (County 704).

Bluegrass Blackjacks. *Bluegrass Blackjacks* (Puritan 5004).

Bluegrass Cardinals. *Livin' in the Good Old Days* (CMH 6229).

The Bray Brothers with Red Cravens. *Prairie Bluegrass* (Rounder 0053).

Connie and Babe. *Connie and Babe (Early Days of Bluegrass, Vol. 10)* (Rounder 1022).

Country Gentlemen. *Joe's Last Train* (Rebel 1559).

Grant, Bill, and Delia Bell. *Bill Grant and Delia Bell* (Kiamichi 101).

Jim and Jesse and the Virginia Boys. *Radio Shows* (Old Dominion 498–10).

Kentucky Colonels. *Kentucky Colonels* (Rounder 0073). Outstanding bluegrass band.

Lilly Brothers and Don Stover. *Lilly Brothers and Don Stover* (County 729).

The Lost and Found. *The First Time Around* (Outlet 1002).

Martin, Jimmy, and the Sunny Mountain Boys. *Country Music Time* (MCA 91).

Martin, Mac, and the Dixie Travelers. *Dixie Bound* (County 743).

McCoury, Del, and the Dixie Pals. *Del McCoury and the Dixie Pals* (Grassound 102).

Monroe, Charlie, and the Dixie Partners. *The Fiddler* (Old Homestead 90052).

Nu-Grass Pickers. *Nu-Grass Pickers* (Pine Tree 512).

Pinnacle Boys. *Award Winning* (Atteiram 1552).

The Seldom Scene. *Old Train* (Rebel 1536).

Sparks, Larry, and the Lonesome Ramblers. *Sings Hank Williams* (County 759).

Stanley Brothers. *The Stanley Brothers and the Clinch Mountain Boys* (Starday/King 615). The Stanley Brothers were—and Ralph Stanley still is—one of the most important musicians in bluegrass. Their style is generally a bit more old-fashioned than that of Bill Monroe, but their music is no less vital.

White, Buck, and the Down Home Folks. *That Down Home Feeling* (Ridge Runner 0006).

Wiseman, Mac, and the Shenandoah Cut-Ups. *New Traditions* (Vetco 508).

BLUEGRASS AND OLD TIME: CONTEMPORARY AND REVIVAL

Any Old Time String Band (Arhoolie 4009). A group comprised of just women.

Arm & Hammer String Band. *Stay on the Farm* (Fretless 136).

Half Shaved. *Down Home, Homemade Old Time Music* (Flying Crow 100).

Highwoods String Band. *No. 3 Special* (Rounder 0074).

Hotmud Family. *Years in the Making* (Vetco 513). Bluegrass.

Hot Rize (Flying Fish 206). Bluegrass.

Joe Val and the New England Bluegrass Boys. *Not a Word from Home* (Rounder 0082).

Major Contay and the Canebrake Rattlers. *Old Familiar Tunes* (Flying Crow 104) and *Songs of the Hills and Plains* (Cinnamon 1201). A group dedicated to recapturing the old string-band sound.

Michael, Walt, and Tom McCreesh. *Dance Like the Waves of the Sea* (Front Hall 017).

New Lost City Ramblers. *Remembrance of Things to Come* (Folkways 31035). Perhaps the seminal revival string band, the Ramblers had their own special sound yet approached their material with the sensitivity of a musicologist. Folkways issues many other Ramblers records, and Mike Seeger, one of the Ramblers, has numerous recordings on his own.

Plank Road String Band. *Vocal & Instrumental Blend* (June Appal 015).

Red Clay Ramblers. *Stolen Love* (Flying Fish 009). Old-timey.

The Wonderbeans. *The Wonderbeans* (Flying Crow 101). Fine string band (with accordion).

Yankee Rebels (Flying Crow 102). Bluegrass.

FEMALE BLUEGRASS SINGERS

"Good female *bluegrass* singers are rare," says Kathy Kaplan, co-host of Moonshine, a popular bluegrass and old-time music show on WKCR in New York City, which is why we've assembled a separate section—to call your attention to some records that do feature women.

Bell, Delia, *Bluer Than Midnight* (County 768).

Belle, Gloria. *Gloria Belle* (Rebel 1479).

Cooper, Wilma Lee. *Daisy a Day* (Leather 7705).

Dickens, Hazel. *Hard Hitting Songs for Hard Hitting People* (Rounder 0126); and Alice Gerrard, *Hazel & Alice* (Rounder 0027) and *Hazel Dickens and Alice Gerrard* (Rounder 0054).

White, Buck, and the Down Home Folks. *Buck White and the Down Home Folks* (County 735 & 760).

ANTHOLOGIES

Both of these anthologies are highly recommended:

Anthology of American Folk Music, Vols. 1–3 (two records each) (Folkways 2951, 2952, 2953).

Will the Circle Be Unbroken (3-United Artists 9801). A superb three-record set featuring the Nitty Gritty Dirt Band with an all-star cast of bluegrass, old-time, and country musicians including Brother Oswald, Vassar Clements, Norman Blake, Merle Travis, Doc Watson, and Maybelle Carter.

THREE VOICES

Guthrie, Woody. *Library of Congress Recordings* (2-Elecktra 271/2), *Woody Guthrie Sings Folk Songs* (2-Folkways 2483/4), and *Dust Bowl Ballads* (Folkways 5212). Guthrie, through those he influenced, was one of the main forces behind the great revival of interest in traditional music in the 1950s and 1960s; without him, too, there would have been no Bob Dylan, and without Dylan there would have been no folk-rock; no Byrds; no Crosby, Stills, Nash and Young; no bearded cowboys. Woody's was a music of protest and social involvement, a synthesis of traditional musical ideas (from the Carter Family, for example) and topical lyrics. Most significant singers or vocal groups do this, but most lyrics are topical in the cultural rather than in the political or social sense—as were Woody's.

Seeger, Peggy, and Ewan McColl. *The Long Harvest: Traditional Ballads in Their English, Scots, and North American Variants* (10-Argo ZDA 66–75). This set is a good example of what these exceptionally fine singers do a lot of: show you, through fine singing and musicianship, how music changes as it passes through and is taken up by various societies or subgroups. Peggy's voice is winning and pure, and her banjo playing always interesting; McColl's voice is strong and stark. Their other records are also highly recommended.

Seeger, Pete. *The Essential Pete Seeger* (Vanguard VSD 97/98). Seeger has so many records (most on Folkways) that two records hardly do justice to his talent for reaching an audience, nor to all the sides of his immense spirit, but this set is a good introduction. Seeger combines the approach of the collector (like the other Seegers) with the spirit and social commitment of Woody Guthrie. Seeger's topicality is wider than Woody's, his voice more urban (in spite of the open-back banjo he usually plays).

❦ APPENDIX B ❦

Books of Songs and Lyrics

Breathnach, Brendan. *Ceol Rince na hEirreann* [*Dance Music of Ireland*]. Oifig an tSolathair, 1963; Vol. 2, 1976. Worth searching for.

Bronson, Bertrand G. *The Singing Tradition of Child's Popular Ballads.* Princeton University Press, 1976. A short version (530 pages) of the famous four-volume set of ballads collected by Francis Child. Recommended, unless you wish to purchase the complete edition.

Cohen, John, Mike Seeger, and Hally Wood. *Old Time String Band Songbook.* Oak, 1964, 1976.

Grossman, Stefan, Hal Grossman, and Stephen Calt. *Country Blues Songbook.* Oak, 1973. Over 120 songs.

Ledbitter, Mike (ed.). *Nothing But the Blues.* Oak, 1971. Collection of blues songs.

Lomax, Alan. *Folk Songs of North America.* Doubleday, 1960. Songs, notes, guitar chords. Recommended.

Lomax, John and Alan (eds.). *The Leadbelly Legend.* TRO, 1965. Leadbelly had a truly remarkable repertoire of songs, shouts, hollers, stories, and miscellanies.

McColl, Ewan, and Peggy Seeger. *Ewan McColl-Peggy Seeger Songbook.* Oak, 1963. Over fifty songs.

Niles, John Jacob. *The Ballad Book of John Jacob Niles.* Dover, 1960, 1961. A good collection of ballads, with comments, by collector/singer Niles.

Ritchie, Jean. *Celebration of Life.* Oak, 1965. Includes seventy-seven songs. Ritchie is one of our best writers on music and a great preserver of tradition.

Ritchie, Jean. *Singing Family of the Cumberlands.* Oak, 1963. Includes forty songs.

Seeger, Mike, and John Cohen. *The New Lost City Ramblers Song Book.* Oak, 1964.

Seeger, Peggy. *Folk Songs of Peggy Seeger.* Oak, 1964. Eighty-eight songs.

Silber, Fred and Irwin. *Folksinger's Wordbook.* Oak, 1973. Chords and lyrics to over one thousand songs.

Silverman, Jerry. *Folk Song Encyclopedia,* 2 vols. Chappell Music, 1975. Almost nine hundred pages of songs. Recommended.

Stricklin, A. (ed.). *Slim Richey's Bluegrass Word Book.* Ridge Runner Publications, 1972. Lyrics to 294 songs.

❈ APPENDIX C ❈

Books for Further Reading

MUSIC AND MUSICIANS

Artis, Bob. *Bluegrass.* Hawthorn Books, 1975. Recommended if you know nothing about bluegrass or want to know more.

Bookbinder, David. *What Folk Music Is All About.* Julian Messner, 1979. Development of American "folk" music—blues, bluegrass, country, etc.

Breathnach, Breandan. *Folk Music and Dances of Ireland.* Belfast: Mercier, 1971; rev. ed., 1977. Mostly text, but some tunes.

Guralnick, Peter. *Lost Highway: Journeys & Arrivals of American Musicians.* Godine, 1979. Sections of interest on Waylon Jennings, Ernest Tubb, Hank Snow, and Howlin' Wolf.

Guthrie, Woody. *Born to Win.* Macmillan, 1965. A kind of scrapbook of Woody's jottings, letters, stories, sketches; invaluable for those for whom Woody is a Great Hero.

Guthrie, Woody. *Bound for Glory.* New American Library, 1970. The autobiography on which the movie was based.

Keil, Carles. *Urban Blues.* University of California Press, 1966.

Lloyd, A. L. *Folk Song in England.* Paladin, 1967.

Lomax, Alan. *Adventures of a Ballad Hunter.* Macmillan, 1947. Lomax was one of the most important figures in American folklore and folk-music studies.

Malone, Bill C. *Country Music U.S.A.: A Fifty-Year History.* University of Texas Press, 1969.

Malone, Bill C. *Southern Music, American Music.* University of Kentucky Press, 1979.

Nettl, Bruno. *An Introduction to Folk Music in the United States.* Wayne State University Press, 1962. Nettl is an ethnomusicologist. A serious work.

O Canainn, Tomás. *Traditional Music in Ireland.* London: Routledge & Kegan Paul, 1978.

Paris, Mike, and Chris Combers. *Jimmie the Kid: The Life of Jimmie Rodgers.* Da Capo, 1977. Rodgers, known as the "singing brakeman" and, among other things, for his "blue yodels," was an important figure in traditional American music.

Porterfield, Nolan. *Jimmie Rodgers: The Life and Times of America's Blue Yodeler.* University of Illinois Press, 1979. According to *The Journal of Country Music,* "the definitive biography."

Roach, Hildred. *Black American Music.* Crescendo, 1973. A good survey of the development of black American music, from its African roots to jazz, blues, pop, and classical.

Seeger, Peter. *The Incompleat Folksinger* (edited by Jo. M. Schwartz). Simon & Schuster, 1972. Seeger's writings on music, music-making, and other matters are intelligent and important.

Shelton, Robert, and Burt Goldblatt. *The Country Music Story.* Castle. 1971.

Shestark, Melvin. *The Country Music Encyclopedia.* Crowell, 1974.

Tunney, Paddy. *The Stone Fiddle: My Way to Traditional Song.* Dublin: Gilbert Dalton, 1978. Tunney is an Irish musician.

Woods, Fred. *Folk Revival: The Rediscovery of a National Music.* Blandford Press, 1979. A book about British music.

MUSICAL INSTRUMENTS

Baines, Anthony (ed.). *Musical Instruments Through the Ages.* Penguin. 1st ed., 1961; 2nd ed., 1976. A good, well-illustrated book.

Buchner, A. *Folk Music Instruments of the World.*

Crown, 1972. Photographs of instruments and musicians (with their instruments); some text.

Diagram Group. *Musical Instruments of the World: An Illustrated Encyclopedia.* Paddington Press, 1976. A very good book that shows, mostly through annotated illustrations (no photographs), the amazing similarities between instruments of different periods and countries. But despite the useful text and good illustrations, you just can't go "wow" the way you can over photographs.

Farrell, Susan. *Directory of Contemporary American Musical Instrument Builders.* University of Missouri Press, 1981. This rather expensive book will help you locate builders and manufacturers around the country. Included are some dubious entries, such as distributors of Japanese-made instruments.

Marcuse, Sybil. *Musical Instruments: A Comprehensive Dictionary.* Norton, 1975. Useful but incomplete. Marcuse's other book is much better.

Marcuse, Sybil. *A Survey of Musical Instruments.* Harper & Row, 1975. Almost nine hundred pages long, this is a very comprehensive book. Unfortunately, there are few illustrations and no photographs.

Panum, Hortense. *The Stringed Instruments of the Middle Ages: Their Evolution and Development* (Jeffrey Pulver, ed. & trans.). Greenwood Press, 1970. Very good.

Sachs, Curt. *The History of Musical Instruments.* Norton, 1940, 1968. This is a classic. Both the Panum and the Sachs are illustrated (photos and/or drawings) in black and white.

ACOUSTICS

Benade, Arthur H. *Horns, Strings, and Harmony.* Doubleday/Anchor, 1960.

MAKING MUSICAL INSTRUMENTS

Cline, Dallas. *Homemade Musical Instruments.* Oak, 1976. From shoebox banjo to coffee-tin bongoes to mouth bow.

Cline, Dallas. *How to Play Nearly Everything.* Oak, 1977. How to make and play spoons, kazoo, musical saw, etc. Both of the Cline books are good to use with children.

Hunter, Ilene, and Marilyn Judson. *Simple Folk Instruments to Make and to Play.* Simon and Schuster, 1977. Also good for working with children but somewhat more advanced than the Cline books.

Roberts, Ronald. *Musical Instruments Made to Be Played.* Leicester, England: The Dryad Press, 1969. Includes instructions for building a psaltery, bowed psaltery, "Nordic lyre" (variation on Finnish kantele, a psaltery-like instrument), zithers, etc. A good selection of instruments, but the instructions leave a lot to the imagination. Some of the instruments are the same as in the other books, but the scope is more advanced.

Sawyer, David. *Vibrations: Making Unorthodox Musical Instruments.* Cambridge University Press, 1977. Drums, flute, percussion, simple stringed instruments. Smaller scope than Roberts book; audience: adult.

READING MUSIC, MUSIC THEORY, CHORDS

Jones, George Thaddeus. *Music Theory.* Barnes and Noble, 1974. Good, and very basic.

Lilienfeld, Robert. *Learn to Read Music.* Barnes and Noble, 1976.

Shanet, Howard. *Learn to Read Music.* Simon and Schuster/Fireside, 1956. The author says he can teach you to read music in just four hours.

Silverman, Jerry. *A Folksinger's Guide to Chords and Tunings.* Oak, 1967. Covers guitar, Dobro, mandolin, ukulele, and banjo. Useful but hard on the eyes.

Skinner, Stephen. *The Bradley Book of Chords, Scales, and Modes* (Richard Bradley, ed.). Bradley, 1980.

OTHER

Rappaport, Diane Sward. *How to Make and Sell Your Own Record.* Quick Fox, 1979.

Sandberg, Larry, and Dick Weissman. *The Folk Music Sourcebook.* Knopf, 1976. Although out of print, worth searching for to add to your reference library.

Weissman, Dick. *The Music Business: Career Opportunities and Self-Defense.* Crown, 1979. Many of the books on careers in the music business sound as if they were written on Madison Avenue; this one is an exception.

Willicutt, J. Robert, and Kenneth R. Ball. *The Musical Instrument Collector* (Steven F. Brines, ed.). The Bold Strummer, 1978. Interviews with fretted-instrument collectors and dealers; photographs. Quite good.

❧ APPENDIX D ❧

Magazines

These magazines are of general interest. A large, somewhat out-of-date list of periodicals can be obtained from the Archive of Folk Song, Library of Congress, Washington, DC 20540, and also found in *The Folk Music Sourcebook* (Knopf, 1976).

The Black Perspective in Music, Afro-American Creative Arts, Inc., P.O. Drawer I, Cambria Heights, NY 11411. $6/year (semiannual). Articles and reviews.

Block, Postbox 244, Almelo, The Netherlands. A Dutch blues and rock magazine.

Blues Unlimited, 217 N. Lincolnway, #224, N. Aurora, IL 60542. $12/year (quarterly). A fine English magazine.

Cadence: The Monthly American Review of Jazz & Blues, Rt. 1, Box 345, Redwood, NY 13679. $15/year (monthly). Reviews, news, interviews, articles, notes.

Canadian Bluegrass Review, P.O. Box 143, Watertown, Ontario, Canada LOR 2HO.

Canadian Folk Music Journal, Canadian Folk Music Society, 5 Notley Pl., Toronto, Ontario, Canada M4B 2M7. $5/year (annual). Scholarly; articles in French and English.

Come for to Sing, 917 Wolfram, Chicago, IL 60657. $6/year (quarterly). American, Canadian, and British "ethnic" music; blues and bluegrass. Articles, songs, how-to, etc.

Folkscene, P.O. Box 64545, Los Angeles, CA 90064. $5/year (bimonthly). Book and record reviews, interviews, articles; folk, bluegrass, country. Nice little magazine.

F.I.G.A. News, Fretted Instrument Guild of America, 2344 S. Oakley, Chicago, IL 60608. Articles, news, photos, etc., mostly on guitar, banjo, and mandolin, and on musicians. Write for further information.

Frets, P.O. Box 28836, San Diego, CA 92128. Of interest to most instrumentalists (see individual chapters) but with a decided emphasis on "new-time," rather than old-time, music. What's newtime? Bluegrass, newgrass, Dawg, jazz, urban sounds.

In the Tradition, P.O. Box 19, Kingston, NJ 08528. $9.50/year (bimonthly); sample: $1.50. Articles on different kinds of music, including Cajun, Jewish, Texas-Mexican, and Irish.

JEMF Quarterly, Folklore and Mythology Center, University of California, Los Angeles, CA 90024. Oriented toward old-time music and very good.

The Journal of Country Music, Country Music Foundation, 4 Music Square East, Nashville, TN 37203. $10/year (triquarterly). Interviews, articles, reviews, etc. Extremely well done.

Mugwumps, 1600 Billman Lane, Silver Spring, MD 20902. $9/year (bimonthly). A serious magazine for people serious about instruments—collecting, identifying, buying and selling, constructing.

Old Time Music, 22 Upper Tollington Park, London N4 3EL, England. $6 (slow) or $9 (airmail)/year; available from Rounder Records, County Sales, Elderly Instruments, and other American outlets. Articles, notes, excellent record reviews, all of interest to the American musician or music lover. Recommended.

Sing Out! 505 Eighth Avenue, New York, NY 10018. $11/year (bimonthly). Articles, reviews, news, ads, tunes, songs; socially and politically aware. In existence for over thirty years, and highly recommended.

Treoir, c/o John Droney, 70 Westminister Dr., West Hartford, CT 06107. $6/year (bimonthly). Promotes Irish music and culture in the U.S.

❧ APPENDIX E ❧

Music Festivals: Bluegrass, Old Time, and Others

For a complete list of festivals, write the National Council for the Traditional Arts, 1346 Connecticut Ave. N.W., Room 1118, Washington, DC 20036. Another excellent source of festival information is the April issue of *Bluegrass Unlimited* (Broad Run, VA 22014). *Frets* magazine (P.O. Box 28836, San Diego, CA 92128) also has a monthly calendar of events. Most of the magazines listed in Appendix B, in fact, have some events listings. For Canadian festivals, see the spring issue (March/April) of *Canadian Bluegrass Review* (P.O. Box 143, Waterdown, Ontario, Canada LOR 2HO).

Annual Border Festival, El Paso, Texas. October. Write: Carlos Chavez, 620 First National Bank Bldg., El Paso, TX 79901.

Bill Monroe's Annual Bean Blossom Bluegrass Festival, Bean Blossom, Indiana. June. Write: Monroe Festival Headquarters, 3819 Dickerson Rd., Nashville, TN 37207.

Bill Monroe's Annual Autumn Bluegrass Festival, Bean Blossom, Indiana. September. Same address as above.

Brandywine Mountain Music Convention, Concordville, Pennsylvania. July. Write: Carl Goldstein, Box 3504, Greenville, DE 19807.

National Folk Festival, Wolf Trap Farm Park, Vienna, Virginia. August. Write: National Council for the Traditional Arts (see above for address).

Old Fiddlers Convention, Galax, Virginia. August. Write: Oscar W. Hall, 328-A Kenbrook Dr., Galax, VA 24333.

Philadelphia Folk Festival, Schenksville, Pennsylvania. August. Write: Philadelphia Folk Song Society, 7113 Emlen St., Philadelphia, PA 19119.

Ralph Stanley's Memorial Bluegrass Festival, Coeburn/McClure, Virginia. May. Write: Ralph Stanley, Rt. 4, Box 226-A, Coeburn, VA 24230.

Walnut Valley Festival, Winfield, Kansas. September. Write: The Walnut Valley Association, P.O. Box 245F, Winfield, KS 67156. Some of the competitions include the National Flatpicking and Fingerpicking Guitar, National Bluegrass Banjo, National Hammered Dulcimer, National Mountain Dulcimer, and Walnut Valley Mandolin.

See individual chapters for other festivals. Most festivals have a wide assortment of music, competitions, and other activities of interest to all kinds of musicians. The fiddlers' conventions have events for banjo, and sometimes "old time" means bluegrass as much as it does old-time music.

GLOSSARY

INSTRUMENT PARTS

Back—the back side of most instruments; acoustically, less important than the top.

Belly—the top of a violin.

Binding—a strip of plastic or wood inlaid around the edges of the body, and sometimes the neck, of almost all flattop guitars, some mandolins, banjos, dulcimers and other instruments. The binding's main functions are to protect the edges from moisture and physical damage and to add decoration.

Body—the soundbox, resonating chamber, predominant part of most musical instruments, which usually means what's left after removing the neck, bridge, strings, fingerboard, and tailpiece. The body of a banjo is called the *pot*.

Bouts—usually, the widest parts of a guitar, violin, or bass; the narrowest part of a violin is called the middle bout.

Braces—strips of wood on the inside back and top of many stringed instruments that reinforce; they control sound.

Bridge—a piece or pieces of wood or other materials that support the strings and transmit vibrations from the strings to the top; acoustically important.

End Pin or Button—on some instruments, the part at the back end to which one end of a strap can be attached; on a violin, the tailpiece is attached to the end button.

Fingerboard—on most fretted instruments, the strip of wood attached to the top of the neck that holds the frets; on a dulcimer, the fingerboard is attached directly to the top since there is no neck; on a violin the fingerboard contains no frets, is attached to the neck at one end and projects up from the body at the other. On instruments with a fingerboard, different pitches are obtained by pressing a string or strings against either the fret or the fingerboard, whereas on an instrument without a fingerboard, such as a harp or hammered dulcimer, different pitches are usually obtainable only by plucking different strings.

Fretboard—a fingerboard with frets, as on a guitar.

Frets—thin bars of metal (gut loops on lutes and viols) that divide the fingerboard and give set pitches.

Friction Peg—see *Tuning Apparatus.*

Guitar Tuners—see *Tuning Apparatus.*

Machine Heads—see *Tuning Apparatus.*

Headstock (Head)—see *Peghead.*

Marquetry—concentric rings of wood, plastic, or abalone inlaid around the soundhole of an instrument.

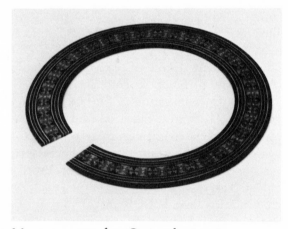

Marquetry rosette from Gurian classic guitar.

Neck—on most fretted instruments the piece of wood or other material extending from the body over which the strings are aligned.

Nut—on most fretted instruments (and also on the violin) a notched piece of some hard material that spaces the strings and forms a stopping point for the vibrating length of the strings at the peg end.

Peghead—the end of the neck where the pegs or tuning machines are mounted.

Pegs—see *Tuning Apparatus.*

Pickguard—a thin sheet of plastic or wood either attached flat to the top of the instrument or suspended above the top, that protects the top from the pick and the hand.

Pin Block—on instruments such as the hammered dulcimer, psaltery, chorded zither, and piano, the blocks of wood in which the tuning and hitch pins are set.

Position Markers or Dots—on some fretted instruments, markers inlaid into the fingerboard (on the top and/or on the edges) to mark the position of certain frets.

Position inlays on Deering banjo.

Purfling—strips of abalone, wood, plastic, etc., inlaid along the edge of an instrument that are mainly decorative but sometimes, as on the violin, func-

tional. *Purfling* and *binding* and often used interchangeably by manufacturers and builders.

Purfling (outside pattern) and soundhole inlays on Gurian guitar. Note herringbone pattern in middle inlay around soundhole.

Rails—the front and back of a hammered dulcimer.

Ribs—on a violin or mandolin, the sides.

Saddle—on a guitar, a thin piece of hard substance inserted into the bridge, on which the strings are supported; on a violin or bass, the piece that the tailpiece goes over.

Soundboard—see *Top.*

Soundhole—a hole or holes in the top of some instruments that connect the air chamber within to the outside air, thereby affecting the sound.

Tailpiece—on some instruments, the part to which the strings are attached at the opposite end from the peghead.

Top—acoustically the most crucial part of a stringed instrument, because most of the vibrations from a plucked or bowed string pass into it through the bridge. Set in motion from the vibrations, the top itself begins to vibrate, like a speaker cone or drumhead, and sets the air in motion.

Tuning Apparatus—devices that hold one end of the strings and allow you to adjust the string tension, thereby changing the pitch of the strings.
Friction pegs are wood or metal pegs that work on

the principle of friction—that is, they are turned by lessening the friction and made fast by increasing the friction (pushing the peg in tight). Metal friction pegs, used primarily on banjos (and thus called banjo pegs) have an adjusting screw in one end. Wood friction pegs are used mostly on violin-type instruments and dulcimers.

Guitar tuners (tuning machines) are another term for machine heads.

Machine heads usually refer to geared guitar-type standard ratio is 4:1—the peg is turned four times tuning machines and are worm-gear machinery. Good ones have ratios of 12:1 or 16:1 (twelve or sixteen rotations of the button for each complete rotation of the post).

Planetary gears (planets, planetary machines) are geared tuning devices used mostly on banjos. The around for each complete revolution of the shaft.

Tuners, Tuning machines usually refer to geared tuning devices.

Waist—on a guitar, the narrowest part of the body.

INSTRUMENT JARGON

Action—string height above the fingerboard (high or low action); ease or difficulty in pressing strings (hard or easy action)—usually measured at the nut and upper end of the fingerboard. The ideal height is as low as the strings will go without buzzing, which will be different for every player and for different playing styles.

Compensated—because of the inherent intonation problems of fretted instruments, the string lengths are often adjusted by compensating the saddle (and sometimes the nut)—adjusting the positions of the notches.

Course—a row containing one or more strings. A six-string guitar has one string per course, six courses; a twelve-string guitar has two strings per course, six courses.

Frontward Curvature (Relief)—on most fretted instruments the fingerboard should exhibit a very slight frontward curvature; otherwise the strings may buzz.

Intonation—how well an instrument plays in tune.

Playability—a catch-all term referring to certain physical and mechanical features of an instrument and also to the relationship between the player and an instrument.

Scale Length—the distance from the nut to the bridge or saddle. Scale length varies according to instrument, manufacturer, and instrument size, but each kind of instrument has a (roughly) standard scale length, usually based on that of a particular instrument. Scale length affects sound and playability. When the scale is long, the strings must be stretched to a greater tension to bring them up to pitch, and the result is more volume, somewhat more brilliance, and strings that are harder to play because of the additional stiffness. A longer scale may also require heavier strings. For the average player, small variations in scale length are negligible. Dulcimers show the greatest variations in scale length—up to about 9 inches.

Setup—setting up an instrument means making it optimally playable: putting on strings, adjusting the neck angle, tightening a banjo head, eliminating string buzz, adjusting the action, etc.

String Buzz—the unwanted rattling of a string or strings against a fret or frets, due to various causes, including incorrect fingerboard curvature, excessively low action, high or low frets, and a nut that is notched too deeply.

MUSICAL TERMS

Chord—two or more pitches sounded at the same time and at a certain interval or intervals. For example, a simple C chord can be made up of C and E, a fuller chord with three notes, CEG.

Chromatic—a chromatic scale is composed of half steps (a step is an interval between pitches). Find a piano, locate middle C, then play every key, white and black, to the next C (thirteen keys altogether)—that's a chromatic scale. The fingerboards of guitars, banjos, and mandolins are chromatic.

Diatonic—a diatonic scale is composed of five whole steps and two half steps, which means fewer notes than in a chromatic scale and five wider spaces. Find middle C on the piano, and play just the white keys—eight of them (do re mi fa sol la ti do). That's the diatonic scale known as C major. The mountain dulcimer has a diatonic scale.

Chromatic scale D-D. Twelve intervals.

Diatonic scale D-D. Seven intervals.

Equal Temperament—the intervals between pitches in a scale are determined mathematically in various ways. One of these is called equal temperament, which makes all the intervals between notes exactly the same. Almost all instruments are tuned in equal temperament. Unfretted instruments like the chorded zither or psaltery can be tuned in other ways, however; and the violin can be played in virtually any temperament.

Key—when you play in the key of C, all the tones in the scale are centered around the note C; when you play in the key of G, all the notes are centered around G. A key is a system of organizing the notes in a scale.

Note—a particular frequency of sound. See *Pitch.*

Pitch—the pitch of a sound is its vibration frequency. A high pitch has many, many vibrations per second; a low pitch has fewer vibrations per

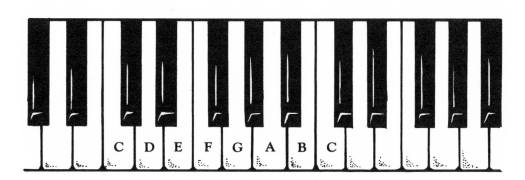

Piano keyboard.

Harmonic— take a fretted instrument, lightly touch any string above the twelfth fret, and then play that note. The bell-like tone is the first harmonic. Touch the same string over the fifth fret and you will hear another harmonic. Now run your finger slowly up the string, stopping over each fret and playing that note. You will hear a whole series of harmonics that may sound mixed up but in fact have a special order.

second. For example, the note A is vibrating at 440 cycles per second (or 440 hertz), so it's called A440; this is also the first A above middle C on the piano keyboard.

Scale—a special arrangement of notes. See *Chromatic, Diatonic,* and *Key.*

Sharp and Flat—when a pitch is sharp, it is higher

in pitch than it should be; when a pitch is flat, it is lower than it should be. Getting in tune means adjusting the pitches of the strings until they are correct.

Tablature and Music—Standard notation (called "music" in the comments on instruction books in individual chapters) is the conventional way of notating music. Contrary to popular belief, reading this music is quite simple and easy to learn.

Tablature is a system for indicating the position of your fingers on a particular instrument; when you read the tablature, the notes ought to be correct—even though you don't know what they are.

Custom — theoretically, a custom instrument is one built to your specifications; in practice, many "custom" instruments only have a choice of options.

Production Model — a loose term meaning a particular instrument model that is always produced the same way. For instance, the Martin D-28 is a production model, but Doug Berch's one-of-a-kind custom dulcimers are not. Even production models, however, have differences, since no two pieces of wood, for example, are exactly the same.

BUSINESS TERMS

Builder, Luthier, Manufacturer—while all three make musical instruments, each has different connotations and denotations. *Manufacturer* generally means a large company, such as CF Martin or Yamaha, and *builder, luthier,* or *individual builder* means one person engaged in building instruments (a luthier builds stringed instruments only). Some luthiers build instruments on their own; others are employed by manufacturers.

✒ FOOTNOTES ✒

Chapter 5

1. David Grisman, "Jethro Burns: Jazz Mandolin Pioneer," *Frets* (October 1979), p. 38.

Chapter 6

1. Joseph Wechsberg, *The Glory of the Violin* (Viking Press, 1973), p. 36.
2. Alberto Bachmann, *An Encyclopedia of the Violin* (Da Capo, 1966), p. 118.

Chapter 8

1. Peter Pickow, *Hammered Dulcimer* (Oak, 1979), p. 7.

Chapter 9

1. A. Doyle Moore, "The Autoharp: Its Origin and Development from a Popular to a Folk Instrument," in *Folkstyle Autoharp* (Oak, 1967; reprinted from New York Folklore Quarterly, Vol. 19, No. 4, December 1963), pp. 11–14.
2. Mike Seeger, quoted in "John Kilby Snow: 1905–1980," *The Autoharpoholic*, Vol. 1, No. 3. (Fall 1980), p. 8.

3. Becky Blackley, "View from the Top: An Interview with Bryan Bowers," *The Autoharpoholic*, Vol. 2, No. 1 (Winter 1981), p. 10.
4. Blackley, "View from the Top," p. 80.
5. Bryan Bowers, quoted in "John Kilby Snow: 1905–1980," *The Autoharpoholic*, Vol. 1, No. 3 (Fall 1980), p. 9.
6. Blackley, "View from the Top," p. 9.

Chapter 17

1. J. Robert Willicutt and Kenneth R. Ball, *The Musical Instrument Collector* (Steven F. Brines, ed.) (The Bold Strummer, 1978), p. 124.
2. Willicutt and Ball, *Musical Instrument Collector*, p. 75.
3. Willicutt and Ball, *Musical Instrument Collector*, p. 13.
4. Willicutt and Ball, *Musical Instrument Collector*, p. 76.

Chapter 18

1. "Tips and Tricks." *The Autoharpoholic*, Vol. 1, No. 2 (Summer 1980), p. 10.
2. "Tips and Tricks," p. 10.

PHOTOGRAPHIC ACKNOWLEDGMENTS

The author is grateful to the following dealers, organizations, and individuals for providing photographs or illustrations of instruments, musicians, and stores.

Chapter 1

Lark in the Morning, Lynn McSpadden (The Dulcimer Shoppe).

Chapter 3

Folklore Productions (Doc Watson), John Gréven, George Gruhn (Epiphone, National), Dixie Gurian, Randy Hess of Ovation Instruments (Adamas, Applause, Ovation), Shot Jackson, Ron Lazar of Original Musical Instrument Co. (Dobro), Randee Ragin of Oz Communications (Guild), Mike Longworth of the CF Martin Organisation (Martin), Dennis O'Brien (Neptune Rising), Lawrence Ostrow (Franklin), Paul Schraub (Santa Cruz), Carl Stark (Bozo).

Chapter 4

Ron Chacey, Janet Deering, Tom Ellis, George Gruhn of Gruhn Guitars (Bacon & Day, Gibson, Vega), Chuck Ogsbury (Ome), Ty Piper (Imperial), Margo N. Rosenbaum (Art Rosenbaum), David Gahr (Tony Triscka), Geoff Stelling, Mike Watson (Stewart-MacDonald). Deering Banjo Co. provided materials on which the illustrations of coordinator rod setup and neck relief adjustment were based; Stewart-MacDonald Mfg. provided the illustration on which the banjo schematic was based.

Chapter 5

Backporch Productions (Flatiron), Mariam Townsley (Los Angeles Mandolin Orchestra), Tom Ellis, George Gruhn, (Gibson, Gilchrist, Martin), Mike Kemnitzer (Nugget), Joe Harris of Buddy Lee Attractions (Bill Monroe), Len MacEachron (Here, Inc.), John Monteleone, Lawrence Ostrow (Givens), John Paganoni, Michael Rugg (Capritaurus), Louis Stiver, Barbara Soloway and Rounder Records (Andy Statman).

Chapter 6

Isabelle Bauret (Kenny Kosek), David Gusset, Reid Kowallis.

Chapter 7

The Roscoe Village Foundation (Dulcimer Days), Bonnie Carol, Janet Deering, (Ron Ewing, L. Harmon, A. W. Jeffreys, Len MacEachron (Here, Inc.), Robert Mize, George Pickow (Jean Ritchie), Michael Rugg (Capritaurus), Jerry Rockwell (Green Mountain), L. O. Stapleton, Keith Young. Black Mountain provided the illustration on which the dulcimer schematic was based.

Chapter 8

The Roscoe Village Foundation (Wes Linenkugel), Ray Mooers (Dusty Strings), Sam Rizzetta, Michael Rugg (Capritaurus), Roger Williams (Rose of Sharon).

Chapter 9

Tom Morgan (Mary Morgan), Rudy Schlacher of Fretted Industries (Autoharp), Keith Young, the Walnut Valley Association (Bryan Bowers).

Chapter 10

M. Hohner Inc.

Chapter 11

Molly Mason.

Chapter 12

George Gruhn.

Chapter 13

Kelischek Workshop for Historical Instruments, Michael Rugg (Capritaurus).

Chapter 14

Alexander Eppler.

Chapter 16

Ron Ewing.

Chapter 17

George Gruhn.

Glossary

Janet Deering, Dixie Gurian.